2008 drivers' champion Lewis Hamilton puts his McLaren through its paces during practice for the 2009 FORMULA 1 PETRONAS MALAYSIAN GRAND PRIX in Kuala Lumpur.

**LONDON, NEW YORK,
MELBOURNE, MUNICH, AND DELHI**

For Tall Tree Ltd:
Editors Rob Colson and Jon Richards
Designer Ben Ruocco

For Dorling Kindersley:
Managing Editor Catherine Saunders
Art Director Lisa Lanzarini
Publishing Manager Simon Beecroft
Category Publisher Alex Allan
Production Editor Clare McLean
Production Controller Inderjit Bhullar

First published in Great Britain in 2009 by
Dorling Kindersley Limited,
80 Strand, London WC2R 0RL

2 4 6 8 10 9 7 5 3 1
175845 – 08/09

A CIP catalogue record for this book
is available from the British Library

ISBN: 978-1-40534-682-5

Colour reproduction by Alta Image, UK
Printed and bound by TBB, Slovakia

Discover more at
www.dk.com

Britain's Jenson Button of Brawn GP leads the field into the first corner of the 2009 FORMULA 1 ING AUSTRALIAN GRAND PRIX in Melbourne.

Formula 1™
THE DEFINITIVE VISUAL GUIDE

WRITTEN BY
Adam Hay-Nicholls

Contents

Finland's Kimi Räikkönen takes his Ferrari around a bend during the 2009 FORMULA 1 GULF AIR BAHRAIN GRAND PRIX.

A plume of spray billows out behind Mark Webber's Red Bull during the 2009 FORMULA 1 CHINESE GRAND PRIX at the Shanghai International Circuit. Webber finished the race second behind team mate Sebastian Vettel.

Foreword

LEWIS: My life is motorsport. Racing is a passion that has consumed my life since I was a small boy – and it still gives me the greatest buzz that I could ever wish for.

Since I was young, I have been fascinated by speed and technology. Before I could even drive, I started my racing career with radio-controlled cars. When I moved into karting, I first experienced the raw excitement of driving on the limit: the thrill of battling wheel-to-wheel and the satisfaction of taking a corner as quickly as you possibly could.

Nothing can ready you for the first time you sit in a Grand Prix car. The sensation of endless drive from the engine and incredible stopping power from the brakes is unforgettable – it is so intense.

For me, motor racing is about both commitment and sacrifice. My family has been totally committed to helping me into Formula 1 – and we have all had to make many sacrifices along the way. These are the qualities that make the sport's participants such strong individuals.

My fascination for Formula 1 burns as brightly as ever: they say you never get used to winning – the incredible elation you feel as you cross the finish line – and you never grow tired of it either.

And that pursuit of victory is the story that you will read again and again in the pages of this magnificent book.

JENSON: The classic theme tune to the BBC's Grand Prix coverage is one of my earliest memories of Formula 1. My dad loves motorsport and was a pretty handy driver in his day so I used to watch every Formula 1 race with him when I was young.

Dad bought me my first go-kart when I was eight years old and had no idea what he was letting himself in for! Formula 1 was a world away then but the fundamentals of racing are the same at every level and my early karting experience taught me so much.

Formula 1 was always my dream and I worked really hard to make it a reality. I've been racing in Formula 1 for a decade now and it's been an unbelievable rollercoaster experience. They say you need self-belief to win but sometimes you need self-belief just to survive. I haven't always had the best car and I haven't always had luck on my side but I have always given my full commitment to the sport and my career.

This book is definitive. It looks at the technology, the glamour, the politics, and the characters that make this sport so electric.

But at its heart is the passion for racing that I felt as a child and feel more strongly than ever. I hope that reading this book inspires a whole new generation of Formula 1 fanatics.

The great race

Toyota's Timo Glock heads the field as the cars approach the first turn of the 2009 FORMULA 1 GULF AIR BAHRAIN GRAND PRIX.

Formula 1 racing is the most competitive and prestigious motor racing series in the world. The ultimate test of man and machine, it pits the most talented drivers in the most technologically advanced cars wheel-to-wheel in all four corners of the globe. The goal is to score the maximum number of points at every race and claim the world championship title.

As soon as the car was invented, its owners wanted to race. In 1887, George Bouton attached an engine to a tricycle and organized what was billed as the world's first motor race. However, he was the only driver to enter. It was 1895 when the first true race was held, from Paris to Bordeaux and back. The cars were painfully slow – 24 km/h (15 mph) was the maximum speed – and the race ran for 48 hours. Nevertheless, thousands of spectators flocked to see these amazing machines and their drivers. It was dangerous, aspirational, and thoroughly modern, and soon it would become professional.

THE ORIGINAL HORSEPOWER

Chariot racing was the ancient world's own version of Formula 1 racing. Homer once wrote of a one-lap race around a tree stump, in which the winner was awarded a slave and a cauldron. In 680 BCE, chariot racing became an Olympic event and a major spectator sport. Teams would pay huge salaries to the best racers, and fights would often break out between opposing fans.

"Szisz passed us by at 149 km/h! A clarion call... it's him... and he passed... a red whirlwind... and gone! I wore out two pairs of gloves with my applause."

AN ANONYMOUS FEMALE OBSERVER, WRITING FOR *PARIS ILLUSTRÉ* MAGAZINE

FIRST GRAND PRIX

The date was 26 June 1906 and 32 cars were fighting the sweltering conditions at the Circuit de la Sarthe in Le Mans, France. A crowd of 180,000 had flocked to see the first Grand Prix. After two days and 1,235 km (768 miles) the winner was Ferenc Szisz (near right), with Nazzaro second (top right), and Albert Clement third (centre right). Temperatures of 40°C (104°F) melted the tarmac on the road and caused 300 cases of sunstroke. One driver, whose eye was torn when a stone hit his goggles, was given a shot of cocaine during his pit stop.

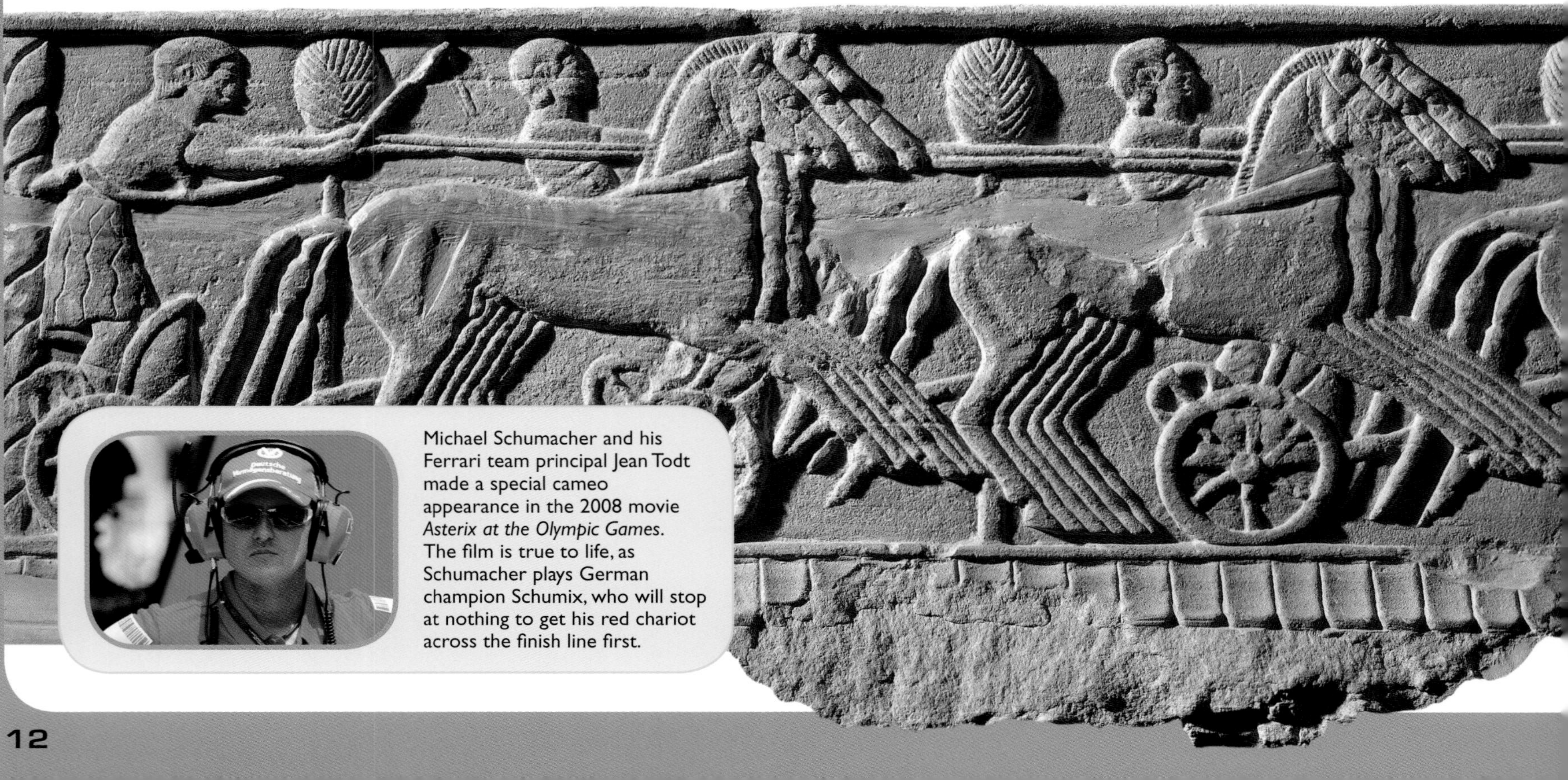

Michael Schumacher and his Ferrari team principal Jean Todt made a special cameo appearance in the 2008 movie *Asterix at the Olympic Games.* The film is true to life, as Schumacher plays German champion Schumix, who will stop at nothing to get his red chariot across the finish line first.

TRIBUTES

LOUIS RENAULT

Louis Renault was 21 when he built his first car, in 1898. Seeing the commercial potential of his ingenuity, he teamed up with his elder brothers Marcel and Ferdinand and established Renault Frères the following year. It would become one of the world's biggest car manufacturers. Louis recognized the marketing value of motor racing, and the marque became dominant in the early city-to-city races. It went on to triumph in front of a French crowd at the first Grand Prix in 1906.

Louis Renault arrives in Bordeaux during the 1903 Paris–Madrid race to learn there has been an accident – his brother Marcel is dead. The company stopped racing for two years until Louis decided to return to competition.

FERENC SZISZ

A locksmith and railway engineer, Ferenc Szisz left his Hungarian homeland to take a factory job with Renault. Louis Renault recognized his talents and invited him to be his riding mechanic. Six years later, Szisz made history by becoming the first Grand Prix winner, aged 32 – it was only his third motor race. He suffered 19 punctures, but managed to claim victory with an average speed of 101.20 km/h (62.88 mph). He was awarded French citizenship and an enormous cash prize of 45,000 francs. It was 80 years before Hungary would host its own Grand Prix, on a circuit dedicated in Szisz's honour.

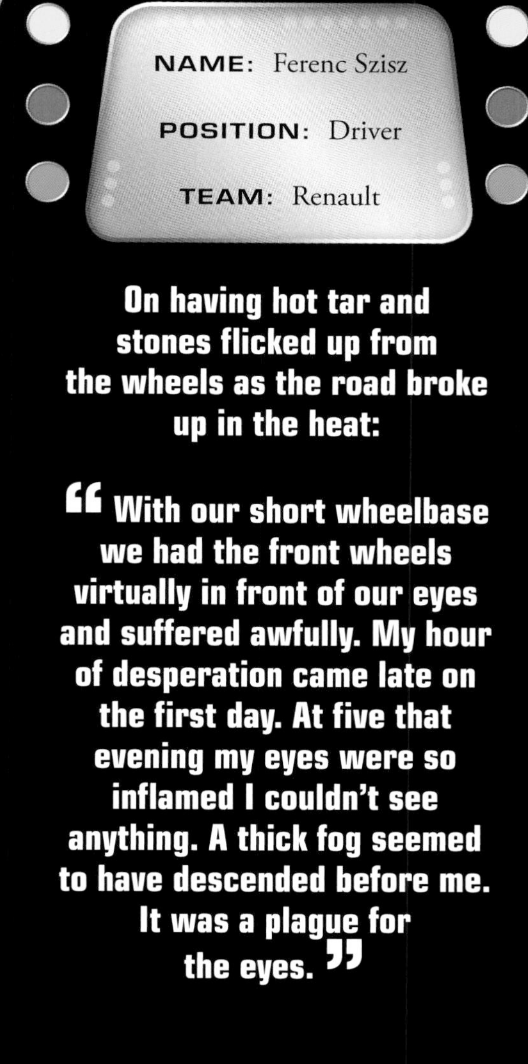

A new era

As motor cars became faster and more accessible, so the sport grew. Racers Rudolf Caracciola and Tazio Nuvolari dominated with the help of manufacturers Mercedes-Benz, Alfa-Romeo, Auto Union, and Bugatti. By the late 1940s, there were seven Grands Prix held annually. Then a technical 'formula' was devised, with which the cars had to comply. Points would be awarded depending on where a driver finished in a race, and the one with the most points at the end of the season would be champion. The Formula 1 World Championship was born.

SILVERSTONE 1950

An old wartime airfield, Silverstone laid out a course flanked by hay bales and the first Formula 1 race track was born. The world's top drivers arrived in Britain to compete for the new official world championship, and King George VI and Queen Elizabeth were on hand to award the trophies, accompanied by Princesses Elizabeth and Margaret (below).

HOW CIRCUITS HAVE CHANGED

When Grand Prix racing first started, it was run on public roads, and the only crash protection was offered by bales of hay. When 86 spectators were killed at Le Mans in 1955, it was clear that safety had to be improved. Slowly, F1 racing adapted long and dangerous circuits like Monza and the Nürburgring into shorter tracks with more 'run-off' areas and more tyre walls to protect drivers and onlookers. The only circuit layout to remain essentially unchanged since those early days is tight and twisty Monaco, which has very little run-off and is rather unsuitable for a modern Formula 1 car – Nelson Piquet used to liken it to 'riding a bicycle around your living room'.

"He's a man of steel, inside and out. But I could never help feeling apprehensive about him. He was like a high-strung thoroughbred, capable of committing the most astonishing follies. As a consequence, he was a regular inmate of the hospital wards."

ENZO FERRARI ON FARINA

GIUSEPPE 'NINO' FARINA

Known as 'the gentleman of Turin', Nino Farina won the first Formula 1 race and became the sport's first world champion. Farina was famous for his stylish driving style – he was very smooth on the steering and throttle. He was also a risk taker, and would regularly trigger accidents. Farina was born into a motoring family – his uncle established the Pininfarina coachbuilding firm that designs Ferrari's road cars to this day.

THE FIRST SPONSORS

Formal sponsorship didn't actually come into Formula I racing until 1968, when Lotus received money from Imperial Tobacco and painted their cars red, white, and gold to promote the Gold Leaf brand. Soon other companies, particularly tobacco rivals, realized that Formula I racing's image of glamour and danger could be used to sell its products.

GARAGISTES

Car manufacturers such as Mercedes and Maserati ruled Formula I racing in the 1950s, but at the end of the decade independent 'garagistes', such as Cooper, BRM, and Lotus, took over. In 1958, the Constructors' World Championship was established.

BIG SCREEN

The 1966 movie *Grand Prix* gave cinemagoers an insight into Formula I racing. The lead character was played by Hollywood heart-throb James Garner, who wore Chris Amon's helmet for the role. Phil Hill and Graham Hill both took acting roles, while director John Frankenheimer attached cameras to the cars and captured thrilling high-speed footage.

IMPROVING SAFETY

Formula I racing was a dreadfully dangerous business in its early years. In the 1970s, drivers Jackie Stewart and Mario Andretti, having lost so many of their colleagues and friends, put pressure on the governing body to improve track and car safety and dramatically reduce the regularity of life-threatening accidents. The 1976 German Grand Prix was to prove a turning point as Niki Lauda (pictured left, with his trainer) escaped a terrifying accident, but emerged with serious burns. Miraculously, he returned to racing just six weeks later.

"We're going to be here forever, don't worry."

BERNIE ECCLESTONE

Thanks to television, today Formula 1 racing is one of the world's most popular sports. It generates billions of dollars for the rights holders and the teams, and top drivers can earn up to US$50 million per season. The cars are tremendously refined, generating incredible speed and grip, and include hybrid technologies and a level of safety that was unimaginable 30 years ago. Yet the racing is as close and as unpredictable as ever.

GLOBAL APPEAL

Lured by the glamour of venues such as Monte Carlo (below), Formula 1 racing has one of the biggest TV audiences of any sport, with approximately 600 million viewers tuning in every race. Only the Olympics and the soccer world cups draw bigger audiences, and they are only held once every four years. China currently enjoys the largest TV audience, but Europe remains the sport's broadcast focus. As a result, races that take place in the East, such as Australia, Malaysia, and Singapore, are scheduled in the late afternoon and evening. This allows live daytime broadcasts in Europe, rather than in the middle of the night.

THE MANUFACTURERS RETURN

Enzo Ferrari used to say, "race on Sunday, sell on Monday". He was referring to how motor racing can be a terrific platform for selling cars, and the manufacturers of the 1950s understood this just as they do today. The independent teams thrived from 1958 to the 1990s, but then the car giants moved in again to start their own teams or purchase existing ones. Car makers, such as BMW (above), had huge budgets and drove up the costs of development. But with a global economic recession biting in 2009, the manufacturers find themselves under pressure to survive, while the 'garagistes' are beginning to thrive again.

NEW SPONSORS

Tobacco sponsorship thrived in the 1970s, '80s, and '90s, but, as a new century came into view and the dangers of smoking became less tolerated, teams were put under pressure to acquire less controversial partners. Instead, Formula 1 racing began to embrace title sponsors who shared a synergy with the sport's appetite for high-tech innovation, such as telecommunications providers (above). Banks and airlines, too, were attracted to the sport's high-income audience and recognized that Formula 1 racing could increase their brand awareness globally.

BUDGETS AND TECHNOLOGY

In 2008, big teams spent up to US$600 million each putting two cars on the grid at 18 races. Some teams would run two full-size wind tunnels 24 hours a day, seven days a week, to optimize aerodynamic efficiency. They would spend millions more on testing, parts machining, and travel. Top teams like McLaren were employing up to 1,000 people. The global recession has brought about efforts to cut costs across the board. Now there is a ban on mid-season testing, and restrictions on wind tunnel use. The governing body, the FIA, is also looking to enforce a budget cap that could see Formula 1 teams shrink in size and more independent teams competing.

THE NEW RULES

In 2009, new regulations were applied to reduce the reliance on aerodynamics and to improve overtaking opportunities. The wider front wing is adjustable, making it easier to overtake if following another car closely. The rear wing is higher and narrower, which creates less 'dirty air'. This refers to the wake turbulence that can disrupt the airflow of a following car – with 'cleaner' air, it is easier to overtake. Slick tyres, which boost mechanical grip, are back for the first time since 1997. Energy that was previously lost by the brakes is now stored in a battery. Drivers have a boost button on their steering wheel, and this releases the stored energy, giving an extra 80 hp – the total power of an average family car.

Slick tyre

Taller, thinner rear wing

DID YOU KNOW?

A total of 64 constructors have competed in Formula 1 racing. Ferrari have competed the longest, having taken part in every season since 1950, while teams such as Spyker and Midland took part in only one season. Three new teams will be introduced in 2010.

Rule makers

"It's not in my nature to walk away from a fight."

MAX MOSLEY

Motor racing is a highly complex sport and, as such, the rule book is as thick as a novel. The governing body of world motorsport is the *Fédération Internationale de l'Automobile* (FIA), which makes and imposes the rules – both sporting and technical – and polices them. Led by former team owner Max Mosley, the Fédération sets the stage and ensures fair play. The FIA is also responsible for safety.

THE ROLE OF STEWARDS

There are three stewards at each Grand Prix, one of whom takes the role of chairman. They are neutral nationalities – not from the same country as any of the competitors. It is their job to referee the race and, should an incident occur, decide if any action should be taken. The stewards can issue a number of punishments for misdemeanours and foul play – anything from fines and drive-though penalties, to grid penalties and race bans.

THE ORGANIZATION

The FIA is the governing body of world motorsport, and its membership is made up of 213 motoring clubs in 125 countries. The organization is based at the famous Place de la Concorde in Paris – where the first guillotine was used! Within its structure is the FIA World Council, which is made up of 26 senior members, including FIA president Max Mosley. Its membership is chosen by the FIA General Assembly. Together they decide on the rules and regulations by which motorsport is governed, and promote continuously improving safety standards. They normally meet three or four times a year, but extraordinary general meetings are common in the event of a major rule infringement, controversy, or other such weighty issue. In 2007, the World Council handed McLaren the biggest fine in sporting history (US$100 million) for bringing F1 racing into disrepute, having been caught with classified Ferrari documents. Should a team or individual want to challenge a decision made by the governing body, there is the independent Court of Appeal.

The FIA headquarters in Paris and its *Salle du Comité* (commitee room).

PROMOTING SAFETY

When Max Mosley took office as president of the FIA he quickly established new standards for car and circuit safety. These have proved extremely effective, and over the last 15 years have led to a zero mortality rate in Formula 1 racing. Funded by the FIA Foundation, the FIA Institute oversees a wide range of projects covering every area of motorsport – from enhancing driver equipment and crash test standards to developing training and education programmes for drivers and safety and medical personnel.

GREEN IDEAS

CLEANER RACING

At a time when natural resources are falling and global warming is an increasing reality, it's a challenge for motor racing to keep on the right side of public opinion. However, the FIA is championing various green strategies, including a 20 per cent reduction in F1 fuel consumption by 2011, and a 50 per cent reduction by 2015. Clean fuels are also under discussion. In 2009, hybrid technology was introduced to F1 cars in the form of the Kinetic Energy Recovery System (KERS).

To promote the FIA's Make Cars Green campaign, designed to encourage cleaner motoring, F1 tyres at the 2008 Japanese Grand Prix had green grooves painted into the tread.

RACE CONTROL

Up in Race Control, FIA Race Director Charlie Whiting and his staff stare at a wall of TV screens, supervising everything that happens in every session. From there they are in radio contact with all the team pit wall stations and team principals, with the safety and medical response car, and the medical centre. Race Control ensures that the whole event runs safely and within the rules, and should a rule or code be broken, will refer it to the race stewards.

Lewis Hamilton gets his hands on the prize – his name is engraved in the silver along with those of his heroes.

FIA GALA

While it's common for most sports champions to receive their prize at the deciding event, that's not the case with FIA championships. Instead, the Formula 1 world champion might have to wait a few months after having won his title before he will finally receive his trophy. Each December at Monte Carlo's Sporting Club, the FIA welcomes champions from across motor racing to a gala dinner and prize-giving ceremony. The select guests – mainly FIA members – applaud winners from all levels of motorsport, from karting upwards. The top three finishers in the F1 championship are expected to attend.

DID YOU KNOW?

While at university in the 1960s, FIA president Max Mosley was secretary of the Oxford Union. Five former British prime ministers have also been officers of the union.

With 600 million Formula 1 fans spread across the world, there is an enormous appetite for words and images every second of a race weekend. Five hundred journalists and photographers attend each race, along with dozens of TV news crews. Cameramen are stationed around the circuit to capture the 'world feed', while some 95 broadcasters take that footage and add their own commentary and interviews as it is broadcast live to their viewers.

Sebastian Vettel is mobbed by photographers on his way to his motorhome, having just won his first race.

The media

DID YOU KNOW?
After the podium, the top three drivers are interviewed live on TV for ten minutes, and then led into a press conference for 20 minutes of questions from print journalists. Finally, a scrum of broadcasters gets to ask another 30 minutes of questions. As if the race wasn't tiring enough!

NAME: Jean Michel Tibi

POSITION: Cameraman

BROADCASTER: FOM

"Ralf Schumacher spun at incredible speed and slammed rearwards into Indianapolis' banked wall. It was about 200 metres before the Williams came to a standstill. I was there, filming Ralf through his open visor. I saw his eyes roll back into his head. They stayed like that for about 12 seconds. Then his head moved slightly, and his eyes rolled back down like the jackpot on a slot machine. It was the most frightening thing I've seen in my 13 seasons of F1."

"This is the sexiest, most thrilling sport. It's all about excess. The drivers are so skilled, the parties are wild... I'm very happy to be here."

SUPERMODEL HELENA CHRISTENSEN

Formula 1 racing is a cocktail of money, danger, and speed. Monaco, in particular, is one of the most prestigious events on the international sporting calendar. On race weekend, the harbour is jammed with luxury yachts, the car park is full of exotic machinery, and celebrity guests drink vintage champagne as the drivers try to keep their cars out of the barriers. In short, F1 racing is the most glamorous sport on the planet and anyone who's anyone wants a trackside seat.

CELEBRITY VISITS

Formula 1 racing attracts A-list celebrities from all walks of life – sporting superstars, screen legends, and business leaders. Regular attendees include, in alphabetical order: Arnold Schwarzenegger, Bono, Brad Pitt, David Beckham, Diego Maradona, Elizabeth Hurley, Eric Clapton, George Clooney, George Lucas, Heidi Klum, Hugh Grant, Jay-Z, Jude Law, Kevin Spacey, Kylie Minogue, Matt Damon, Naomi Campbell, Nicolas Cage, Ozzy Osbourne, P Diddy, Pelé, Penelope Cruz, Prince William, Quentin Tarantino, Robert Plant, Rod Stewart, and Sylvester Stallone.

THE GRID GIRLS

Forty grid girls attend every race, and their job is to provide beauty and calm to a strip of tarmac filled with busy mechanics and bustling TV crews. These girls are sourced from modelling agencies. One stands in front of each car with that driver's number board, while another stands next to the car with her driver's national flag. No matter how busy they are before a race, it's traditional for each driver to give his grid girls a peck on the cheek before he jumps in his car.

THE OTHER HALF

Lewis Hamilton wasted no time when he arrived in F1 racing. Within a year, he was dating one of the most beautiful women in the world, Pussycat Dolls frontwoman Nicole Scherzinger (right). Rival Fernando Alonso's wife Raquel del Rosario is a pop star in Spain, and Kimi Räikkönen's wife, Jenni, was Miss Scandinavia 2001.

THE PLAYBOY DRIVERS

Just as every era has a dominant driver, so every era has its character. Mike Hawthorn wore a bow tie when racing, while Graham Hill was known to drive without his trousers. James Hunt would show up with a bottle of wine in one hand and a girl in the other. Gerhard Berger had an agreement with Ayrton Senna that the Brazilian would give female fans Gerhard's room number. Eddie Irvine once bought an apartment in Milan because it was close to a nightclub, while Kimi Räikkönen likes to enter speedboat races under his *nom de plume*, 'James Hunt'.

Pictured from left to right: Mike Hawthorn, Graham Hill, James Hunt, Gerhard Berger, Eddie Irvine, Kimi Räikkönen

1950s

1960s

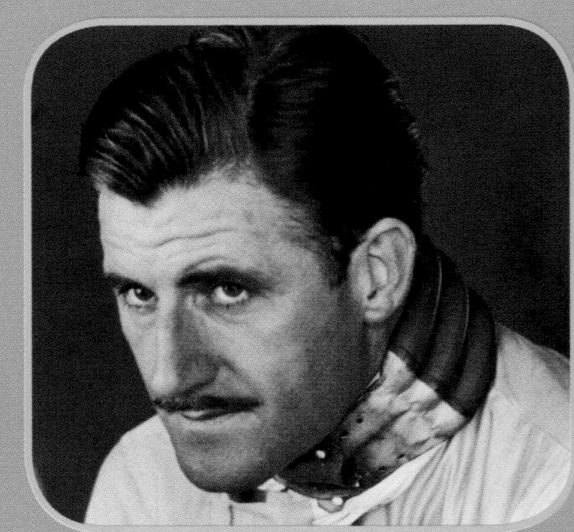

DIAMOND HEIST

Jaguar Racing placed flawless diamonds in the nosecones of their cars at the 2004 Monaco Grand Prix (right). Christian Klien hit the barriers on the first lap, and when the car was returned to the pits the US$250,000 rock was nowhere to be found. It seems a fan walked away with a very valuable souvenir.

HOLLYWOOD

In recent years, team motorhomes have become like film sets. At Monaco in 2005, the Red Bull Energy Station was given a Star Wars makeover. The Red Bull pit crew even wore white suits and Storm Trooper helmets during the race. The following year the team promoted *Superman Returns* – their motorhome was turned into the Daily Planet HQ and David Coulthard wore a red cape on the podium. In 2009, the Brawn GP garage had a special guest – the Terminator robot.

Rock band KISS takes to the stage at the end of the Australian Grand Prix in Melbourne in 2008.

MUSIC TIME

While the teams pack up after a race, many don't want the party to stop. Circuits sometimes organize post-race concerts, and the Australian Grand Prix has hosted some particularly rocking shows. KISS and The Who have both performed there, while the French Grand Prix hosted Pink Floyd's Roger Waters and Malaysia Jamiroquai. F1 parties also draw top DJs to the decks, including David Morales, Gorillaz, Maxi Jazz from Faithless, Carl Cox, and David Guetta.

Formula 1 racing is fuelled by the passion and dedication of those who follow it and those who run it. The men you see here found great success in the sport. It made them rich, powerful, and famous. Yet they've put more into the sport than they've taken out. They've helped to make F1 racing what it is today – the most elite motorsport championship.

BERNIE ECCLESTONE

Known as the 'ringmaster', Bernie is F1 racing's commercial rights holder and is effectively in charge of the show. He does billion-dollar deals on a handshake and, legend has it, learned to hustle selling cupcakes to his school friends at inflated prices when he was 12. He started his business life selling cars and motorcycles, and raced at weekends. He tried to qualify for the 1958 Monaco Grand Prix but then turned his attention to management, purchasing the Brabham team. He took charge of the Formula One Constructors' Association (FOCA) in 1978, and negotiated the TV deals that have helped to make F1 racing into a huge money maker. He left team management behind in the late '80's to concentrate on his Formula One Group of companies, masterminding the expansion of F1 racing to all corners of the globe, bringing it to the Middle East and Asia, with plenty more to come.

MAX MOSLEY

Max was a barrister and amateur racing driver before co-founding the March Formula 1 team in 1969. He then became Bernie Ecclestone's legal adviser, settling a long-running dispute between FOCA and the *Fédération Internationale du Sport Automobile* (FISA). Since 1993, Max has been the president of the *Fédération Internationale de l'Automobile* (FIA). As such, he presides over the rules, both sporting and technical, and has done a lot to shape F1 racing as we know it, championing safety and environmental technologies.

"No driver, no person, will ever be bigger than Formula 1 itself."

BERNIE ECCLESTONE

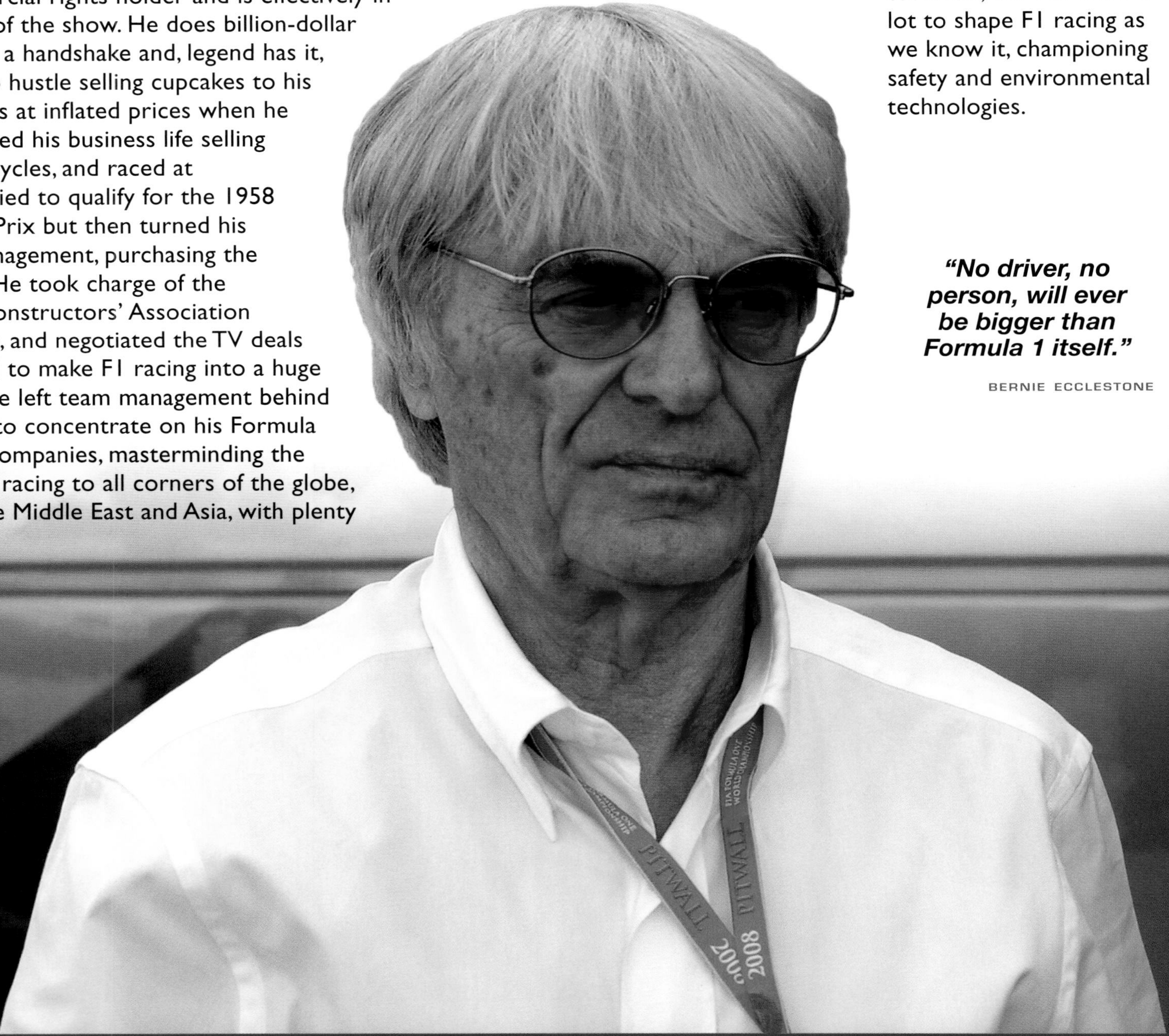

COLIN CHAPMAN

The founder of Team Lotus, Chapman was one of F1 racing's most influential engineers. When other cars ran chassis made of several different parts, Lotus introduced the single-shell monocoque and composite materials. The resulting body was both lighter and stronger. Colin also developed wings to create aerodynamic downforce, and his was the first team to run advertising on its cars. All these innovations remain in the sport today. Colin died in 1982, at the age of 54, from a heart attack. During his tenure, Lotus achieved six drivers' titles and seven constructors' titles.

ENZO FERRARI

Having been a mule-shoer for the Italian army during World War I, Enzo fell in love with cars and started to race and build them for Alfa Romeo. He established Ferrari in 1947, and the team competed in the inaugural 1950 Formula 1 championship. The 'Commendatore' died in 1988, a week before his cars scored a glorious 1-2 at the Italian Grand Prix. His team has achieved a record 15 drivers' titles and 16 constructors' titles in nearly 60 years of F1 competition. Politically the most powerful team in F1 racing, Ferrari is practically a religion in Italy. Whenever Ferrari wins, the church bells ring at its Maranello base.

RON DENNIS

Aged 18, Ron took a job as a mechanic with the Cooper team, and went on to work for Sir Jack Brabham. He then headed several teams in the lower formulae before taking control of McLaren in 1981. Known for his fastidious attention to detail, legend has it that he cleans the gravel in his driveway with a toothbrush and changes his shirts four times a day. It's that level of perfectionism that won seven constructors' titles and ten drivers' titles during his tenure as team principal, which came to an end at the start of 2009.

FRANK WILLIAMS

After a brief career as a driver and mechanic, funded by his work as a travelling grocery salesman, Frank founded his first racing team in 1966. Struggling for money, his office was based out of a public telephone box. In 1977, he established Williams Grand Prix Engineering with designer Patrick Head. The team went on to win nine constructors' titles and seven drivers' titles, dominating the sport between 1992 and 1997. Frank was left paralysed after a car crash in 1986. One of the sport's great survivors, Williams F1 has competed in over 600 Grands Prix, and Sir Frank remains at the helm.

The championships

Grid girls parade national flags at the front of the grid before the start of the 2008 Australian Grand Prix in Melbourne.

The eight-month-long season starts in Australia and takes the chequered flag in Abu Dhabi. The prizes everyone works towards are the drivers' and constructors' world championship trophies, etched with immortal names from the past. The pursuit of glory often goes down to the wire. In 2008, it was decided on the very last lap, so there is huge pressure on every driver to make every race count.

DID YOU KNOW?
Sixty-eight circuits have hosted world championship Grands Prix. Since 1950, the British Grand Prix has been held at three different circuits: Silverstone, Aintree, and Brands Hatch. And in 1993 Donington hosted the European Grand Prix.

BELGIUM
Spa-Francorchamps
Race 12

BRITAIN
Silverstone
Race 8

MONACO
Monte Carlo
Race 6

SPAIN
Catalunya
Race 5

EUROPE
Valencia
Race 11

BRAZIL
Sao Paulo
Race 16

Formula 1 racing is a global championship and it is spreading, picking up exciting new venues in Asia and the Middle East. As a result, historic venues in Europe are under threat. In 2009, for only the second time in F1 history, the French Grand Prix was absent from the calendar. The teams will cover 130,000 km (80,000 miles) as they travel from circuit to circuit, grabbing as many championship points as they can along the way.

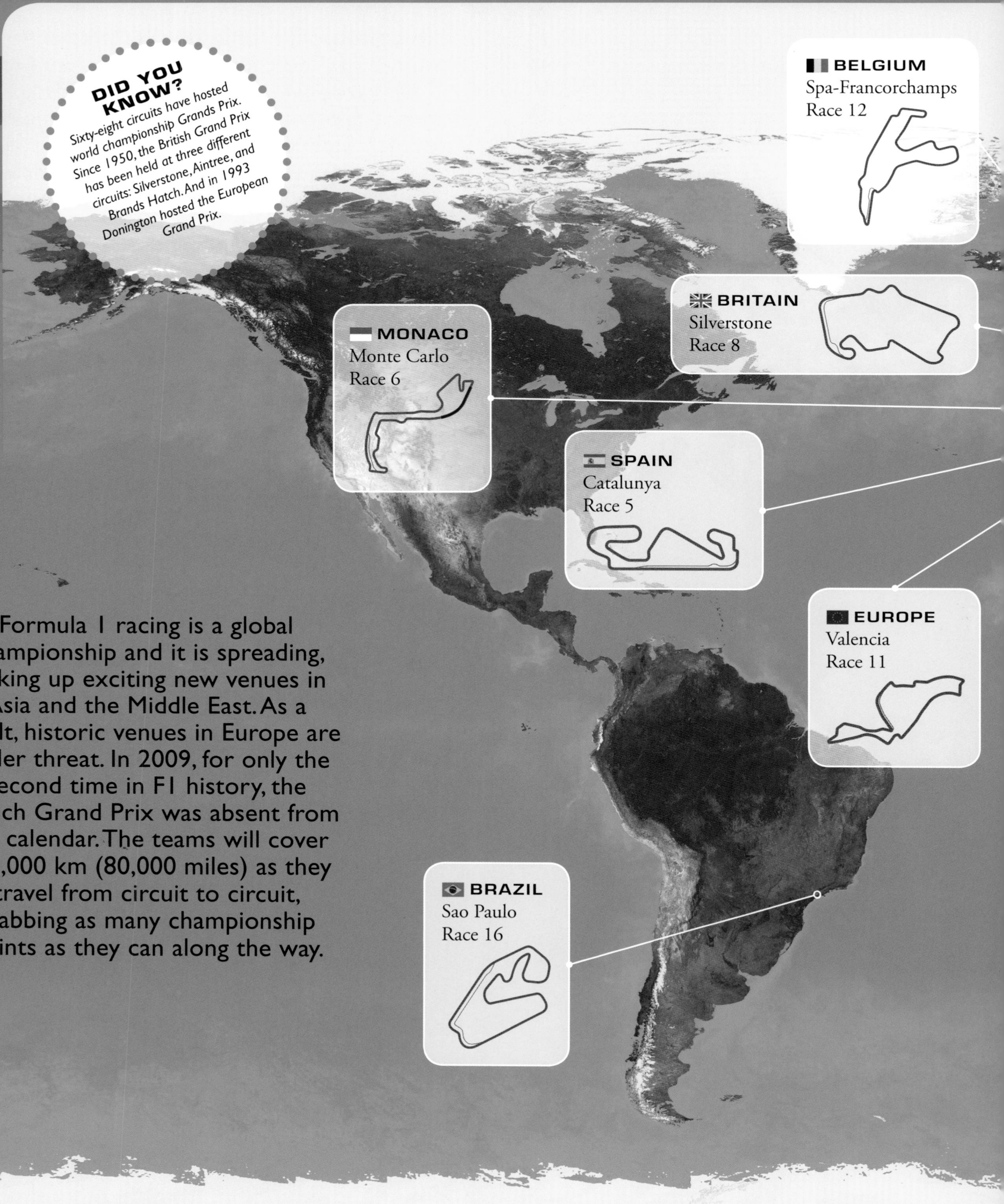

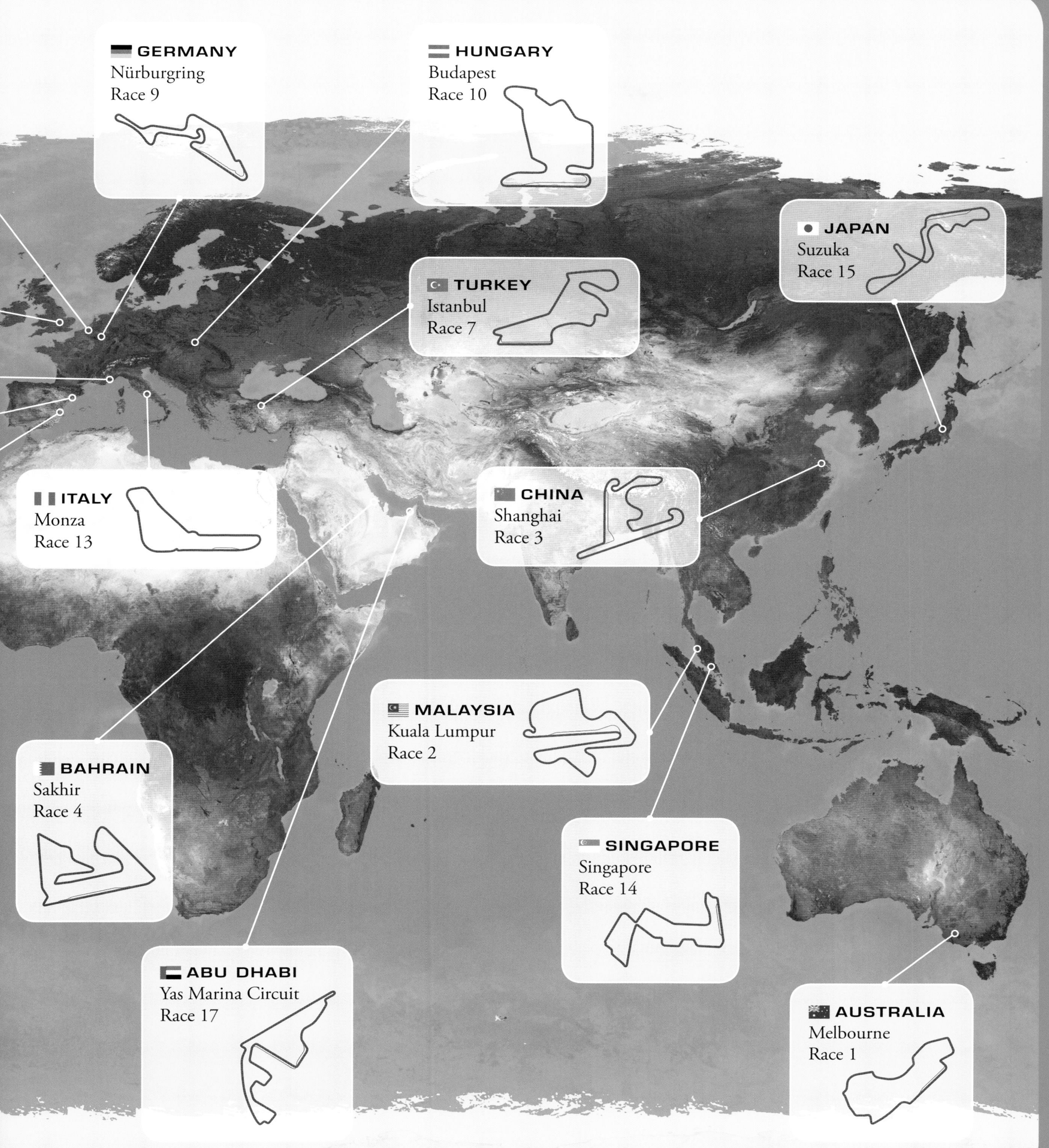
GERMANY
Nürburgring
Race 9
HUNGARY
Budapest
Race 10
JAPAN
Suzuka
Race 15
TURKEY
Istanbul
Race 7
ITALY
Monza
Race 13
CHINA
Shanghai
Race 3
MALAYSIA
Kuala Lumpur
Race 2
BAHRAIN
Sakhir
Race 4
SINGAPORE
Singapore
Race 14
ABU DHABI
Yas Marina Circuit
Race 17
AUSTRALIA
Melbourne
Race 1

Grand Prix victories are always a glorious occasion, but they are an hors d'oeuvre to the more satisfying meal that is the world championship. To win, drivers need to finish at the front consistently, make the most of every opportunity, and finish the season with more points than anyone else.

DID YOU KNOW?

To celebrate his record seven world championship titles, there are plans to erect seven skyscrapers – Michael Schumacher Towers – in locations across the globe. The first, in Dubai, has already been completed.

POINTS SYSTEM

The top eight finishers in each Grand Prix score points according to the following scale:

1st place: 10 points **2nd place:** 8 points
3rd place: 6 points **4th place:** 5 points
5th place: 4 points **6th place:** 3 points
7th place: 2 points **8th place:** 1 point

The only exception to this is when a race has been suspended and cannot be restarted. If less than 75 per cent of the race distance has been completed, only half points are awarded. So first place earns 5 points, second 4 points, and so on.

RECORD BREAKER

THE YOUNGEST CHAMPION

In 1972, Emerson Fittipaldi became Formula 1 racing's youngest-ever world champion, at the age of 25 years and 274 days. That record stood for 33 years, until Fernando Alonso won his first title in 2005, aged 24 years and 59 days. Most recently, though, Lewis Hamilton broke the record by becoming world champion in 2008, aged 23 years and 301 days, having only just missed out on winning the championship by a single point the year before.

PODIUM LEGENDS

Thirty different men have won the Formula 1 World Championship (see the F1 statistics on pages 178–185). There have been 58 opportunities to win one so far, and the gentlemen you see on this podium have claimed 16 titles between them. The record holder is Michael Schumacher, the Red Baron (a nickname first given to the World War I flying ace Manfred von Richthofen), who took seven titles between 1994 and 2004. To his right is Juan Manuel Fangio, El Maestro, who won five titles between 1951 and 1957. He held the record until Michael equalled him in 2002. And on the third step is Alain Prost, the Professor (nicknamed for his mental discipline), who seized four titles between 1985 and 1993. Incidentally, Schumacher has scored the most points (1,369), the most victories (91), and the most podiums (154) of all time.

NAME: Fernando Alonso

CHAMPION: 2005, 2006

TEAM: Renault

"I came from a country with no tradition in Formula 1 and I fought alone, basically. I think this title is the maximum I can achieve in my life, in my career, and it is thanks to three or four people, no more than that. Winning my first world championship is a very emotional moment for me."

Constructors

The Formula 1 constructors' championship is the teams' prize. Teams earn championship points from each top eight finish they achieve, so it's important for the team to have two strong pilots capable of consistently bringing their cars home in the points. And there's more than honour to winning the title. The higher a team finishes in the world championship, the greater the share of the television revenues it takes, and this can run into hundreds of millions of pounds.

POINTS SYSTEM

Teams earn points based on the combined total of their drivers. So if one of their cars finishes second and the other sixth, the team earns 11 points. The perfect score for a team is 18 points. Initially, both the constructors' and the drivers' championships offered points only down to sixth place, but in 2003 the system was changed in order to make the championships more competitive and help more teams get on the points board.

DID YOU KNOW?
The constructors' championship is 50 years old, and in that time only three countries have won the title. All 12 winning constructors come from either the UK, France, or Italy. UK teams are by far the most successful, having won 32 titles between them.

VANWALL
1 constructors' title

MATRA
1 constructors' title

BENETTON
1 constructors' title

COOPER
2 constructors' titles

TYRRELL
1 constructors' title

BRM
1 constructors' title

RENAULT
2 constructors' titles

BRABHAM
2 constructors' titles

RIVALRIES

FERRARI V MCLAREN

Over time, Ferrari's greatest adversary has proved to be McLaren. They first did battle in 1974, McLaren beating the Scuderia by eight points. Their tussles of the modern era started in 1998, Ferrari's Michael Schumacher going head-to-head with McLaren's Mika Häkkinen. On occasion, the battle for supremacy between the two teams has reached the courtroom. Since the animosity of 2007's spying scandal, when a McLaren employee was caught with secret Ferrari design documents, the teams appear to be on cordial terms. As the saying goes, keep your friends close and your enemies closer.

LOTUS
7 constructors' titles

WILLIAMS
9 constructors' titles

FERRARI
16 constructors' titles

McLAREN
8 constructors' titles

MELBOURNE, AUSTRALIA

The lakeside track in Albert Park is a real challenge on which to overtake, as there are few long straights. Even so, there's plenty of action thanks to the walls that line the narrow circuit, punishing the slightest error – and this means that safety car periods are almost guaranteed. The track is used just once a year and therefore has very little grip. As this is the first race of the season, the drivers are still getting used to their machinery, and teams usually plan for accidents and bring a decent set of spares with them.

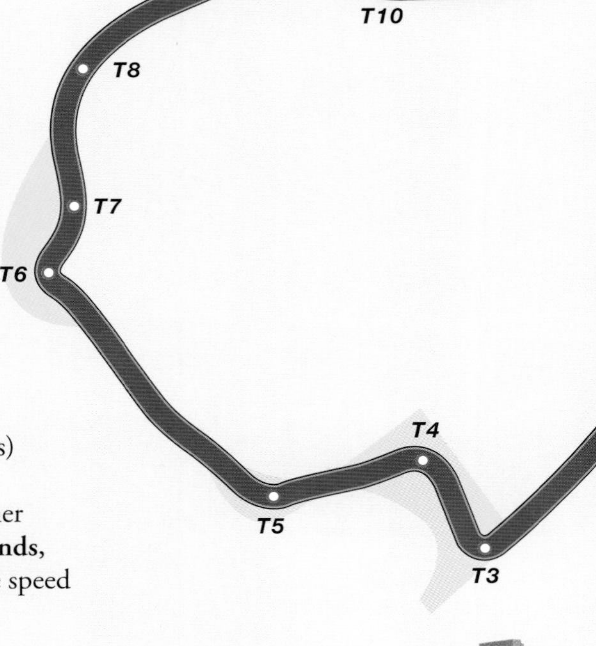

NUMBER OF LAPS: 58

CIRCUIT LENGTH: 5.303 km (3.295 miles)

RACE DISTANCE: 307.574 km (191.110 miles)

LAP RECORD: Michael Schumacher (Ferrari, 2004), **1 minute 24.125 seconds,** 226.933 km/h (141.016 mph) average speed

1998: GENTLEMEN'S AGREEMENT

David Coulthard and Mika Häkkinen had an agreement prior to the race that whoever made it into Turn 1 first would be allowed to win the race. McLaren knew they had a quick car, and didn't want their two drivers to jeopardise victory by fighting each other. Häkkinen got the better start, and despite the Finn botching his pit stop and Coulthard leading, the Scot was forced to yield to Mika in the closing laps.

KUALA LUMPUR, MALAYSIA

Malaysia is the hottest event on the calendar. Ambient temperatures of up to 40°C (104°F) and a track hot enough to fry an egg mean the drivers, wrapped up in their Nomex® suits and helmets, are close to fainting after 56 laps. The palm-tree-like grandstand provides an awesome backdrop. The sweeping high-speed curves demand a well-balanced car. The two long straights provide a great opportunity for the drivers to get a tow, and the generous track width encourages drivers to take chances.

MEMORIES

2001: RAIN MASTER

Weather can be a major factor at any track and rain can change a race instantly. When the heavens opened on lap 2, Michael Schumacher spun off the track. He rejoined in 11th place, and had to queue for tyres behind his team mate. The opposition went for full wet tyres, but Schumacher gambled on intermediates. It was the right decision. The Ferrari driver was five seconds a lap quicker than the McLarens and went on to win the race.

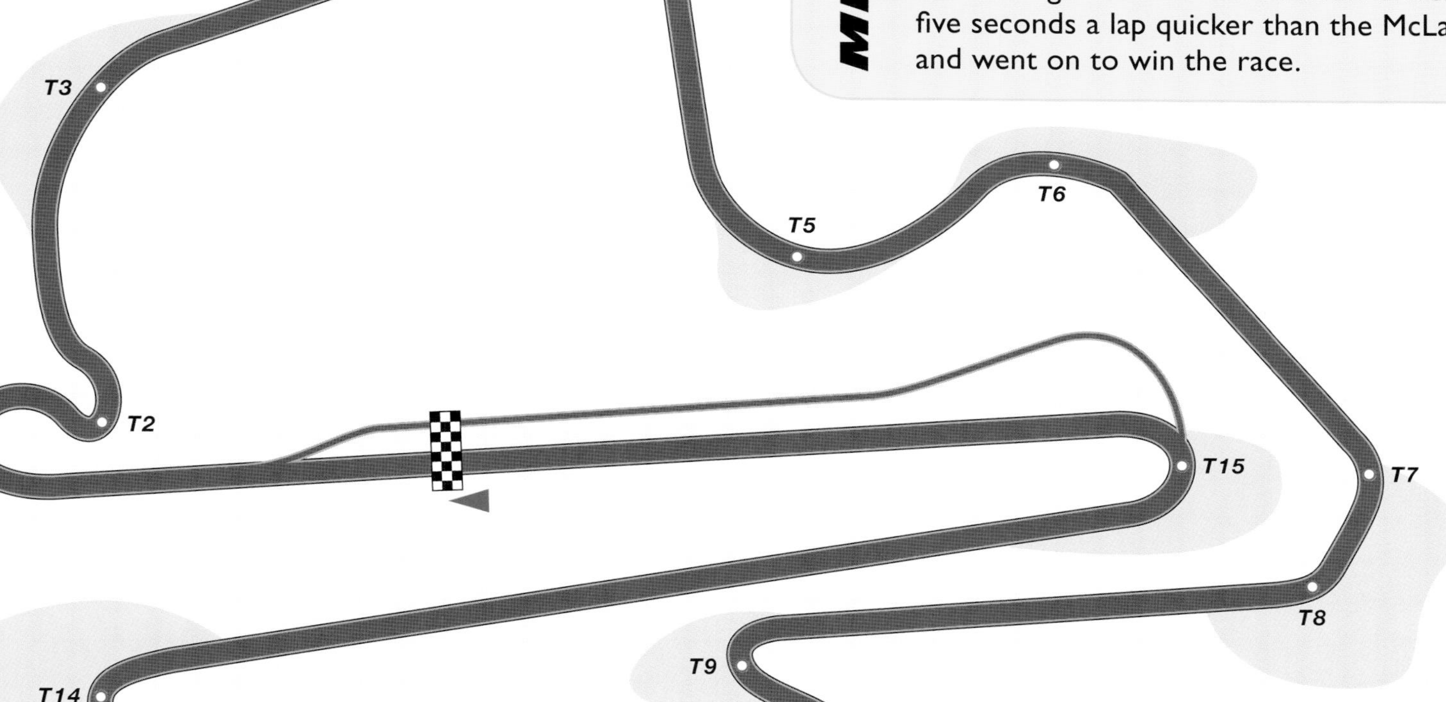

NUMBER OF LAPS: 56

CIRCUIT LENGTH: 5.543 km (3.444 miles)

RACE DISTANCE: 310.408 km (192.887 miles)

LAP RECORD: Juan Pablo Montoya (Williams, 2004), **1 minute 34.223 seconds,** 211.782 km/h (131.595 mph) average speed

NUMBER OF LAPS: 56

CIRCUIT LENGTH: 5.451 km (3.387 miles)

RACE DISTANCE: 305.066 km (189.568 miles)

LAP RECORD: Michael Schumacher (Ferrari, 2004), **1 minute 32.238 seconds**, 212.749 km/h (132.202 mph) average speed

T1 T2 T3 T4 T5 T6 T7 T8 T9 T10 T11 T12 T13 T14 T15 T16

SHANGHAI, CHINA

Laid out to resemble the Chinese character 'Shang' – meaning 'high' – this circuit cost approximately US$450 million to construct. It has a vast main grandstand with viewing suites suspended above the start/finish straight. The first corner complex is among the trickiest in Formula 1 racing – a demanding 270 degree right-handed corner combination that requires an aggressive flat-out entry and braking through the corner, which tightens up towards the end. Then there's a sudden change of direction, and the bend unwinds itself.

MEMORIES

2007: COMPLETELY TYRED OUT

Lewis Hamilton was en route to winning the world title in his rookie year. He was way in the lead, but McLaren, thinking the weather would turn, wanted to keep him out on tyres that were well past their sell-by date. When they did finally call him into the pits, Lewis slid off the circuit and into the gravel. Ultimately, he'd have to wait another year for championship glory.

MEMORIES

2009: JENSON'S FLYING FIRST LAP

Jenson Button lined up fourth on the grid in his Brawn and knew he had to make up a place if his race strategy was to work. At the start, he was passed by Lewis Hamilton, but he held fourth by taking Sebastian Vettel around the outside of Turn 1. Then he went to pass Hamilton on the exit of the final corner. The McLaren driver pressed his KERS button, but Jenson was still able to outbrake him and take third en route to victory.

SAKHIR, BAHRAIN

This Middle Eastern venue features some remarkable architecture, most notably a ten-storey VIP tower overlooking the paddock. The circuit's design encourages overtaking, and there are also large run-off areas, which make this track one of the safest in the world. To keep sand off the track, the surrounding dunes have been coated in adhesive. Because alcohol is illegal in many Islamic states, this podium doesn't feature champagne. Instead, drivers spray themselves with fragrant, non-alcoholic rose water.

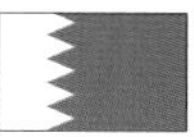

NUMBER OF LAPS: 57

CIRCUIT LENGTH: 5.412 km (3.363 miles)

RACE DISTANCE: 308.238 km (191.539 miles)

LAP RECORD: Michael Schumacher (Ferrari, 2004), **1 minute 30.252 seconds,** 216.074 km/h (134.268 mph) average speed

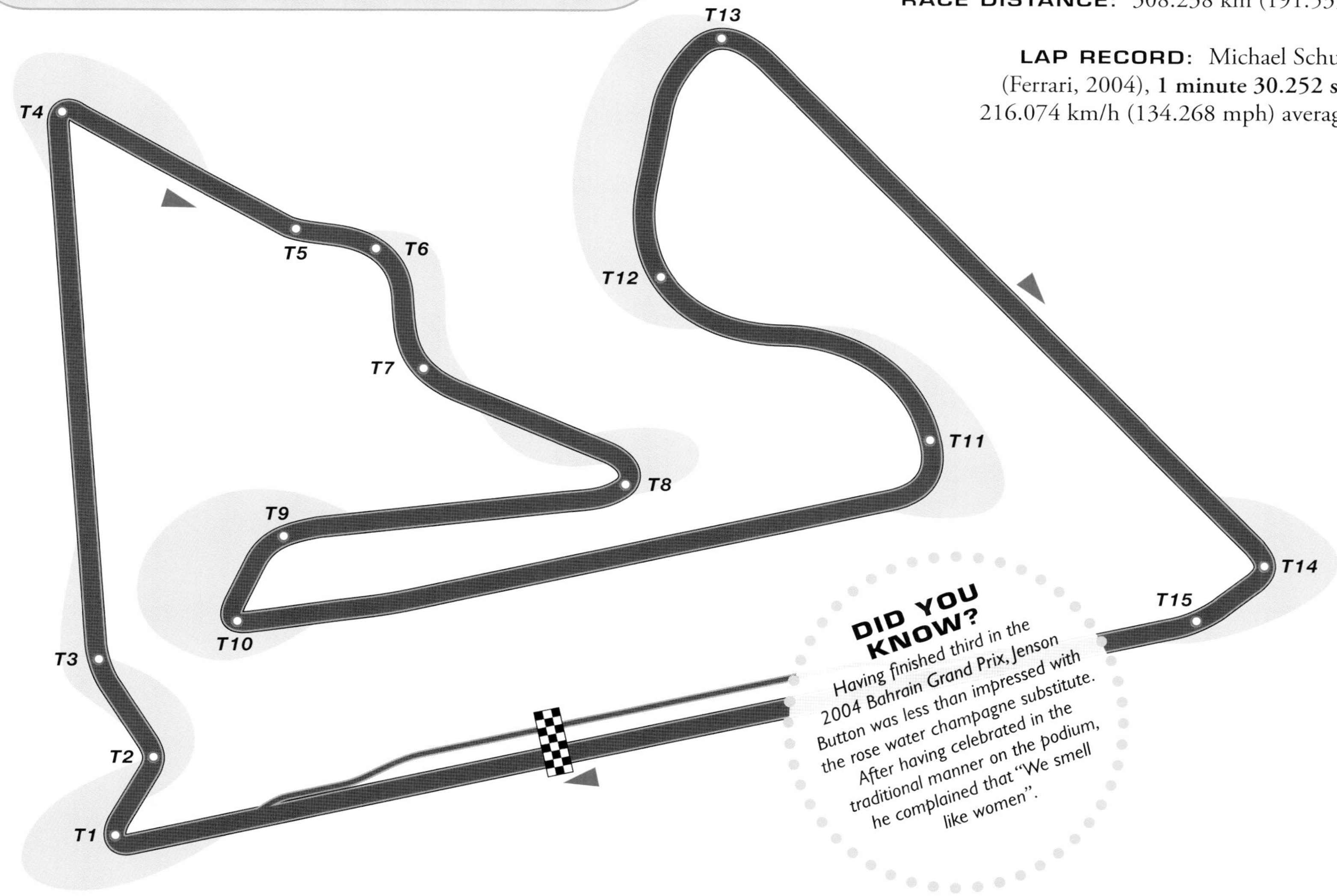

DID YOU KNOW?

Having finished third in the 2004 Bahrain Grand Prix, Jenson Button was less than impressed with the rose water champagne substitute. After having celebrated in the traditional manner on the podium, he complained that "We smell like women".

CATALUNYA AND VALENCIA, SPAIN

With long straights and a variety of corners, the Circuit de Catalunya is seen as an 'all-rounder' circuit, and is used by teams for testing. As a result, the drivers know the track so well that they seldom make mistakes, leading to a lack of overtaking. Overtaking is difficult on the Valencia Street Circuit, too. The winding track makes its way around a port and across a swing bridge.

CATALUNYA
NUMBER OF LAPS: 66

CIRCUIT LENGTH: 4.655 km (2.892 miles)

RACE DISTANCE: 307.104 km (190.825 miles)

LAP RECORD: Kimi Räikkönen (Ferrari, 2008), **1 minute 21.670 seconds,** 205.191 km/h (127.505 mph) average speed

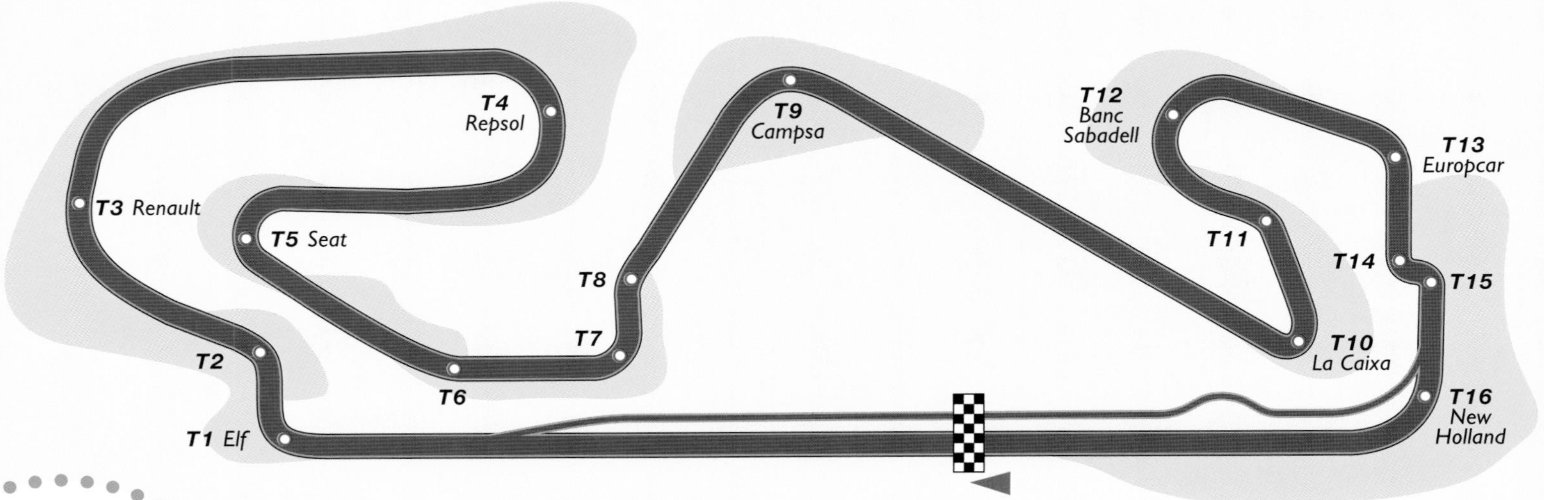

T1 Elf
T2
T3 Renault
T4 Repsol
T5 Seat
T6
T7
T8
T9 Campsa
T10 La Caixa
T11
T12 Banc Sabadell
T13 Europcar
T14
T15
T16 New Holland

DID YOU KNOW?
The swing bridge at the entrance to Valencia's marina is welded shut before each race. As a result, any yacht captains who want a berth during the race have to ensure that they are in the harbour before any track action starts.

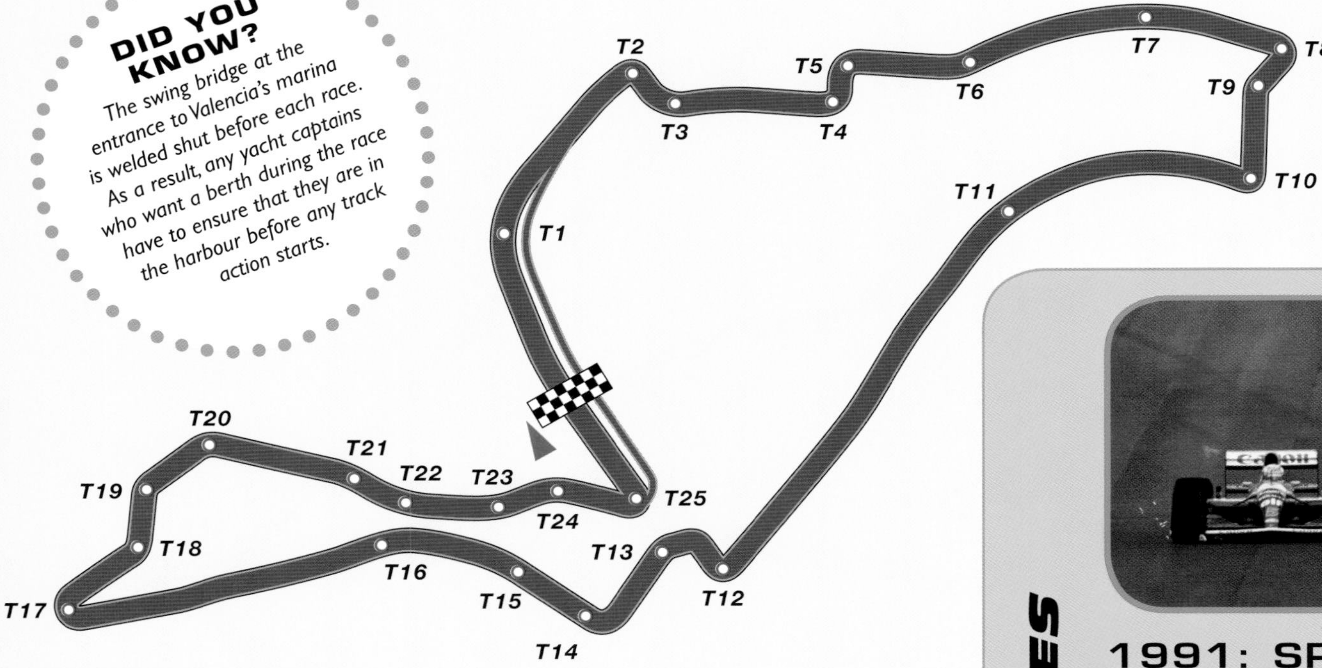

T1
T2
T3
T4
T5
T6
T7
T8
T9
T10
T11
T12
T13
T14
T15
T16
T17
T18
T19
T20
T21
T22
T23
T24
T25

VALENCIA
NUMBER OF LAPS: 57

CIRCUIT LENGTH: 5.419 km (3.367 miles)

RACE DISTANCE: 308.883 km (191.919 miles)

LAP RECORD: Felipe Massa (Ferrari, 2008), **1 minute 38.708 seconds,** 197.637 km/h (122.811 mph) average speed

MEMORIES

1991: SPARKS FLY

Nigel Mansell and Ayrton Senna raced neck and neck the full length of the start/finish straight at the Circuit de Catalunya, neither willing to yield until the last second. Sparks shot out from behind both cars as their floors touched the tarmac. Mansell ended up taking the position and the win.

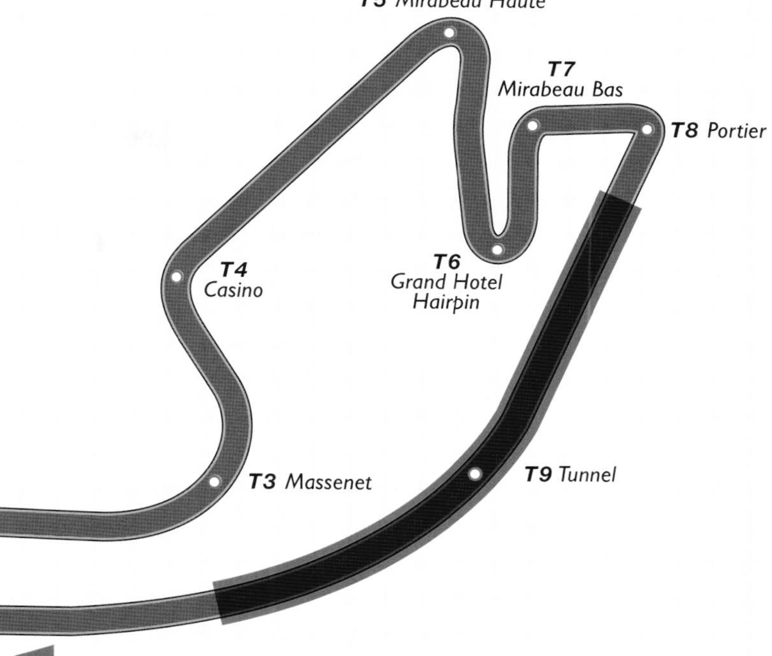

NUMBER OF LAPS: 78

CIRCUIT LENGTH: 3.340 km (2.075 miles)

RACE DISTANCE: 260.520 km (161.887 miles)

LAP RECORD: Michael Schumacher (Ferrari, 2004), **1 minute 14.439 seconds,** 161.528 km/h (100.373 mph) average speed

MONTE CARLO, MONACO

First held in 1929, the Monaco Grand Prix is the most prestigious race on the calendar. Racing on the streets of the Principality and around its harbour, this circuit is extremely tight and twisty, making overtaking almost impossible. High downforce settings and low gear ratios are the order of the day. The highlights of the lap include racing past Monte Carlo's famous casino and plunging in and out of darkness through Formula 1 racing's only tunnel. Overall, this circuit requires total concentration from all the drivers, as the slightest mistake could ruin their weekend.

MEMORIES

1982: CH-CH-CH-CHANGES

The leader changed five times in the final three laps of this incredible race, and the eventual winner didn't believe he'd won! Alain Prost was in the lead as it rained, but then crashed heavily at the chicane. Riccardo Patrese then led, but spun at the hairpin. That gave Didier Pironi the lead, but on the final lap he ran out of fuel. The same happened to the next leader, Andrea de Cesaris. Patrese was able to bump-start his car and complete the lap to take the win.

MEMORIES

2006: FELIPE'S FIRST

Felipe Massa's first win came at a track on which he would continue to dominate for years to come. It was a perfect weekend for the Brazilian. He took pole position ahead of team mate Michael Schumacher and left him in the shade during the race, forcing the German to queue behind him following a safety car period and demoting Schumacher to third.

ISTANBUL, TURKEY

Istanbul Park's 14 curves were inspired by other famous turns, such as Interlagos' 'Senna S', Suzuka's 'Spoon Curve', and Spa's 'Eau Rouge'. The highlight is Turn 8 – a very fast triple-apex curve which, for the drivers, provides great reward. Through this corner the drivers endure a load of 5G (five times the force of gravity) for approximately four seconds. The circuit runs anti-clockwise, a rarity shared only with Brazil, Singapore, and Abu Dhabi, and therefore puts extra strain on the drivers' necks.

NUMBER OF LAPS: 58

CIRCUIT LENGTH: 5.338 km (3.317 miles)

RACE DISTANCE: 309.396 km (192.250 miles)

LAP RECORD: Juan Pablo Montoya (McLaren, 2005), **1 minute 24.770 seconds,** 226.693 km/h (140.867 mph) average speed

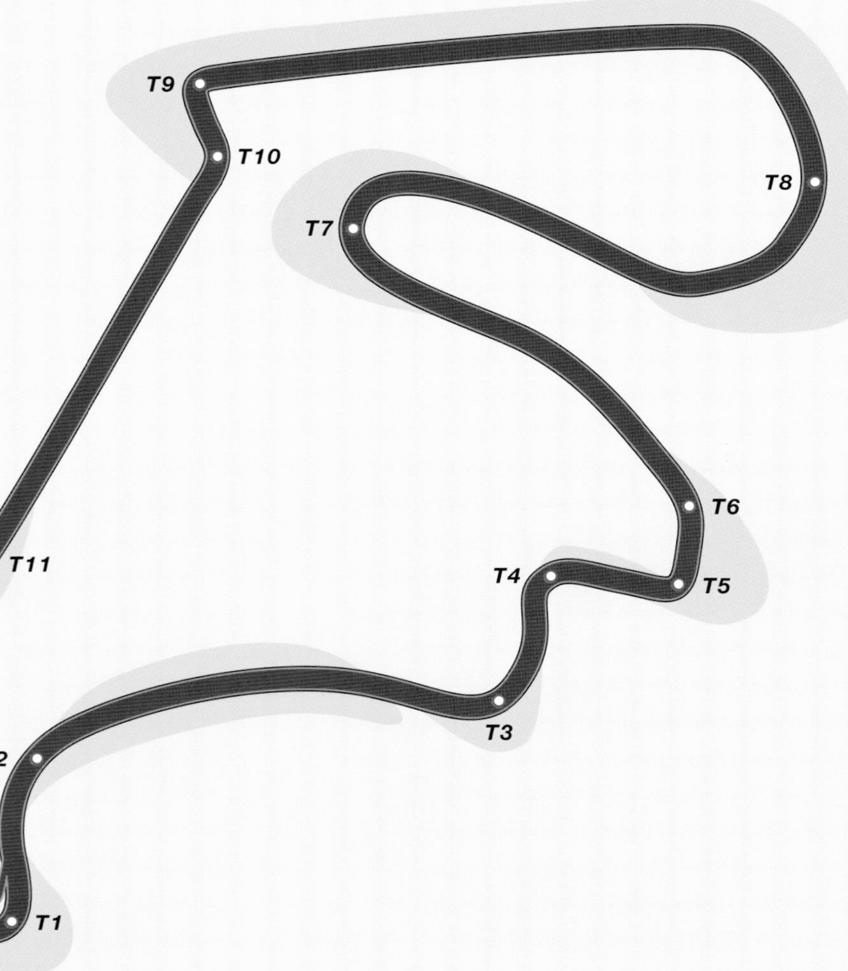

SILVERSTONE, GREAT BRITAIN

Silverstone was previously a wartime airfield and remains open to the elements; it is often victim to rain and crosswinds that threaten a car's balance. It is a power circuit with a challenging flow of high-speed corners that the drivers love. However, the track's facilities cannot match those of the most modern circuits, and 2009 was the last time F1 racing visited for the foreseeable future.

NUMBER OF LAPS: 60

CIRCUIT LENGTH: 5.141 km (3.194 miles)

RACE DISTANCE: 308.355 km (191.600 miles)

LAP RECORD: Michael Schumacher (Ferrari, 2004), **1 minute 18.739 seconds,** 235.049 km/h (146.059 mph) average speed

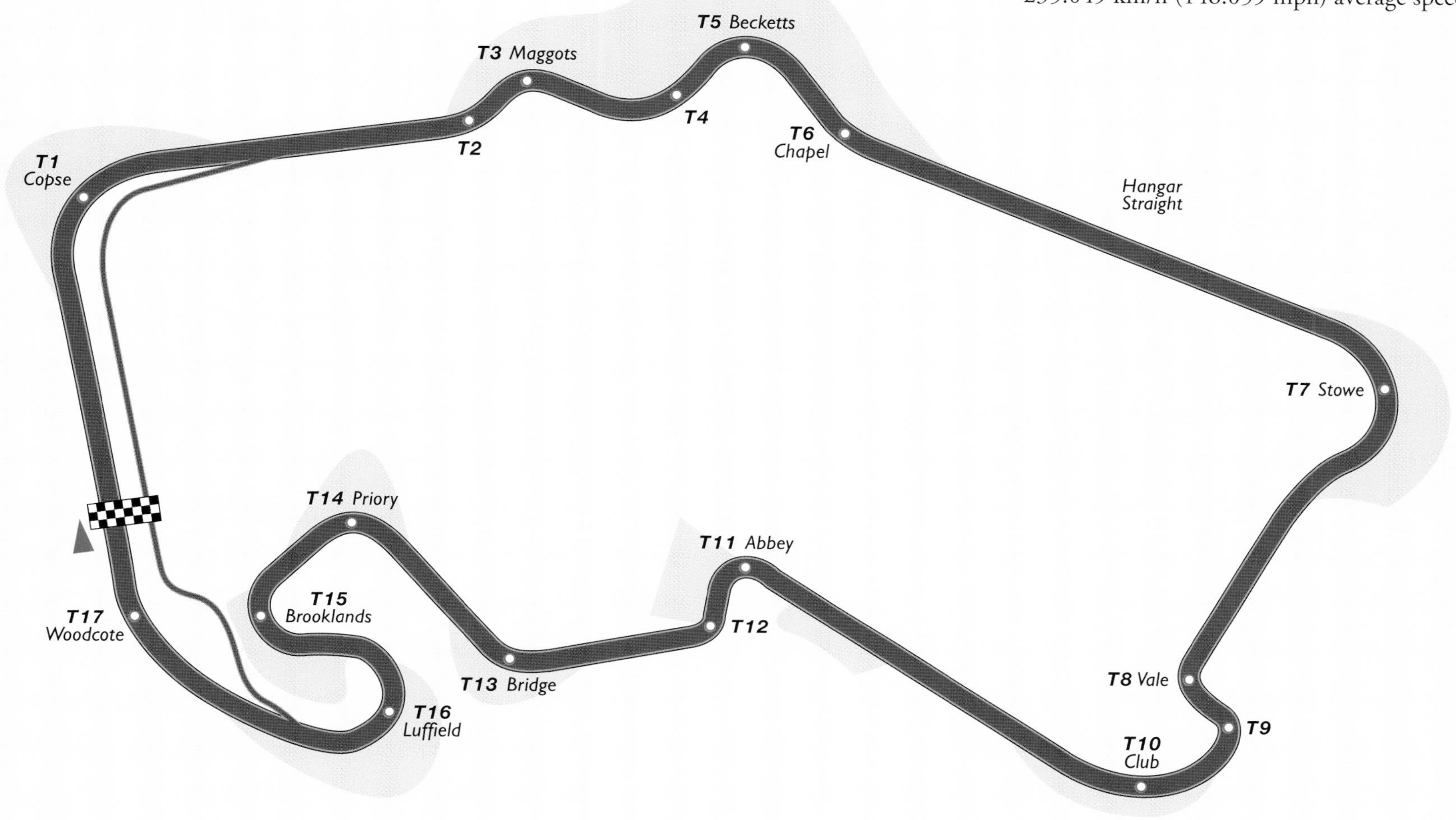

T1 Copse
T2
T3 Maggots
T4
T5 Becketts
T6 Chapel
Hangar Straight
T7 Stowe
T8 Vale
T9
T10 Club
T11 Abbey
T12
T13 Bridge
T14 Priory
T15 Brooklands
T16 Luffield
T17 Woodcote

MEMORIES

2003: TRACK INVASION

This race is best remembered for an Irish priest, wearing a kilt, who ran down the Hangar Straight while the race was on and had to be rugby tackled by a marshal. What's often overlooked is that Rubens Barrichello drove the race of his life, pressuring Kimi Räikkönen into a mistake at Bridge to take a fabulous win. Unfortunately for the Brazilian, his skills behind a luggage trolley aren't so hot. At Heathrow Airport that evening he hit a pillar and smashed his winning trophy.

MEMORIES

1999: STEWART'S ONE AND ONLY

During the race, the lead changed five times before the Stewart Grand Prix team claimed its only win. Heinz-Harald Frentzen led from pole, but his race was ended by an electrical problem. David Coulthard picked up the baton, but spun off in the rain. Ralf Schumacher was leading when he pitted, giving first position to Giancarlo Fisichella, but he spun too. This left Britain's Johnny Herbert clear to take the chequered flag for a popular victory.

NÜRBURGRING, GERMANY

The original Nürburgring, dubbed 'The Green Hell' by Jackie Stewart, had 22.5 km (14 miles) of endless turns and crests that threw all four wheels off the ground – it was perilously dangerous. Since 1984, the German Grand Prix has been run on a neutered circuit. This was built to the highest safety standards, but that has cost it some of the character of the original 'Ring. The German Grand Prix now alternates between here and the Hockenheimring. The Eifel region encounters unpredictable weather, which can turn carefully considered strategy into a lottery.

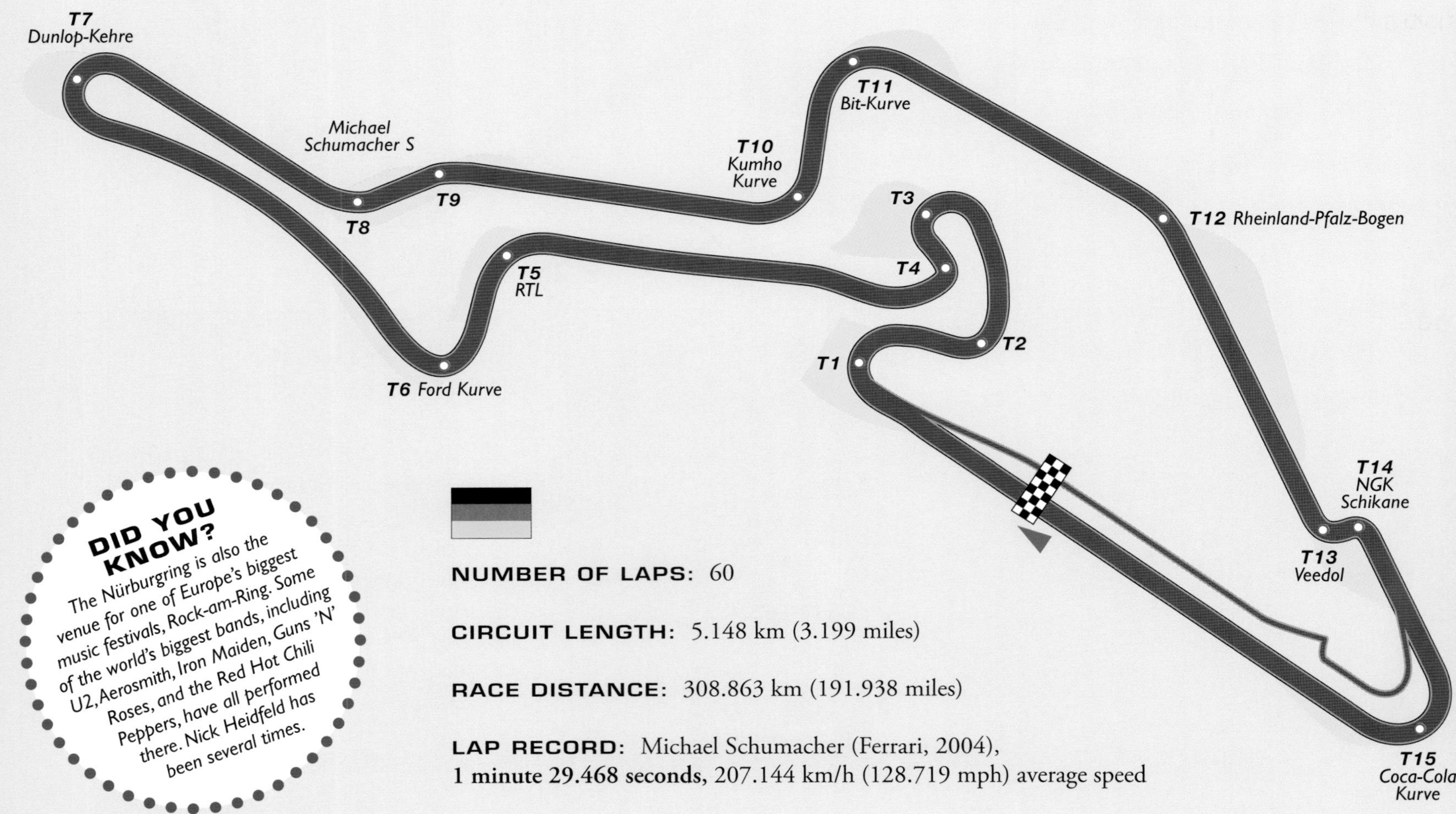

DID YOU KNOW?
The Nürburgring is also the venue for one of Europe's biggest music festivals, Rock-am-Ring. Some of the world's biggest bands, including U2, Aerosmith, Iron Maiden, Guns 'N' Roses, and the Red Hot Chili Peppers, have all performed there. Nick Heidfeld has been several times.

NUMBER OF LAPS: 60

CIRCUIT LENGTH: 5.148 km (3.199 miles)

RACE DISTANCE: 308.863 km (191.938 miles)

LAP RECORD: Michael Schumacher (Ferrari, 2004), **1 minute 29.468 seconds,** 207.144 km/h (128.719 mph) average speed

MEMORIES

1997: SO CLOSE FOR ARROWS

Switching from Williams to Arrows for the 1997 season had seen reigning champion Damon Hill suffer a reversal of fortune. The car qualified at the back of the grid at the opening race, but Hungary proved magical. Hill passed his old nemesis, Michael Schumacher, to take the lead, and was cruising to victory when, two and a half laps from the end, he suffered a hydraulics glitch and limped home in second place behind Jacques Villeneuve.

BUDAPEST, HUNGARY

The Hungaroring is often compared to a go-kart track, due to its lack of straights. In fact, it has been dubbed 'Monaco without the buildings'. As a result, races can be processional, but it's also true that this circuit has hosted some truly remarkable results. It's at the first corner that the only real chance of a passing move lies. The final section of curves forces cars to bunch up tightly. Precision is of key importance, with each corner leading into the next. And it can be hard on tyres. Cars require mechanical grip and a torquey engine.

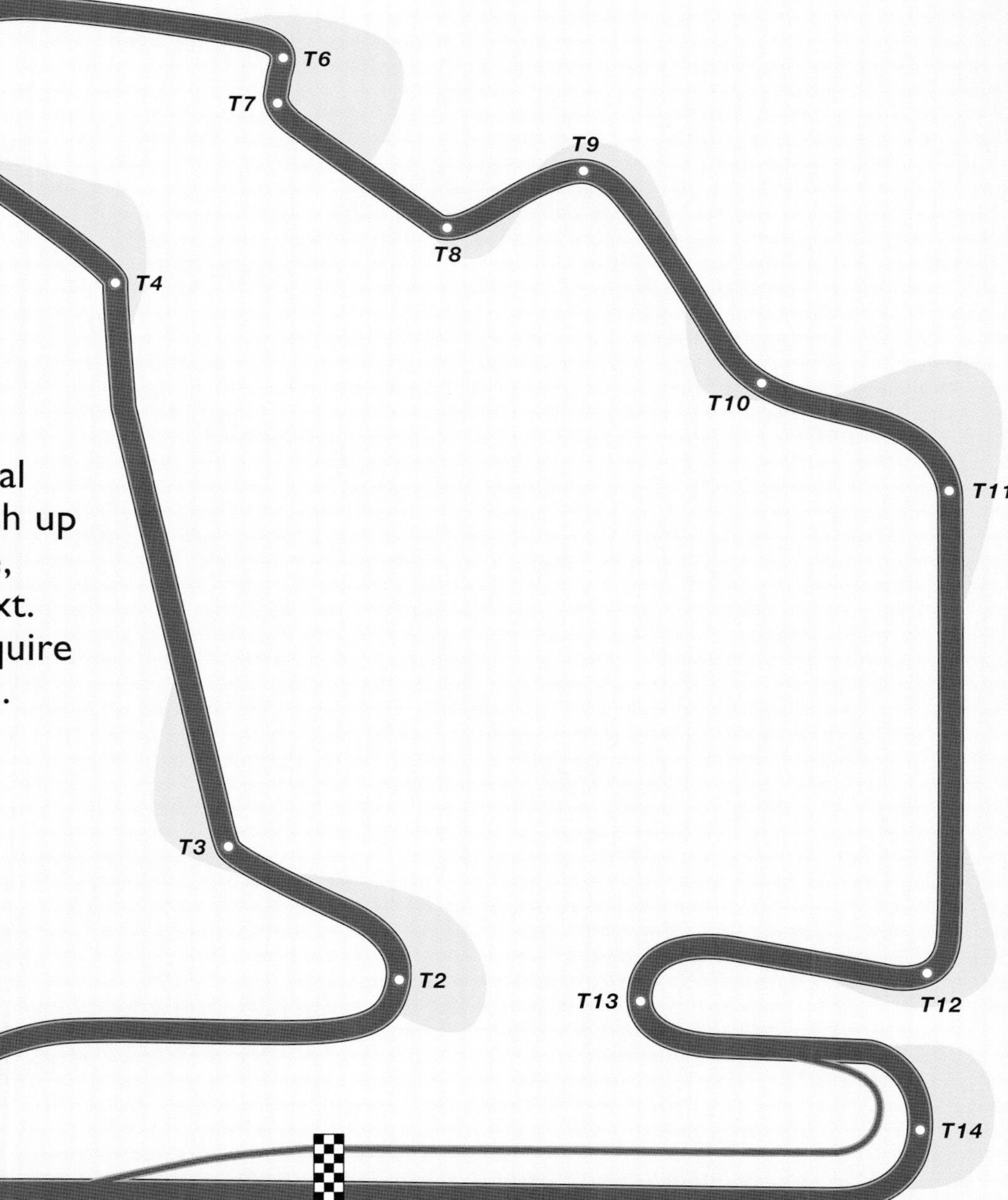

NUMBER OF LAPS: 70

CIRCUIT LENGTH: 4.381 km (2.722 miles)

RACE DISTANCE: 306.458 km (190.420 miles)

LAP RECORD:
Michael Schumacher (Ferrari, 2004),
1 minute 19.071 seconds,
199.461 km/h (123.945 mph) average speed

SPA-FRANCORCHAMPS, BELGIUM

Spa is exactly as a Grand Prix track should be – fast, fearsome, and full of atmosphere, with undulating asphalt ploughing through dense forest and sweeping around mountains. For the drivers it's a test, and for the strategists it's a nightmare, as the weather in the Ardennes is wildly unpredictable. It can be bone dry at the far side of the circuit and flooded in the pits. The signature corner is Eau Rouge, a valley that features an uphill kink with a blind crest taken at 298 km/h (185 mph).

NUMBER OF LAPS: 44

CIRCUIT LENGTH: 7.004 km (4.352 miles)

RACE DISTANCE: 308.052 km (191.410 miles)

LAP RECORD: Kimi Räikkönen (McLaren, 2004), **1 minute 45.108 seconds,** 238.931 km/h (148.471 mph) average speed

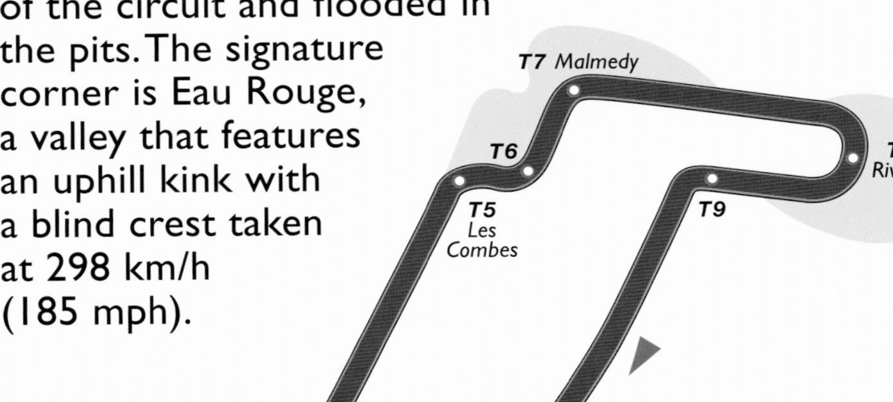

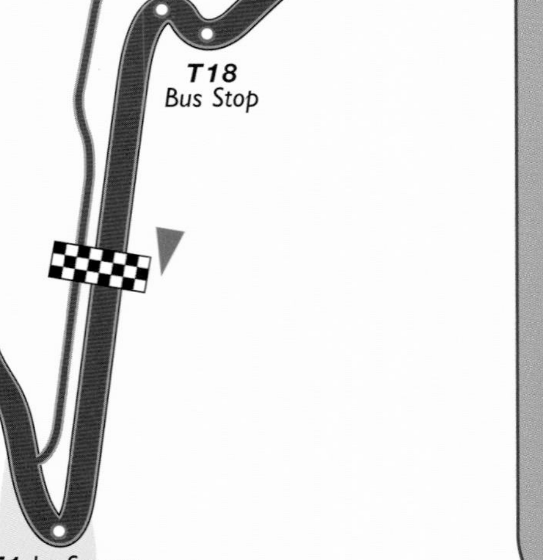

1998: CARNAGE AT THE START

David Coulthard spun into the wall after Turn 1, triggering a 13-car pile-up – the biggest in Formula 1 history. After the restart, Michael Schumacher built up a 40-second lead in the wet before slamming into the back of Coulthard as he went to lap the McLaren. Schumacher was furious, claiming Coulthard had tried to kill him. Damon Hill went on to take Jordan's first win, with team mate Ralf Schumacher in second.

MEMORIES

MEMORIES

1971: ALMOST TOO CLOSE TO CALL

Race finishes don't get any closer or more exciting than the 1971 Italian Grand Prix. The first five drivers home were covered by just 0.61 seconds! It was the closest finish ever, and gave BRM's Peter Gethin his only Grand Prix win. He beat Ronnie Peterson across the line by 0.01 seconds, followed by François Cevert, Mike Hailwood, and Howard Ganley.

NUMBER OF LAPS: 53

CIRCUIT LENGTH: 5.793 km (3.600 miles)

RACE DISTANCE: 306.720 km (190.596 miles)

LAP RECORD: Rubens Barrichello (Ferrari, 2004), **1 minute 21.046 seconds,** 257.320 km/h (159.898 mph) average speed

MONZA, ITALY

A cathedral of speed, Monza has hosted Grands Prix since 1922, and while the circuit no longer utilizes its now crumbling, historic banking, the experience is still epic. This is the fastest circuit in Formula 1 racing, and can be taken at an average speed of up to 257 km/h (160 mph). This is a power circuit, so cars run with almost no wing and get to fully utilize KERS. Because the start/finish straight is so long, there's an approximate 25-second penalty for making a pit stop – and that means most teams run a one-stop strategy.

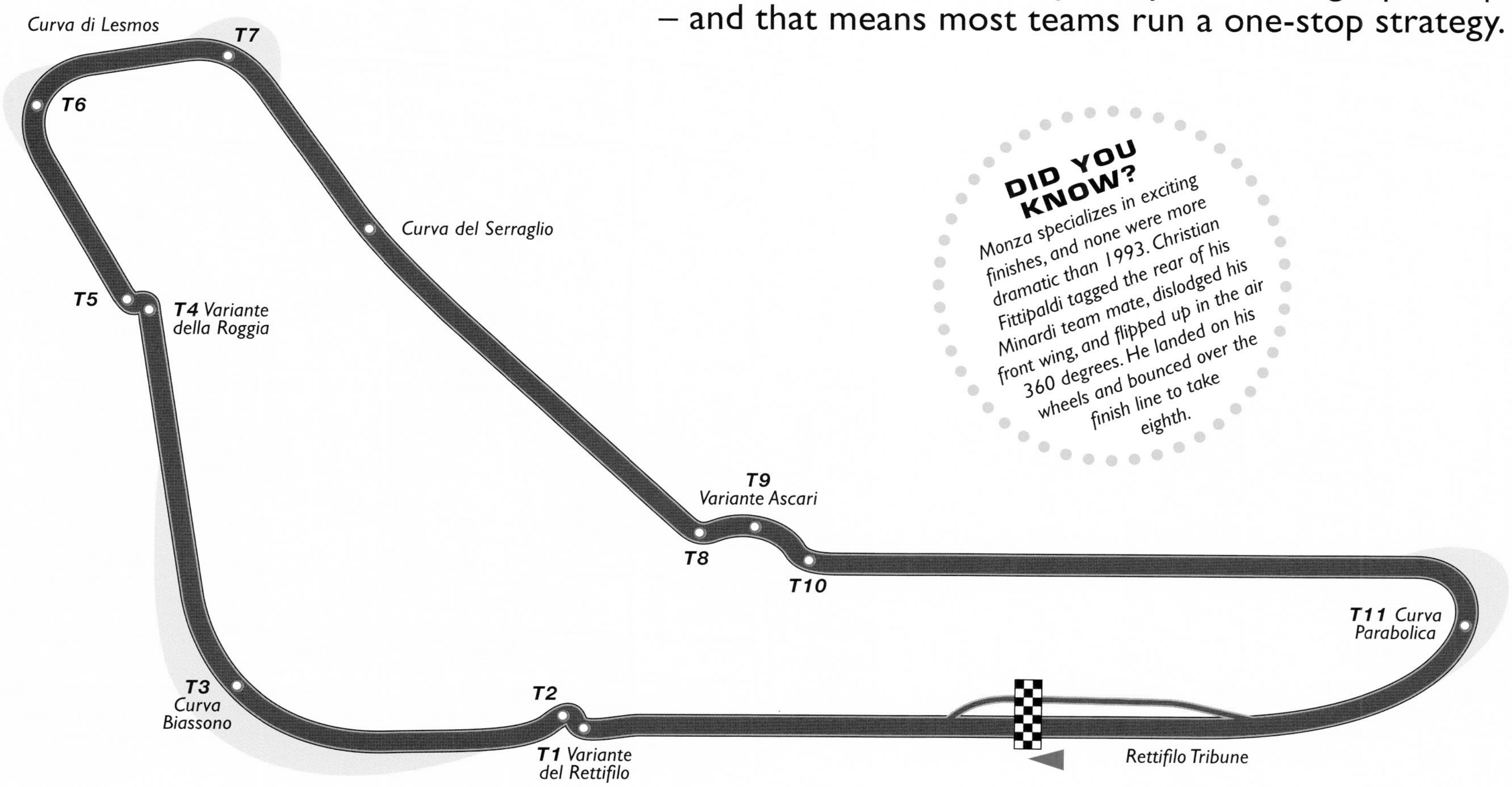

Curva di Lesmos
T7
T6
Curva del Serraglio
T5
T4 *Variante della Roggia*
T9 *Variante Ascari*
T8
T10
T11 *Curva Parabolica*
T3 *Curva Biassono*
T2
T1 *Variante del Rettifilo*
Rettifilo Tribune

DID YOU KNOW?

Monza specializes in exciting finishes, and none were more dramatic than 1993. Christian Fittipaldi tagged the rear of his Minardi team mate, dislodged his front wing, and flipped up in the air 360 degrees. He landed on his wheels and bounced over the finish line to take eighth.

SINGAPORE

Formula 1 racing's only night race is a great spectacle with a fantastic backdrop. It does threaten to throw the drivers' body clocks though, so they maintain European time and sleep late, often with their hotel bedroom windows blacked out. The circuit is characterized by bumps and cambers, and as the street sections differ from the smooth asphalt of the designated racing circuit, it provides a set-up conundrum. In 2008, Mark Webber's car is believed to have suffered an electrical surge when a subway train passed underneath the track!

NUMBER OF LAPS: 61

CIRCUIT LENGTH: 5.067 km (3.150 miles)

RACE DISTANCE: 309.087 km (192.066 miles)

LAP RECORD: Kimi Räikkönen (Ferrari, 2008), **1 minute 45.599 seconds,** 172.740 km/h (107.340 mph) average speed

T1
T2
T3
T4 Republic Boulevard
T5
T6 Raffles Boulevard
T7
Nicoll Highway
T8
Stamford Road
T9
St Andrews Road
T10
T11
T12
Anderson Bridge
T13
Esplanade Drive
T14
Raffles Avenue
T15
T16
T17
T18
T19
T20
T21
T22
T23

MEMORIES

2008: ALONSO'S GOOD NIGHT

Having raced an uncompetitive car aggressively all season, Renault finally gave Fernando Alonso a car he could fight with in Singapore. However, technical problems in qualifying meant he had to start in 15th place on the grid. Nevertheless, when his Renault team mate Nelson Piquet hit the wall, Alonso was able to capitalize on the safety car, and take his first win of the year.

MEMORIES

2005: THE NEW GENERATION

Fernando Alonso was out to prove himself a worthy champion, and what he did at Suzuka was startling. He passed Schumacher around the outside of the terrifying 130R corner to claim third. It was one of the finest moves ever. Meanwhile, showman Kimi Räikkönen waited until the final lap before passing Giancarlo Fisichella around the outside of Turn 1, in a nail-biting finale.

SUZUKA, JAPAN

Suzuka is a truly technical circuit with a lot of character. It features some wonderfully rewarding corners and enthusiastic Japanese fans. This figure-eight circuit looks a bit like a toy car track and is the only F1 track to cross itself. The highlight of the lap is 130R, a 130-degree, 306-km/h (190-mph) flat left-hander that can give a driver goosebumps. After the race, the drivers retire to the circuit's Log Cabin bar to blast out some karaoke tunes.

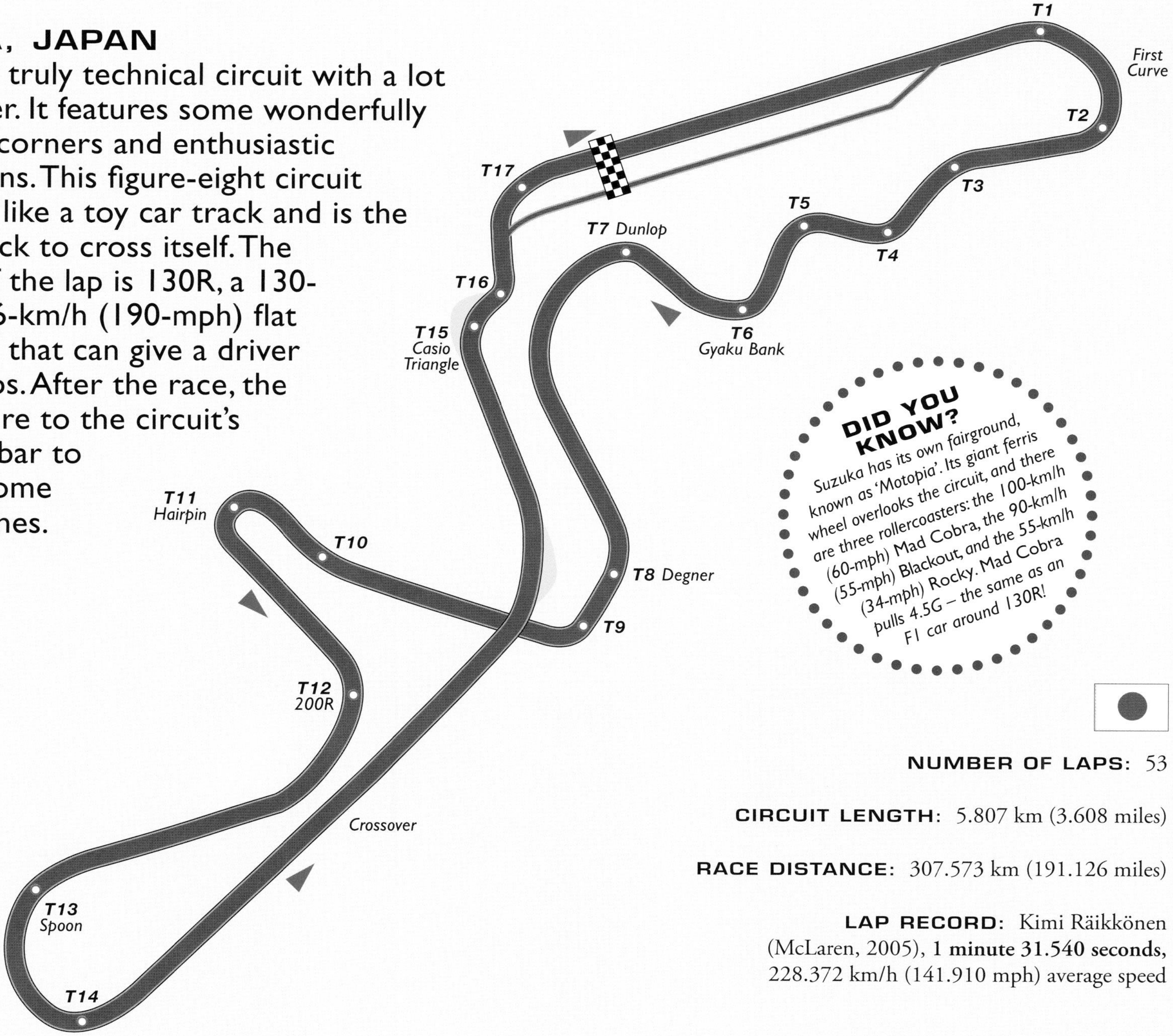

T1
First Curve
T2
T3
T4
T5
T6 Gyaku Bank
T7 Dunlop
T8 Degner
T9
T10
T11 Hairpin
T12 200R
Crossover
T13 Spoon
T14
T15 Casio Triangle
T16
T17

DID YOU KNOW?

Suzuka has its own fairground, known as 'Motopia'. Its giant ferris wheel overlooks the circuit, and there are three rollercoasters: the 100-km/h (60-mph) Mad Cobra, the 90-km/h (55-mph) Blackout, and the 55-km/h (34-mph) Rocky. Mad Cobra pulls 4.5G – the same as an F1 car around 130R!

NUMBER OF LAPS: 53

CIRCUIT LENGTH: 5.807 km (3.608 miles)

RACE DISTANCE: 307.573 km (191.126 miles)

LAP RECORD: Kimi Räikkönen (McLaren, 2005), **1 minute 31.540 seconds,** 228.372 km/h (141.910 mph) average speed

T14
Subida dos Boxes

T10
Bico de Pato

T13

T15

T8

T12
Junçao

T11
Mergulho

T9
Pinheirinho

T7
Curva do Laranjinha

T5

Des cida do Lago

T4

T6
Ferra Dura

T1
Senna S

Reta Oposta

T2

T3
Curva do Sol

NUMBER OF LAPS: 71

CIRCUIT LENGTH: 4.309 km (2.677 miles)

RACE DISTANCE: 305.909 km (190.067 miles)

LAP RECORD: Juan Pablo Montoya (Williams, 2004), **1 minute 11.473 seconds** , 217.038 km/h (134.867 mph) average speed

SAO PAOLO, BRAZIL

Formula 1 racing is more popular in Brazil than in almost any other country. The fans that fill the grandstands are also the loudest, cheering on the Brazilian drivers and banging their samba drums. The Interlagos circuit isn't short on atmosphere. What it is short on are the state-of-the-art facilities that most other circuits on the calendar provide. The first left-right-left corner, a steep downhill complex known as the 'Senna S', is a great overtaking spot. The drivers will try to avoid going off at Turn 3, as it's swampland and full of snakes!

MEMORIES

2008: DOWN TO THE WIRE

McLaren's Lewis Hamilton had a seven-point lead over Ferrari's Felipe Massa going into the last race of the season. He just needed to finish fifth or better. Three laps from the end, though, Hamilton slid wide and let Sebastian Vettel through into fifth. With Massa crossing the line first, Hamilton needed to find a way past. Eventually, on the approach to the final corner of the last lap, Timo Glock ran wide and Lewis took fifth place and the title by the tightest of margins.

YAS MARINA CIRCUIT, ABU DHABI

A new addition to the roster of circuits in 2009, Abu Dhabi plans to host the most opulent racing spectacle of the year. Set on Yas Island east of the city, the circuit is essentially split into three sections – a high-speed section, a street section, and then a marina section to complete the lap. It hopes to combine the best bits of Monaco, Monza, and Hockenheim.

NUMBER OF LAPS: 55

CIRCUIT LENGTH:
5.554 km (3.451 miles)

RACE DISTANCE:
305.470 km (189.819 miles)

LAP RECORD:
n/a

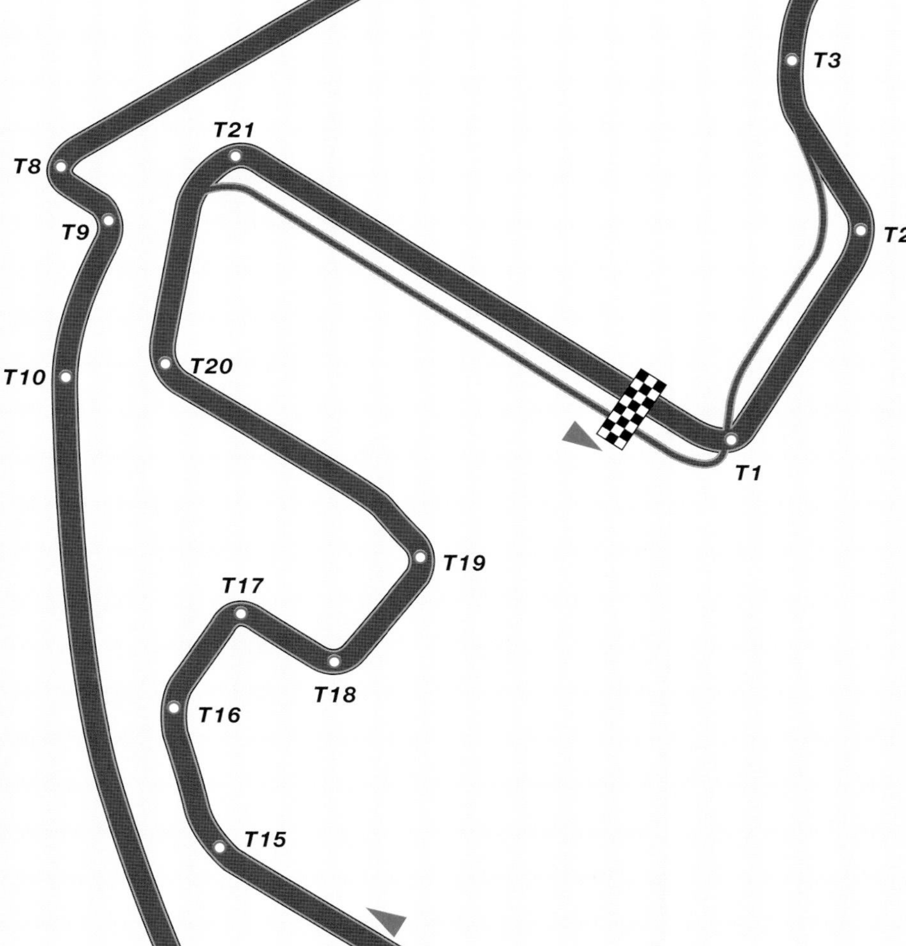

FACILITIES

LUXURY RACING

Built on an opulent waterfront setting, the Yas Marina Circuit is a luxury leisure destination in itself, and much more than just a race track. The venue features a shopping mall, the marina, a Ferrari theme park, apartments, driving school, kart centre, stunning entertainment suites, a solar-powered sun tower reserved for VIPs, and a 500-room luxury hotel through which the circuit actually passes.

The teams

Toro Rosso's Sebastian Vettel waves to his team as he takes the chequered flag at Monza to win the 2008 Italian Grand Prix.

There is more to F1 racing than the cars and the drivers. It's about teamwork. No driver, no matter how talented, can win a race on his own. Teams employ between 400 and 1,000 highly skilled staff to make sure the whole operation performs at its best, from the designers and mechanics through to the person who prepares the driver's lunch. And just like the drivers, they are driven to win.

"If someone said to me that you can have three wishes, my first would have been to get into racing, my second to be in Formula 1, my third to drive for Ferrari."

GILLES VILLENEUVE

Ferrari, or *Scuderia Ferrari* as they are properly known, is the most famous and successful team in F1 history. Originally formed as the works race team for Alfa Romeo, Ferrari is the only team to have competed in every season of the Formula 1 world championship since its inception in 1950. If it was ever to leave the sport, F1 racing just wouldn't be the same.

The distinctive scarlet paint, or *rosso corsa*, of the Scuderia harks back to the early days of Grand Prix racing when cars raced in national colours. Back then the British cars were all dark green, the French blue, and the Italian cars – Fiats, Alfa Romeos, Maseratis, and Ferraris – were, of course, red.

THE PRANCING HORSE

The prancing horse symbol was first used by World War I fighter ace Francesco Baracca. During the conflict, the Italian pilot shot down 34 enemy planes. After he was killed in 1918, his parents asked Enzo Ferrari – with whom they were friends – to paint the logo on his racing cars and continue Baracca's daredevil tradition.

TEAM VIPs

Stefano Domenicali (below) joined Ferrari in 1991 and quickly rose through the team's ranks. In 1995, he was made head of personnel, and then promoted to the position of team manager just a year later. At the end of the 2007 season, Ferrari announced he was to be made director of the Formula 1 team. Aldo Costa (right) joined Ferrari from Minardi in 1989, rising to become technical director in 2007.

THE CAR

Named to celebrate Ferrari's 60th year in Formula 1 racing, the F60 is the Scuderia's 2009 contender and the 55th model to wear the prancing horse badge. Its engine is built in-house – a department steeped in heritage. As old Enzo used to say: "Aerodynamics are for those who cannot manufacture good engines."

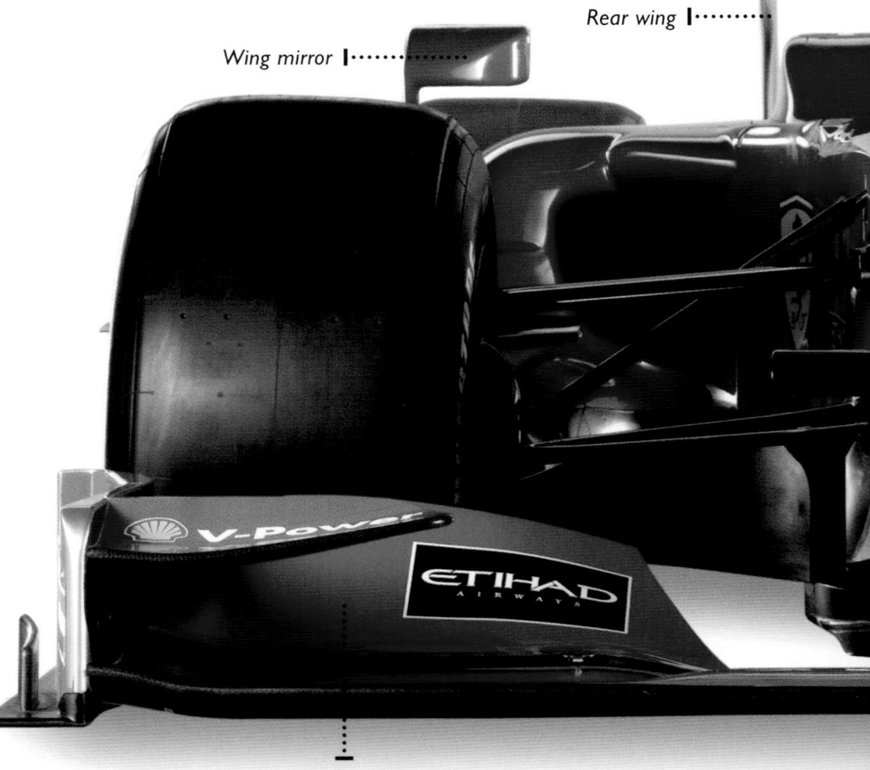

MOMENTS

Enzo Ferrari, the founder of the Scuderia, died on 14 August 1988. A week later, Gerhard Berger and Michele Alboreto completed a 1-2 victory at the Italian Grand Prix, and dedicated the win to their late team chief.

On the last lap of the 2002 Austrian Grand Prix at the A1 Ring, race leader Rubens Barrichello was ordered by Ferrari to pull over and let his team mate Michael Schumacher overtake and win the race. Both drivers were booed as they approached the podium, and an embarrassed Schumacher pushed Barrichello onto the top step. As a result of this incident, team orders during Formula 1 races were promptly banned.

THE TIFOSI

Ferrari boasts some of the most loyal fans in sport – the *tifosi*. The grandstands at most tracks appear painted red, with fans dressed in Ferrari colours. At Monza, fans bring along a 100 sq m (1,076 sq ft) Ferrari flag.

FACT FILE: FERRARI

DRIVERS: Felipe Massa, Kimi Räikkönen

BASE: Maranello, Italy

DEBUT: 1950 Monaco Grand Prix

RACES COMPETED: 785

CONSTRUCTORS' CHAMPIONSHIPS: 16 (1961, 1964, 1975, 1976, 1977, 1979, 1982,1983, 1999, 2000, 2001, 2002, 2003, 2004, 2007, 2008)

DRIVERS' CHAMPIONSHIPS: 15 (1952, 1953, 1956, 1958, 1961, 1964, 1975, 1977, 1979, 2000, 2001, 2002, 2003, 2004, 2007)

RACE VICTORIES: 209

POLE POSITIONS: 203

FASTEST LAPS: 219

FAMOUS DRIVERS:
Michael Schumacher (1996–2006)
Niki Lauda (1974–1977)
John Surtees (1963–1966)
Mike Hawthorn (1953–1955, 1957–1958)
Alberto Ascari (1950–1954)

information correct up to FORMULA 1 GROSSER PREIS SANTANDER VON DEUTSCHLAND 2009

The second most successful team in Formula 1 history, McLaren has a reputation for unflinching attention to detail – so much so that some feel it has quite a cold, austere image. But beneath the grey uniform lies the beating heart of a red-blooded race team. The team's state-of-the-art facilities make it one of the most resourceful engineering companies on the planet, but the focus has and always will be F1 racing.

INNOVATION

Outside racing, McLaren has created supercars including the McLaren F1 road car. In addition, McLaren has developed a pod to measure and relay healthcare information to doctors (left), bomb-resistant seats for armoured personnel carriers, and composites for the *Beagle 2* space probe.

TEAM VIPs

In 2009, after 28 years at the top, team principal Ron Dennis (far right) handed control over to his deputy Martin Whitmarsh (near right), who joined McLaren in 1989. Whitmarsh oversees managing director Jonathan Neale and engineering director Paddy Lowe. Norbert Haug, vice president of Mercedes-Benz Motorsport, is also omnipresent in the garage.

MOMENTS

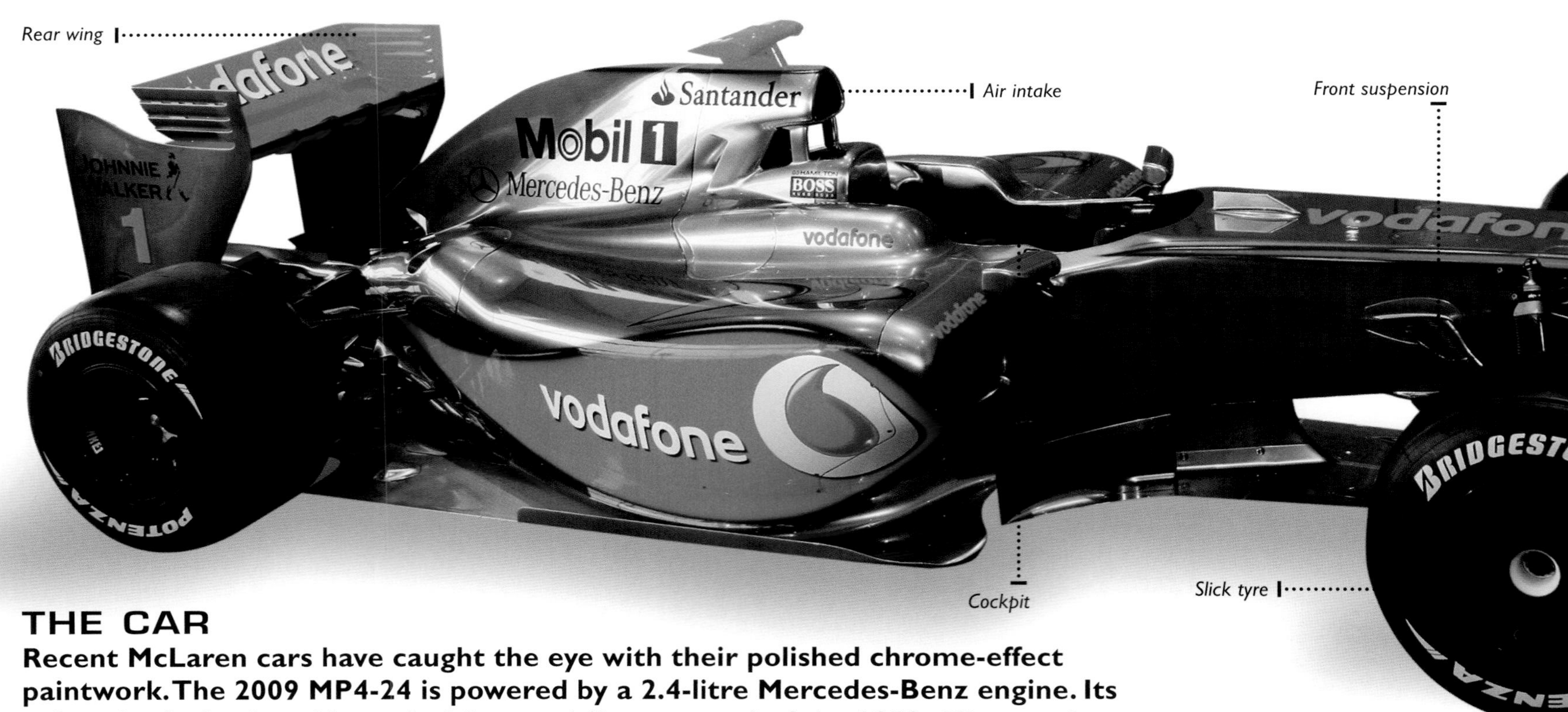

THE CAR

Recent McLaren cars have caught the eye with their polished chrome-effect paintwork. The 2009 MP4-24 is powered by a 2.4-litre Mercedes-Benz engine. Its colour harks back to Mercedes' famous 'silver arrows' of the 1950s. The number '1' on the nose and rear wing honours Lewis Hamilton's title victory in 2008.

HQ

For McLaren's new headquarters, architect Norman Foster designed a 'yin'-shaped, environmentally friendly building, which is low and flat with subterranean labs, wind tunnel, and engineering facilities. Opened in 2004, the state-of-the-art facility is thought to have cost £300 million to construct.

BRUCE McLAREN

In 1959, 22-year-old New Zealander Bruce McLaren became the youngest winner of an F1 race at that time. He founded Bruce McLaren Motor Racing in 1963 with a group of friends. He died at the wheel of one of his own cars in 1970.

Mika Häkkinen won the 1998 world championship three years after a crash saw him lying in a coma. Häkkinen crashed during practice for the 1995 Australian Grand Prix in Adelaide. An emergency tracheotomy had to be performed on him at the side of the track to save his life. Remarkably, he was back racing for the start of the 1996 season, won his first race in 1997, and the first of two world drivers' championships a year later.

McLaren's chief designer, Mike Coughlan, was found in possession of secret Ferrari documents in 2007. The team was fined US$100 million by the FIA, and had its constructors' points for that year taken away.

"If you cut me I'd bleed McLaren, but it goes beyond that. The DNA of McLaren is in me and I'm in the DNA of McLaren."

RON DENNIS

Front wing

TROPHY KEEPING

McLaren is very proud of its trophy collection, and drivers have to settle for replicas. An exception was made when Lewis Hamilton won the 2008 Monaco Grand Prix and was allowed to keep the trophy. Ironically, the Monaco trophy is the most inexpensive to reproduce.

FACT FILE: McLAREN

DRIVERS: Lewis Hamilton, Heikki Kovalainen

BASE: Woking, UK

DEBUT: 1966 Monaco Grand Prix

RACES COMPETED: 657

CONSTRUCTORS' CHAMPIONSHIPS: 8 (1974, 1984, 1985, 1988, 1989, 1990, 1991, 1998)

DRIVERS' CHAMPIONSHIPS: 12 (1974, 1976, 1984, 1985, 1986, 1988, 1989, 1990, 1991, 1998, 1999, 2008)

RACE VICTORIES: 162

POLE POSITIONS: 141

FASTEST LAPS: 137

FAMOUS DRIVERS:
Kimi Räikkönen (2002–2006)
Mika Häkkinen (1993–2001)
Ayrton Senna (1988–1993)
Alain Prost (1984–1989)
Niki Lauda (1982–1985)
James Hunt (1976–1978)

information correct up to FORMULA 1 GROSSER PREIS SANTANDER VON DEUTSCHLAND 2009

"We wanted to be in the points in our first year, 2006; to be on the podium in '07; to win our first race in '08; and to fight for the championship in 2009 onwards. We have achieved all these targets in the previous years, so it is clear what we have to go for this year."

DR MARIO THEISSEN

The Sauber team was a well-run, highly respected team that launched the careers of several great drivers, but never came close to winning... until BMW took over. Now the team has the resources it needs to challenge for the championship, and a methodical team boss with a history of always meeting his targets.

Driver Nick Heidfeld knows the team inside and out. He was at Sauber between 2001 and 2003. Then, after a year at Jordan, he raced with a BMW engine at Williams in 2005. Then it was back to Hinwil after the German car giant had bought Sauber.

TEAM VIPs

Dr Mario Theissen (on the right) joined BMW straight from university in 1977, and became motorsport director in 1999. Theissen persuaded BMW to buy the Sauber team and install him as team principal. He kept on Sauber's Willy Rampf (left) to act as technical director.

HOME FROM HOME

BMW Sauber has one of the most attractive motorhomes in the F1 paddock, and its simple design, rich in natural light, is also quick to put up and take down. The central entertaining area is built around four trucks, with a glass frontage and canvas roof, and takes 13 hours to erect and dismantle.

THE CAR

The team focused on its 2009 car in the middle of 2008, particularly its complex Kinetic Energy Recovery System (KERS). However, the weight of the system presented a problem, and during the 2009 season the team was forced to create a lighter chassis to overcome ballast issues. The F1.09 is powered by a BMW V8 engine manufactured in Munich, Germany, while the chassis was made in Switzerland.

MOMENTS

Twelve months after suffering a horrendous accident at Montreal in 2007, Robert Kubica returned to Canada to take his and the team's maiden victory. Kubica and Kimi Räikkönen were sitting at the end of the pitlane, waiting for the green light, when Lewis Hamilton arrived behind them at speed, skidded, and hit Räikkönen's Ferrari. "I have to thank him for choosing Kimi rather than me," joked Kubica afterwards. And to make the day even better, Nick Heidfeld finished second to give BMW Sauber a 1-2.

SIDE SHOW

In 1979 and 1980, Grands Prix were supported by BMW's Procar event – a race made up of 500-hp BMW M1 supercars. The top five F1 qualifiers on Saturday would then battle it out against 15 other racers. The thrilling '79 season was won by Niki Lauda, and the '80 title by Nelson Piquet Sr.

ALBERT 3

The fastest supercomputer in industrial use in Europe, 'Albert 3' powers BMW Sauber's computational fluid dynamics (CFD) department, which simulates airflow and heat around the car. The machine has a total memory of 8,448 GB and a maximum power of 50,700 GigaFlops. That's the equivalent of 48,000 home PCs.

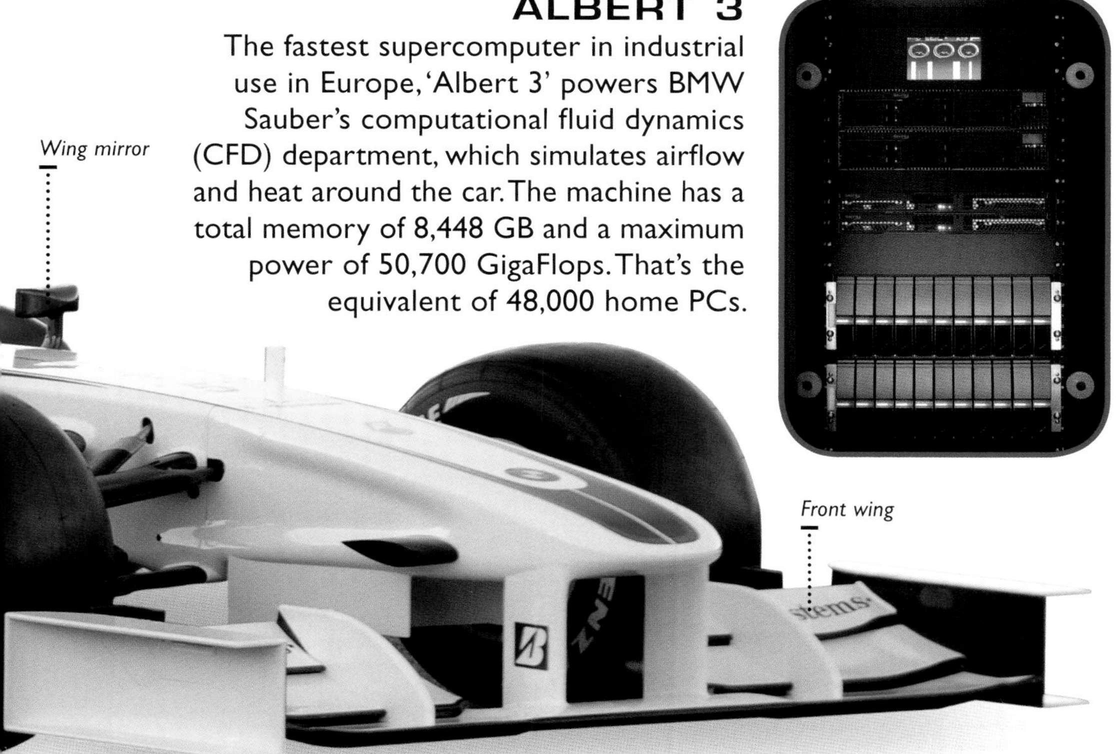

FACT FILE: BMW SAUBER

DRIVERS: Robert Kubica, Nick Heidfeld

BASE: Hinwil, Switzerland

DEBUT: 1993 South African Grand Prix *(as Sauber)*

RACES COMPETED: 279

CONSTRUCTORS' CHAMPIONSHIPS: 0

DRIVERS' CHAMPIONSHIPS: 0

RACE VICTORIES: 1

POLE POSITIONS: 1

FASTEST LAPS: 2

FAMOUS DRIVERS:
Jacques Villeneuve (2005–2006)
Felipe Massa (2002, 2004–2005)
Heinz-Harald Frentzen (1994–1996, 2002)
Kimi Räikkönen (2001)
Jean Alesi (1998–1999)
Johnny Herbert (1996–1998)

information correct up to FORMULA 1 GROSSER PREIS SANTANDER VON DEUTSCHLAND 2009

"We only exist to race."

SIR FRANK WILLIAMS

Williams is as traditional a racing team as you'll find anywhere in motorsport. It exists for one purpose only: to race. Whereas other teams are backed by car manufacturers or drinks companies, or have their drive-train constructed by another team, Williams is truly independent. The team came from humble beginnings, but was a force in the 1980s and dominant during the '90s. It's hoping to rekindle that magic.

TEAM VIPs

Perhaps the ultimate racer among team chiefs, Sir Frank Williams (below left) established Williams Grand Prix Engineering in 1977 with technical director Patrick Head (below right). Patrick, a no-nonsense character, has remained the team's technical overlord ever since, and is a 30 per cent shareholder in the team. "Is Patrick intimidating? I didn't find him so at first, but back then I was the boss," jokes Sir Frank.

FAMILY TIES

If you want to race for Williams, it'll help if your dad was an F1 driver. Nico Rosberg and Kazuki Nakajima both have F1 dads. So did Jacques Villeneuve and Damon Hill. And Ralf Schumacher was related to someone famous too.

ALAN JONES

Asked to nominate their favourite driver, Frank and Patrick always point to 'AJ'. The Australian won the title in a Williams in 1980. He wore red underpants for good luck, but won races not through good fortune but by fighting. He once punched a sponsor – something modern drivers are discouraged from doing.

THE CAR

The Williams FW31 is powered by a Toyota V8 engine. While the other teams that chose to run Kinetic Energy Recovery Systems (KERS) in 2009 decided to base their system around super-capacitor batteries, Williams has developed a more unusual flywheel method, where braking energy is used to turn a flywheel, which spins when extra power is needed.

It was fitting that this most patriotic of British teams should take its first victory at Silverstone. The FW07 was rapidly improving, and Alan Jones proved that by taking pole position. However, on lap 39 his engine overheated, handing victory to his team mate Clay Regazzoni (left).

Formula I racing was never the same again after I May 1994. Leading the San Marino Grand Prix, Ayrton Senna's Williams-Renault went off the track at Tamborello and slammed into a concrete wall. The 34-year-old – a hero to millions – suffered fatal head injuries. Ayrton's state funeral was the biggest public event in Brazilian history. His coffin was driven through the streets aboard a fire engine, while fighter jets roared overhead. The wrecked car was impounded by Italian authorities while they investigated the crash and what caused it. Those causes remain a mystery and, ultimately, Frank Williams was absolved of responsibility.

SPORTING LIFE

Although English, Frank Williams attended school in Scotland, and played rugby for Scotland's Under-15 team, while Patrick Head has an enduring love of the sea, having studied at the Royal Naval College in Dartmouth. Perhaps as a result, Williams employs a number of ex-professional rugby players and experienced sailors in engineering and marketing roles. Every year, Williams enters a boat in the famous Cowes Week yachting regatta, where team manager and helmsman Tim Newton puts team work to the test.

FACT FILE: WILLIAMS

DRIVERS: Nico Rosberg, Kazuki Nakajima

BASE: Grove, UK

DEBUT: 1977 Spanish Grand Prix

RACES COMPETED: 576

CONSTRUCTORS' CHAMPIONSHIPS: 9 (1980, 1981, 1986, 1987, 1992, 1993, 1994, 1996, 1997)

DRIVERS' CHAMPIONSHIPS: 7 (1980, 1982, 1987, 1992, 1993, 1996, 1997)

RACE VICTORIES: 113

POLE POSITIONS: 125

FASTEST LAPS: 129

FAMOUS DRIVERS:
Jacques Villeneuve (1996–1998)
Damon Hill (1993–1996)
Ayrton Senna (1994)
Alain Prost (1993)
Nigel Mansell (1985–1988, 1991–1992, 1994)
Alan Jones (1978–1981)

information correct up to FORMULA I GROSSER PREIS SANTANDER VON DEUTSCHLAND 2009

Toro Rosso

It was meant to be the 'B' team to Red Bull's main team, but in 2008 Scuderia Toro Rosso – formerly perennial minnows Minardi – outpaced its big brother to take its first victory. While Italy's preferred team may be Ferrari, Toro Rosso enjoys its status as the nation's favourite underdog. The next challenge for the Faenza team is to become a fully fledged constructor, as in the Minardi days. But now the team has tasted success and won't settle for the back of the grid.

EXPERIENCED NEWCOMER

Driver Sebastien Buemi is 2009's only rookie, while Sebastien Bourdais is in his second season. However, the Frenchman won four successive Champ Car titles in the US from 2004 to 2007, taking 31 wins and 27 poles along the way. He has also competed in the Le Mans 24-hour race seven times, finishing second in 2007 and 2009.

TEAM VIPs

Previously Ralf Schumacher's assistant manager, Franz Tost (below right), joined BMW as track operations manager and was there when the team first tested young Sebastian Vettel. A couple of years later, Tost was put in charge of the new Scuderia Toro Rosso and set his sights on recruiting the German *wunderkind*. Tost once reportedly lost his temper with driver Scott Speed, and a scuffle ensued. Another no-nonsense character is technical director Giorgio Ascanelli (below left), who was Ayrton Senna's engineer at McLaren.

THE CAR

The Toro Rosso STR4 is the same as Red Bull Racing's RB5. Almost. Both cars were designed by Adrian Newey and constructed by Red Bull Technology. Aerodynamically they're nearly identical. However, the RB5 uses Renault power, whereas Toro Rosso gets its engines from up the road in Maranello – from Ferrari. In 2008, this engine helped give Toro Rosso a faster car than Red Bull's 'A' team.

MOMENTS

The Faenza-based team had not troubled the podium in the 23 years since it was first established (Minardi's best result was fourth), so the 2008 Italian Grand Prix was a dream come true. Sebastian Vettel achieved pole position and then led the wet race lights to flag, becoming at the age of 21 the sport's youngest winner. The mechanics carried their driver down the pitlane on their shoulders, and then headed back to the factory for a party to remember.

MINARDI

Founded by Giancarlo Minardi, his eponymous team made its F1 debut in 1985 and contested 345 races. In that time they failed to win a single race, and scored just 38 points. It didn't matter – they had the best espresso in the paddock. They also gave Fernando Alonso his big break.

RAGING BULLS

The charging bull livery of the Toro Rosso cars was designed and painted by 81-year-old artist Professor Jos Pirkner. A fellow Austrian and close friend of Red Bull owner Dietrich Mateschitz, Pirkner is known largely for his metal sculptures, and also designed the trophies for the World Stunt Awards.

"Buemi faces a steep learning curve, but we should not forget he's still very young – he makes Vettel look like a veteran!"

FRANZ TOST

FACT FILE: TORO ROSSO

DRIVERS: Sebastien Bourdais, Sebastien Buemi

BASE: Faenza, Italy

DEBUT: 2006 Bahrain Grand Prix

RACES COMPETED: 62

CONSTRUCTORS' CHAMPIONSHIPS: 0

DRIVERS' CHAMPIONSHIPS: 0

RACE VICTORIES: 1

POLE POSITIONS: 1

FASTEST LAPS: 0

FAMOUS DRIVERS:
(**as Minardi*)
Sebastian Vettel (2007–2008)
Mark Webber (2002)*
Fernando Alonso (2001)*
Giancarlo Fisichella (1996)*
Pierluigi Martini (1985, 1988–1991, 1993–1995)*

information correct up to FORMULA 1 GROSSER PREIS SANTANDER VON DEUTSCHLAND 2009

"When Red Bull Racing entered F1, we grabbed headlines by offering a new take on what had become a very stuffy sport."

CHRISTIAN HORNER

Red Bull arrived in F1 racing with a bang. Having sponsored other teams for a decade, they bought the Jaguar team from Ford for £1. Then they went on a mission to recruit the best engineering brains they could find. They built the biggest motorhome in the paddock, and threw parties whether they'd scored points that day or not. Finally, in 2009, the efforts of those brains bore fruit and the team became winners.

TEAM VIPs

At 35, Christian Horner is the youngest team principal in F1 racing. Previously, he'd been a driver in the lower formulae and founded the F3000 title-winning Arden International team, which continues to compete in GP2. In 2005, he was tasked with turning the poorly performing team that was Jaguar Racing into the front-running Red Bull Racing.

Genius is an overused word, but most people would agree that designer Adrian Newey possesses an incredible mind when it comes to science and engineering. Previously at McLaren and Williams, his cars dominated the '90s, winning a total of 12 world titles. An enthusiastic amateur racer, he's known as 'crasher' behind his back.

For ten years Red Bull sponsored the Sauber team. But while buying that team was a possibility, Peter Sauber and Red Bull had a disagreement over drivers. In 2001, Sauber signed the inexperienced Kimi Räikkönen, while Red Bull favoured Brazilian Enrique Bernoldi. Where is Bernoldi now?

24HR PARTY PEOPLE

The team is famous for its huge, star-studded parties. At the team's Melbourne launch in 2005, pop star Pink (below) was invited to perform. At the end of the year, the team recreated a Chinese village, floated it on the river in Shanghai, and had a party. Then, at the season-closing party in Sao Paulo in 2006, Red Bull took over the vast Morumbi football stadium and invited several thousand of the team's friends.

In 2009, Red Bull finally got the win it had been working towards, taking a 1-2 finish in wet Shanghai. Sebastian Vettel (left) won the race. But Red Bull's first taste of champagne came in Monaco in 2006, when David Coulthard finished third. Team boss Christian Horner fulfilled a bet by jumping into the Energy Station's swimming pool wearing only a superman cape.

After 14 seasons and 246 Grands Prix, the 2008 finale in Brazil should have been a glorious day for Coulthard. He had a special white car made for him, which he crashed 10 seconds into the race.

THE ENERGY STATION

The Energy Station is Red Bull's travelling operations and hospitality centre at all European races. The three-storey structure takes 50 riggers over two days to build. It contains three bars and two kitchens, relaxation rooms and showers for the drivers, offices for management, dining areas for both Red Bull Racing and Toro Rosso personnel, and 300 square metres (3,230 square feet) of entertaining space upstairs, including a sun terrace and dance floor. In Monaco, the Energy Station is floated in the harbour and features a swimming pool. Over the weekend, Red Bull's chefs will prepare up to 13,500 meals for 7,500 guests, and the bar staff will mix 1,845 vodka Red Bulls.

THE CAR

New aerodynamic restrictions – wide front wings and narrow rear wings – threatened to make 2009's cars look ungainly and primitive. However, the Red Bull RB5 is an elegant car. While most cars are designed with computers, the original lines were sketched by Adrian Newey's own hand. Newey has always been skilled at capitalizing on technical changes, and the RB5 is a great example of his work.

FACT FILE: RED BULL

DRIVERS: Sebastian Vettel, Mark Webber

BASE: Milton Keynes, UK

DEBUT: 2005 Australian Grand Prix

RACES COMPETED: 80

CONSTRUCTORS' CHAMPIONSHIPS: 0

DRIVERS' CHAMPIONSHIPS: 0

RACE VICTORIES: 3

POLE POSITIONS: 4

FASTEST LAPS: 1

FAMOUS DRIVERS:
(**as Jaguar Racing, **as Stewart Grand Prix*)
David Coulthard (2005–2008)
Eddie Irvine (2000–2002*)
Johnny Herbert (1999**, 2000*)
Rubens Barrichello (1997–1999**)

information correct up to FORMULA 1 GROSSER PREIS SANTANDER VON DEUTSCHLAND 2009

"We have to stand up to Ferrari and take them on and beat them."

JOHN HOWETT

Toyota entered the Formula 1 world championship with one aim: to win. That, and beat Honda. Having succeeded in the World Rally Championship, it turned its Cologne factory into a state-of-the-art F1 facility, and spent a full year testing before entering the championship in 2002. In that first year, it scored just two points despite having the biggest budget of any team. However, it has made steady progress since then and in 2009 it had one of the most capable cars on the grid.

Jarno Trulli's grandfather was a winemaker, and the Italian racer now owns 35 hectares (85.5 acres) of vineyards in Pescara, his home town. "You have more time to reflect on what you are doing," says Jarno. "In F1 you are just flat-out all the time, it is a big rush."

TEAM VIPs

Tadashi Yamashina (above left) is Toyota Motorsport's chairman and team principal. Previously, he was president of Toyota's technical operations in the US, where he was called 'George' because it was easier for his colleagues to pronounce, and in deference to the country's incumbent president. Englishman John Howett (above right) joined Toyota's rally team in 1977, before going to work in road car marketing. He has been president of Toyota Motorsport since 2003.

THE CAR

The livery of Toyota's TF109 car features the team's signature red on white brushstroke, just like its previous cars, but this car is very different from its predecessors. Like Red Bull, the team has gone for a narrow front nose, pointing downwards to collect as much downforce as possible. It is powered by Toyota's RVX-09 2,398 cc engine, which is identical to the one found in the Williams cars.

MOMENTS

Timo Glock scored a magnificent second place at the 2008 Hungarian Grand Prix just two weeks after he had been stretchered away from the Hockenheimring in Germany. His car smashed into the pit wall after a rear suspension failure. Budapest gave the amiable German the first F1 podium finish in his career, four years after his F1 debut. It was also the team's best result in 61 races.

During Friday practice at the 2005 United States Grand Prix, Ralf Schumacher's Toyota suffered a puncture and was thrown into the wall at Turn 13. On Sunday, the teams using Michelin tyres pulled out and only the six Bridgestone-shod cars raced.

MULTICULTURAL TEAM

Formula 1 racing is a global business, and companies don't come more international than Toyota Motorsport. It is a Japanese company, based in Germany, with a workforce comprising over 40 different nationalities. The staff canteen has a varied menu of world food to suit every palate come lunchtime.

FACT FILE: TOYOTA

DRIVERS: Jarno Trulli, Timo Glock

BASE: Cologne, Germany

DEBUT: 2002 Australian Grand Prix

RACES COMPETED: 131

CONSTRUCTORS' CHAMPIONSHIPS: 0

DRIVERS' CHAMPIONSHIPS: 0

RACE VICTORIES: 0

POLE POSITIONS: 3

FASTEST LAPS: 2

FAMOUS DRIVERS:
Ralf Schumacher (2005–2007)
Olivier Panis (2003–2005)
Cristiano da Matta (2003)
Mika Salo (2002)

information correct up to FORMULA 1 GROSSER PREIS SANTANDER VON DEUTSCHLAND 2009

Cockpit

Front wing

FUJI SPEEDWAY

Toyota actually has its very own Grand Prix circuit. The Fuji Speedway has hosted the Japanese Grand Prix for the past two years. It was struck from the F1 calendar in 1977 after two spectators were killed, but returned in 2007 having had an extensive overhaul. It was the first track to feature in an arcade video game – Namco's *Pole Position*, back in 1982.

Having won back-to-back titles in 2005 and 2006, Renault has since struggled to produce a car that is a front-runner. However, thanks to the lead driver Fernando Alonso, around whom the team is increasingly built, anything is possible. Few drivers are capable of squeezing so much potential from a car. If they're to hold onto Alonso, though, Renault needs to give him the car he deserves.

"After his experience at McLaren, Fernando needed to be somewhere where he would feel good and feel settled. There was a lot of competition for his services, but in the end he chose what he knew."

FLAVIO BRIATORE

THE BOY IS BACK

Triple world champion Nelson Piquet saw out his career at Benetton, the forerunner to this team, in 1991. Back then his six-year-old son watched in the garage, propped up on Flavio Briatore's shoulders. These days Nelson Junior is an F1 driver in his own right.

TEAM VIPs

Flamboyant Flavio Briatore (above) claims he doesn't like motor racing, and it's true that he only entered the sport at the behest of the Benetton family. Nevertheless, he has achieved considerable success as a team principal and adds an air of showmanship to the paddock. Pat Symonds (right) is a died-in-the-wool engineer and utterly loyal to the team – he's been with them since they were called Toleman way back in 1982!

THE CAR

The Renault R29, with its shark-like nose and vivid paintwork, isn't traditionally beautiful. However, the most unusual thing about this car is that it's built in two different factories in two different countries. The Renault RS27 engine is built in Viry-Chatillon in France, while the car itself is designed and constructed in Enstone, UK, to the north of Oxford. Note the huge 'anvil' engine cover, which was first developed by Red Bull last year to aid high-speed stability.

MOMENTS

Despite running a fully French team between 1977 and 1985, Renault never finished higher than runner-up in the championship – the cars were quick but unreliable. In 2005, though, the R25 car had bombproof reliability and Fernando Alonso was as consistent as a Swiss watch. He took the title at Interlagos, with two races still to go, and became the sport's youngest-ever world champion at 24, a record since beaten by Lewis Hamilton.

F1 RACING'S FOOTBALL FANATIC

Briatore is now even bigger news in the back pages of British newspapers following his investment in Queens Park Rangers football club. He and Bernie Ecclestone masterminded a £14 million takeover. Many observers expect a spending spree on players.

SMOOTH OPERATOR

Flavio Briatore has dated some of the world's most beautiful women, including Heidi Klum and Naomi Campbell. In 2008, he tied the knot with Italian underwear model Elisabetta Gregoraci – 30 years his junior! Chauffeuring the newlyweds' vintage Rolls Royce at the wedding was Fernando Alonso.

BENETTON

Before 2002, the Enstone-based team went by the name of Italian fashion house Benetton. The team was established in 1986 and won championships with Michael Schumacher in 1994 and 1995. The team's first and last wins both came courtesy of Gerhard Berger – 11 years apart!

Wing mirror

Front wing

FACT FILE: RENAULT

DRIVERS: Fernando Alonso, Nelson Piquet Jr

BASE: Enstone, UK

DEBUT: 1977 British Grand Prix

RACES COMPETED: 254

CONSTRUCTORS' CHAMPIONSHIPS: 2 (2005, 2006)

DRIVERS' CHAMPIONSHIPS: 2 (2005, 2006)

RACE VICTORIES: 35

POLE POSITIONS: 50

FASTEST LAPS: 28

Note that these figures do not include the 238 races the team ran as Benetton

FAMOUS DRIVERS:
Giancarlo Fisichella (2005–2007)
Jarno Trulli (2002–2004)
Jenson Button (2002)
Alain Prost (1981–1983)
Rene Arnoux (1979–1982)

information correct up to FORMULA 1 GROSSER PREIS SANTANDER VON DEUTSCHLAND 2009

Brawn GP is the phoenix that rose from the ashes of Honda Racing. When the Japanese manufacturer pulled out, the staff of the Brackley-based team were left to fend for themselves. They knew they had a fast car, having focused on the 2009 model throughout the previous year. Team principal Ross Brawn led a management buy-out, the drivers accepted a pay cut, and the team arrived at the first race in Melbourne with only six days' worth of testing. Brawn GP won pole position and finished 1-2. It was the perfect start to the season.

VIRGIN TERRITORY

Having looked for some time at getting involved in F1 racing, entrepreneur Sir Richard Branson seized the opportunity with Brawn. According to Branson, whose Virgin Group will soon be sending paying passengers into space, "Virgin loves to invest in great engineers. In space we have Bert Ratan building Virgin Galactic spaceships for us. Ross [Brawn] is the genius of engineering down here on Earth."

TEAM VIPs

Team principal Ross Brawn (below right) was the technical director who took Michael Schumacher to all seven of his drivers' championships, first at Benetton and then at Ferrari. In 2007, he took a sabbatical, but returned with the ambition to run a team. He joined Honda alongside chief executive Nick Fry (below left). When Honda decided to quit at the end of 2008, the pair pulled off a management buy-out.

"We deserve this after the tough times we've had."

JENSON BUTTON

"This is the start of a very exciting journey for us."

RUBENS BARRICHELLO

Wing mirror

Slick tyre

Front wing

THE CAR

When the Brawn BGP 001 emerged for its debut test just two weeks before leaving for its first race, it was clear it was much faster than the opposition. While other teams had focused on '09 development six months previously, the Brawn car had a full 15 months' worth of development. The BGP-001 had been designed around a Honda engine, but at the last minute was adapted to take a Mercedes-Benz FO108W – the same engine used by McLaren.

MOMENTS

It was a fairytale. Having faced redundancy just a few weeks previously, Jenson Button led his team mate Rubens Barrichello across the line to win the 2009 FORMULA 1 ING AUSTRALIAN GRAND PRIX. Button got on the radio to his engineer and said he needed pinching. On the podium, Ross Brawn was rendered speechless. It was the first time a team had scored a 1-2 on its debut since Mercedes-Benz won the 1954 French Grand Prix.

THE PHOENIX

British American Racing vowed to win on its F1 debut in 1999. In fact, neither car finished and the team failed to score a single point that whole year. Honda bought the team outright in 2006 and it took one win. The manufacturer withdrew at the end of 2008, but the team carried on as Brawn GP. Winning in Australia in 2009 Button scored more points in that single race than he had in the previous two seasons.

Brawn found itself in court in 2009 over interpretation of the F1 rules. The matter concerned a three-tier diffuser, which helps suck the car to the ground and provide grip. In the end, the court declared the aerodynamic device legal.

AN EXPERIENCED PAIRING

Brawn has the most experienced driver pairing of any team. Before this season started, Button and Barrichello had between them competed in 421 Grands Prix. Rubens made his F1 debut at the 1993 South Africa Grand Prix and is the only current driver to have raced Ayrton Senna. At 37, he still believes he can be drivers' world champion. Driving the super-quick Brawn, who would bet against it?

FACT FILE: BRAWN GP

DRIVERS: Jenson Button, Rubens Barrichello

BASE: Brackley, UK

DEBUT: 2009 FORMULA 1 ING AUSTRALIAN GRAND PRIX

RACES COMPETED: 9

CONSTRUCTORS' CHAMPIONSHIPS: 0

DRIVERS' CHAMPIONSHIPS: 0

RACE VICTORIES: 6

POLE POSITIONS: 4

FASTEST LAPS: 4

FAMOUS DRIVERS:
(**as B.A.R*)
Takuma Sato (*2003–2005)
Jacques Villeneuve (*1999–2003)
Olivier Panis (*2001–2002)

information correct up to FORMULA 1 GROSSER PREIS SANTANDER VON DEUTSCHLAND 2009

Formula 1 fanatic Dr Vijay Mallya wanted to create a team that India's enormous population would support, and to find an F1 superstar with an Indian passport. Well, he's achieved one out of two so far, and the search for an Indian driver continues. Mallya, a billionaire industrialist, bought a share in the team that was previously Jordan, and aims to return it to the glory days it enjoyed in the late 1990s. He also throws the F1 paddock's most lavish yacht parties. Graham Hill may have been 'Mr Monaco', but Vijay is catching up fast.

As well as driving F1 cars, Adrian Sutil knows what he's doing behind the ivories, having trained as a concert pianist. His father, Jorge, is a famous conductor, and the young Adrian was set for musical stardom until he tried go-karting and ditched the piano.

TEAM VIPs

Team principal Dr Vijay Mallya (right) co-owns the team with Dutch IT millionaire Jan Mol. Brewery heir Vijay is responsible for Kingfisher beer, the most popular in India, and Whyte & MacKay whisky. He also owns Kingfisher Airlines and, for fun, the Bangalore Royal Challengers cricket team. In India, he is known as 'the king of good times'.

PARTY BOAT

Mallya throws F1 parties aboard his 95-metre (312-foot) yacht, *Indian Empress*. He bought the floating palace in 2006 and it is still one of the largest private yachts in the world.

"In a country of more than a billion, there has to be a Lewis Hamilton somewhere. Yes, it's my dream to see an Indian driving a Force India car."

DR VIJAY MALLYA

THE CAR

For 2009, Force India entered into a five-year partnership with McLaren-Mercedes. The VJM02 has the same Mercedes-Benz FO108W engine as McLaren and Brawn GP, and also shares McLaren's gearbox, hydraulic systems, and KERS. Also, McLaren man Simon Roberts has taken the position of Force India's chief executive, overseeing the partnership.

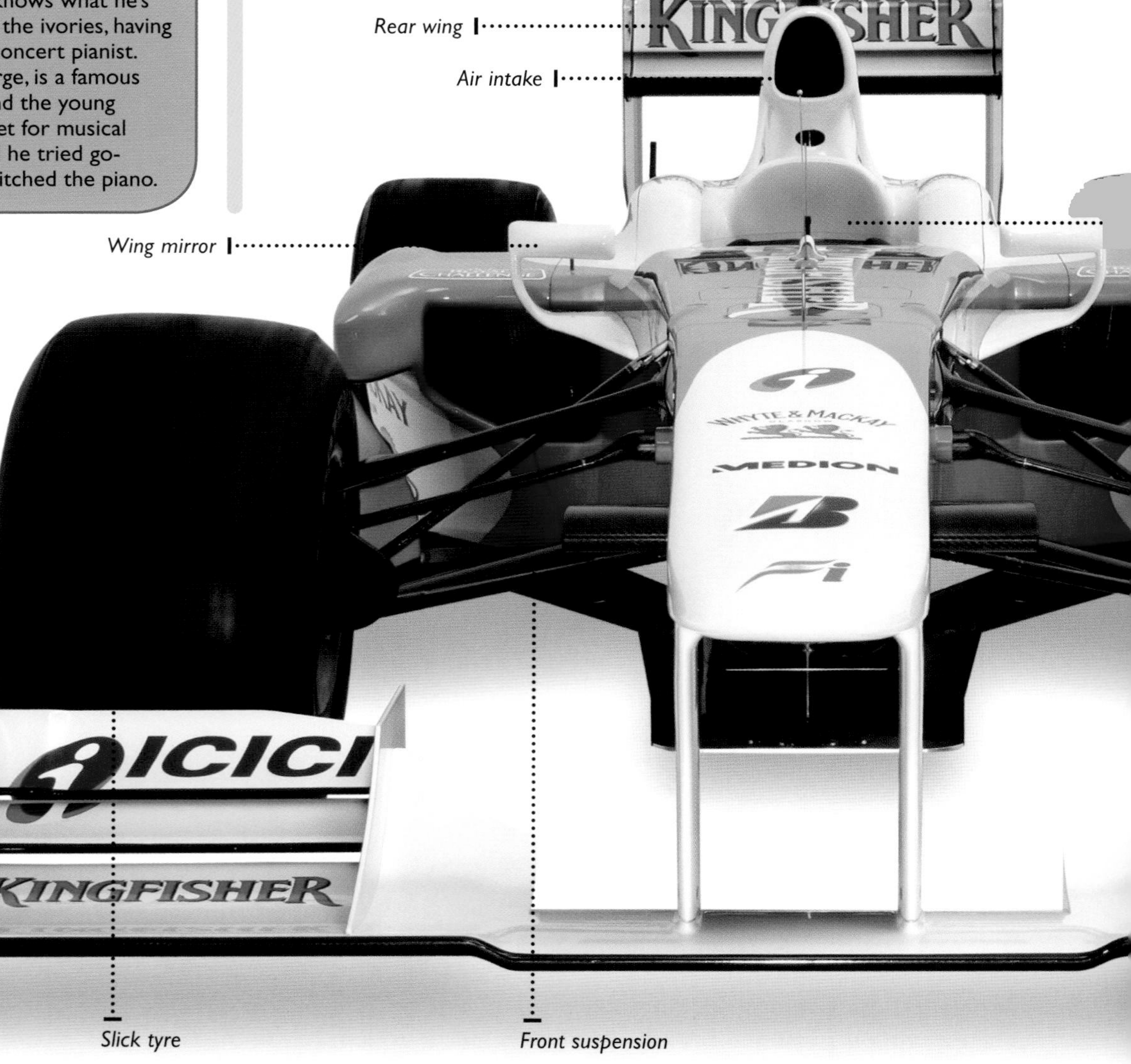

MOMENTS

Nine laps from the end of the 2008 Monaco Grand Prix, Adrian Sutil was running a fantastic fourth. The Force India team had a first-ever points finish within its grasp, having started 18th on the grid. But then, just behind Sutil, Ferrari's Kimi Räikkönen lost control coming out of the tunnel and careened into the back of the Force India. Sutil returned to the pits and wept. "I can't believe it," he said, "it feels like a pain in my heart."

WHO'S THAT?

This team has gone by four different names in four years. First it was known as Jordan, before changing its name to Midland MF1 in 2006. That name lasted less than a year, and towards the end of the 2006 season it became Spyker, before finally settling on Force India in 2008.

KING OF BLING

Vijay surrounds himself with the trappings of wealth. He owns 42 homes around the globe, including a castle in Scotland. He has four private jets at his disposal and a collection of 260 cars, including a Rolls Royce garbage truck! Indian movie stars, such as *Celebrity Big Brother* winner Shilpa Shetty, are a frequent sight in the Force India garage. Vijay has even produced Bollywood films, including the acclaimed *Dance Like a Man*.

Cockpit

Slick tyre

Front wing

FACT FILE: FORCE INDIA

DRIVERS: Giancarlo Fisichella, Adrian Sutil

BASE: Silverstone, UK

DEBUT: 2008 Australian Grand Prix

RACES COMPETED: 27

CONSTRUCTORS' CHAMPIONSHIPS: 0

DRIVERS' CHAMPIONSHIPS: 0

RACE VICTORIES: 0

POLE POSITIONS: 0

FASTEST LAPS: 0

FAMOUS DRIVERS:
Jean Alesi (2001*)
Jarno Trulli (2000–2001*)
Heinz-Harald Frentzen (1999–2001*)
Damon Hill (1998–1999*)
Rubens Barrichello (1993–1996*)
Eddie Irvine (1993–1995*)
Michael Schumacher (1991*)
(*as Jordan Grand Prix)

information correct up to FORMULA 1 GROSSER PREIS SANTANDER VON DEUTSCHLAND 2009

Lotus remains arguably the most innovative team in Formula 1 history, introducing new methods of car construction and even corporate sponsorship to the sport. The team established itself in the 1950s by building simple, lightweight sports cars with sublime handling. It stuck with that same philosophy as it became the dominant force in Grand Prix racing in the 1960s and '70s, and had many of racing's greatest drivers pilot its machines.

HISTORY

Team founder Colin Chapman entered his first F1 race at Monaco in 1958, with Graham Hill and Cliff Allison driving. A victory of sorts came the following year with Stirling Moss in a customer Lotus. Team Lotus had to wait until 1961 when Innes Ireland earned the Norfolk-based gang its first win. The team had recruited ace Scottish driver Jim Clark, and he recorded a remarkable seven wins in 1963, earning the team's first constructors' title. Soon the cars' iconic green livery with a yellow stripe gave way to sponsorship. In the 1970s, Lotus's black and gold John Player Special cars continued to win, thanks to their ground-breaking aerodynamics and fearless drivers. In the 1980s, Team Lotus's performance was less consistent, despite Ayrton Senna taking an epic 15 pole positions from 32 races between 1985 and 1986. At the end of the decade, the cars were not a success and the engines were underpowered. In 1994, debts caught up, and while Lotus continued to race in other categories, its time in F1 racing had come to an end.

Despite bent suspension, Jim Clark's Lotus 49 takes victory at the 1967 United States Grand Prix. Legendary Watkins Glen flag-waver Tex Hopkins leaps in the air as the Flying Scotsman crosses the finish line.

TEAM VIPs

Lotus founder Colin Chapman was an ingenious engineer who experimented with lightweight materials and relied heavily on his knowledge of aeronautical engineering, which he had gained while in the Royal Air Force. Both Team Lotus and Lotus Cars – makers of the Elite, Elan, and Esprit road cars – were a great success under his leadership. After his death in 1982, the team's management was overseen by fellow Englishman Peter Warr.

"He was the computer. If the car wasn't handling well on the Friday, he would go back to the garage and call the mechanics. By Saturday morning the car would be fantastic. Only Colin Chapman could do that. He was a genius."

EMERSON FITTIPALDI

ACHIEVEMENTS

Between 1963 and 1978, Team Lotus won seven constructors' titles and six drivers' titles. The team was runner-up five more times. Success came Stateside too. The Lotus 29 almost won the Indianapolis 500 at its first attempt in 1963. In 1965, Jim Clark won the biggest prize in US auto racing. Much of Lotus' legacy is still to be found in F1 racing today. The Lotus 25 had the first F1 monocoque chassis, the 49 was the first car of note to use the engine as a stressed member, and the 72 broke new ground in aerodynamics. Lotus was also the first team to have corporate sponsorship, way back in 1968.

DID YOU KNOW?

When Colin Chapman was creating a name for his racing team, he looked no further than his wife, Hazel. Her nickname was 'Lotus blossom'.

FACT FILE: LOTUS

BASE: Hethel, UK

DEBUT: 1958 Monaco Grand Prix

FINAL RACE: 1994 Australian Grand Prix

RACES COMPETED: 491

CONSTRUCTORS' CHAMPIONSHIPS: 7
(1963, 1965, 1968, 1970, 1972, 1973, 1978)

DRIVERS' CHAMPIONSHIPS: 6
(1963, 1965, 1968, 1970, 1972, 1978)

RACE VICTORIES: 79

POLE POSITIONS: 107

FASTEST LAPS: 71

FAMOUS DRIVERS:
Mika Häkkinen (1991–1992)
Nelson Piquet Sr (1988–1989)
Ayrton Senna (1985–1987)
Nigel Mansell (1980–1984)
Mario Andretti (1968–1969, 1976–1980)
Emerson Fittipaldi (1970–1973)
Graham Hill (1958–1959, 1967–1969)
Jim Clark (1960–1968)

The most rock 'n' roll outfit of the 1990s, led by a wheeler-dealing Irish entrepreneur, Jordan was the little team that could. It gave Michael Schumacher his break in F1 racing, schooled some of the sport's brightest young engineers, brought fun and glamour back to a sterile corporate paddock, and even came close to winning the title one year.

"I think we can be proud of what we achieved. It's the right time to close the book."

EDDIE JORDAN

Damon Hill was lured to Jordan in 1998 and gave the team its first win. A guitar player, he also found a place in Eddie Jordan's band. Here, the Englishman is seen kicking off his final year racing in Melbourne in 1999. Note the hornet's eye on the nose of the EJ199.

HISTORY

Eddie Jordan Racing was a successful Formula 3 and F3000 team with grand ambitions. In 1991, it became Jordan Grand Prix and went F1 racing. Despite a lack of funds, Jordan proved reliable midfielders and, in the second half of the decade, began punching above its weight. In 1999, Heinz-Harald Frentzen scored two Grand Prix wins and was even in the running for the world title. But as more manufacturers came into the sport, it proved impossible for Jordan to match their resources. In 2004, the team finished ahead of only Minardi and Eddie Jordan decided to sell. Twelve months later, the Jordan name was laid to rest.

TEAM VIPs

Eddie Jordan had been a driver in the 1970s and then started his own team, running racers Martin Brundle, Johnny Herbert, and Jean Alesi. EJ was a fun-loving boss who worked hard and played hard, often entertaining fans with his band, or throwing parties on his yacht. When the team won its first race, it's said the party lasted for seven days.

ACHIEVEMENTS

Jordan won four Grands Prix and finished third in the constructors' championship in 1999. The team's strangest victory was at the Brazilian Grand Prix in 2003, when the race was stopped early due to a crash, and the victory given to McLaren's Kimi Räikkönen. However, when the stewards counted back the laps to before the incident, they found the win belonged to Jordan's Giancarlo Fisichella, and the Italian was awarded his trophy ten days later. Perhaps the team's greatest contribution to F1 history was Michael Schumacher. The team was paid US$150,000 to run the German in the 1991 Belgian Grand Prix. He qualified an impressive seventh. A fortnight later, Flavio Briatore seized Schumacher from Jordan and he spent the remainder of the season driving for Benetton.

FACT FILE: JORDAN

BASE: Silverstone, UK

DEBUT: 1991 United States Grand Prix

FINAL RACE: 2005 Chinese Grand Prix

RACES COMPETED: 250

CONSTRUCTORS' CHAMPIONSHIPS: 0

DRIVERS' CHAMPIONSHIPS: 0

RACE VICTORIES: 4

POLE POSITIONS: 2

FASTEST LAPS: 2

FAMOUS DRIVERS:
Jean Alesi (2001)
Jarno Trulli (2000–2001)
Heinz-Harald Frentzen (1999–2001)
Damon Hill (1998–1999)
Ralf Schumacher (1997–1998)
Rubens Barrichello (1993–1996)
Eddie Irvine (1993–1995)
Michael Schumacher (1991)

"Please be reasonable. Do it my way."

BERNIE ECCLESTONE

Originally set up to build cars for customer teams in lower formulae, Brabham went on to become a powerhouse team in its own right. Led by racer-owner Jack Brabham in the 1960s, and then powerful entrepreneur Bernie Ecclestone in the '70s and '80s, Brabham set new standards for professionalism, design ingenuity, and an appetite for winning.

DID YOU KNOW?

Brabham's design guru Gordon Murray went on to design the McLaren F1 road car. Powered by a BMW V12 engine, the F1 was capable of reaching an astonishing 388 km/h (241 mph), making it, at the time, the fastest production car in the world.

Northern Ireland's John Watson on his way to fourth place at the 1978 Monaco Grand Prix behind the wheel of a Brabham BT46, which was powered by an Alfa Romeo engine.

HISTORY

Racing in the Australian colours of green and gold, American Dan Gurney took Brabham's first win at the 1964 French Grand Prix. Already a double world champion, Jack Brabham was 40 when he took his third title in a car of his own making. Prior to the 1966 Dutch Grand Prix, he hobbled onto the grid wearing a long false beard and holding a cane. His laughing mechanics helped him into the car, and he went and won the race. During the '70s, under the ownership of Bernie Ecclestone, the team took eight wins, but lost its star driver Carlos Pace to an air crash. Nelson Piquet joined the team in 1978 and the team enjoyed success until 1986, when the radically long and low BT55 scored only two points and driver Elio de Angelis was killed testing. Ecclestone sold the team the following year and it drifted into anonymity, finally ceasing to trade in 1992.

TEAM VIPs

Known as 'Black Jack', for he was the strong silent type, Jack Brabham won three world championships as a driver. He set up his team with fellow Australian Ron Tauranac, a designer. In 1971, the team was sold to Bernie Ecclestone. Bernie had been managing drivers, as well as trading in bikes, cars, and real estate. He promoted a young Gordon Murray as chief designer, and the two set about revolutionizing F1 racing.

ACHIEVEMENTS

Jack Brabham's 1966 drivers' championship remains the only victory by a car bearing the driver's name. In 1963, Brabham were the first team to use a wind tunnel. In 1978, the team created the BT46B, a car that was sucked to the ground by a fan. For the BT49C, Gordon Murray pioneered hydropneumatic suspension, soon copied by Brabham's rivals.

FACT FILE: BRABHAM

BASE: Milton Keynes, UK

DEBUT: 1962 German Grand Prix

FINAL RACE: 1992 Hungarian Grand Prix

RACES COMPETED: 394

CONSTRUCTORS' CHAMPIONSHIPS: 2 (1966, 1967)

DRIVERS' CHAMPIONSHIPS: 4 (1966, 1967, 1981, 1983)

RACE VICTORIES: 35

POLE POSITIONS: 39

FASTEST LAPS: 40

FAMOUS DRIVERS:
Damon Hill (1992)
Nelson Piquet Sr (1978–1985)
Niki Lauda (1978–1979)
Carlos Reutemann (1972–1976)
Graham Hill (1971–1972)
Jack Brabham (1962–1969)
Jochen Rindt (1968)
Denny Hulme (1965–1967)

Tyrrell's blue cars dominated racing in the late 1960s and early 1970s, driven by a man with large sideburns and a helmet with a tartan band. That man was Jackie Stewart, and his alliance with team boss 'Uncle Ken' brought success and stardom. The death of Stewart's team mate, the charismatic Parisian François Cevert, at Watkins Glen in 1973, had a huge affect on both Stewart and Tyrrell. Stewart retired at the peak of his career, while Ken continued but slipped into the midfield and, eventually, out of Formula 1 racing.

"Motor racing is a disease. The only way you get rid of it is to die. I just love it."

KEN TYRRELL

Tyrrell's most successful driver, Jackie Stewart, in the team's Ford-powered car at a one-off F1/F5000 race at Oulton Park in August 1970. Defending champion Stewart struggled that year, finishing the championship in fifth, but he regained his crown the following season.

HISTORY

The Tyrrell Racing Organisation was established in 1960, running factory Coopers in Formula Junior and then competing in the new Formula 3 series with Jackie Stewart. Stewart entered the F1 championship in 1965 with BRM, but when Tyrrell entered F1 racing in 1968, Stewart was to be its driver. Back then, the team was racing a Matra chassis and Stewart won his first title with a Matra-Ford in 1969. By the end of 1970, though, Tyrrell had developed its own car and the following season the team won the constructors' championship. Stewart showed himself to be the class of the field, taking two more titles for himself before retirement in 1973 – prompted, in part, by the death of his team mate François Cevert. The era of Tyrrell's dominance was over, and it only picked up occasional wins from then on. In 1998, the team was sold to British American Racing.

TEAM VIPs

Ken Tyrrell served in the Royal Air Force during World War II and subsequently entered the family timber business. He indulged his interest in cars by buying a Cooper and racing in F3. There, he met Jackie Stewart and engineered his car, and soon both men were in F1 racing. 'Uncle Ken', as he was known, was affected by the death of driver François Cevert, and afterwards the team slipped down the field. By the early '90s the team was struggling, and Tyrrell handed control over to Dr Harvey Postlethwaite, whose design genius gifted the team a few more podiums against far better-funded rivals. In 1999, Postlethwaite suffered a fatal heart attack while testing in Barcelona, aged 55. In 2001, Ken Tyrrell died from cancer, aged 77.

FACT FILE: TYRRELL

BASE: Ockham, UK

DEBUT: 1968 South African Grand Prix

FINAL RACE: 1998 Japanese Grand Prix

RACES COMPETED: 463

CONSTRUCTORS' CHAMPIONSHIPS: 1 (1971)

DRIVERS' CHAMPIONSHIPS: 3 (1969, 1971, 1973)

RACE VICTORIES: 23

POLE POSITIONS: 14

FASTEST LAPS: 20

FAMOUS DRIVERS:
Johnny Herbert (1989)
Martin Brundle (1984–1986)
Stefan Bellof (1984–1985)
Ronnie Peterson (1977)
Jody Scheckter (1974–1976)
Francois Cevert (1970–1973)
Jackie Stewart (1968–1973)

ACHIEVEMENTS

Jackie Stewart became the first driver to win three drivers' championship crowns with one team. In 1976, Tyrrell became the only team to win a Grand Prix with a six-wheeled car. The unusual-looking machine was the best-selling Corgi die-cast model of the period. In 1990, Tyrrell's 019 car was the first to set the precedent for high noses, which remain in F1 racing to this day.

Grand Prix racing was invented in France, and in the late 1970s the French fell in love with Formula 1 racing. During that period, and into the early 1980s, France saw 14 of its countrymen take part in F1 racing, and the national team was Ligier – its cars painted in French blue. 'Les Bleus' established themselves as a top team during a very competitive period, won nine Grands Prix, but ultimately could do no better than second place in the constructors' championship, finishing as runner-up in 1979.

HISTORY

Equipe Ligier entered the Formula 1 World Championship in 1976 with a Matra V12-powered car, winning its first race the following year in the hands of Jacques Laffite. Between 1979 and 1981, Ligier established itself as a top team, with an impressive portfolio of sponsors. The team brokered a free engine deal with Renault, running turbocharged V6s between 1984 and 1986. Then it struggled with poor engines and poor cars until reuniting with Renault from 1992 to 1994, when they were powered by the same engines that took Williams to victory. By then, Guy Ligier had sold the team and Flavio Briatore had rescued it. Then, in 1996, came a result no one was expecting, least of all driver Olivier Panis – a win on the streets of Monaco. At the end of the season the team was sold to Alain Prost, but Prost Grand Prix would go bust in 2001. The four-times world champion described it as "a disaster for France".

TEAM VIPs

An orphan, Guy Ligier began his professional life as a butcher's assistant. He later went on to play international rugby for France before making his fortune with a road construction company that built most of France's autoroutes. He was also an enthusiastic racer, who competed in F1 racing in 1966–67, and came second in the 1975 Le Mans 24-hour race. When tobacco company Gitanes voiced their F1 ambitions, Ligier offered to help, and hired designer Gerard Ducarouge. He built the JS5 – named after Ligier's great friend Jo Schlesser – and entered the 1976 championship, with French Formula 2 star Jacques Laffite in the driver's seat. Laffite raced for the team for nine seasons, until an accident at Brands Hatch in 1986 brought his career to a close.

ACHIEVEMENTS

It wasn't obligatory to be French to drive for Ligier, but nonetheless, 17 of the team's 28 drivers were. Ligier was not only a patriotic team – famed for its long lunches lubricated with lashings of Bordeaux – but a well-connected one. French president François Mitterrand helped put in place some big sponsorship deals with French companies. But despite France's proud F1 history, to date Olivier Panis remains the last Frenchman to win a Grand Prix, some 13 years ago.

FACT FILE: LIGIER

BASE: Vichy, France

DEBUT: 1976 Brazilian Grand Prix

FINAL RACE: 1996 Japanese Grand Prix

RACES COMPETED: 326

CONSTRUCTORS' CHAMPIONSHIPS: 0

DRIVERS' CHAMPIONSHIPS: 0

RACE VICTORIES: 9

POLE POSITIONS: 9

FASTEST LAPS: 11

FAMOUS DRIVERS:
Olivier Panis (1994–1996)
Martin Brundle (1993–1995)
René Arnoux (1986–1989)
Jacques Laffite (1976–1982, 1985–1986)
Jean-Pierre Jabouille (1981)
Jean-Pierre Jarier (1977, 1981)

DID YOU KNOW?
Ligier is still in the business of building four-wheeled machines, but instead of racing cars, it now makes inexpensive microcars aimed at young people and pensioners. Drivers of these vehicles need to be aged over 16, but don't require a car licence.

"Maybe it was a mistake to stay with Ligier for so long, but I don't care. I was driving a French car – a blue car – and we were successful. The team was like a family."

JACQUES LAFFITE

French driver Jacques Laffite in his Ligier JS5 takes a corner ahead of Alfa Brabham's Carlos Reutemann during the 1976 United States Grand Prix at Long Beach, California. Despite only having one driver, Ligier finished the season with 20 points, recording three podium finishes and one pole position.

The cars

The car is the star in Formula 1 racing. Drivers at this level are quite evenly matched – it's the cars that set them apart. While many of the skills needed to drive these cars remain, the designs themselves have changed. Firstly engines moved backwards, wings sprouted, construction materials changed, electronics and computers came in, and, perhaps most importantly, safety improved exponentially. But one thing has always held true – Formula 1 cars are the fastest and most sophisticated racing machines in the world.

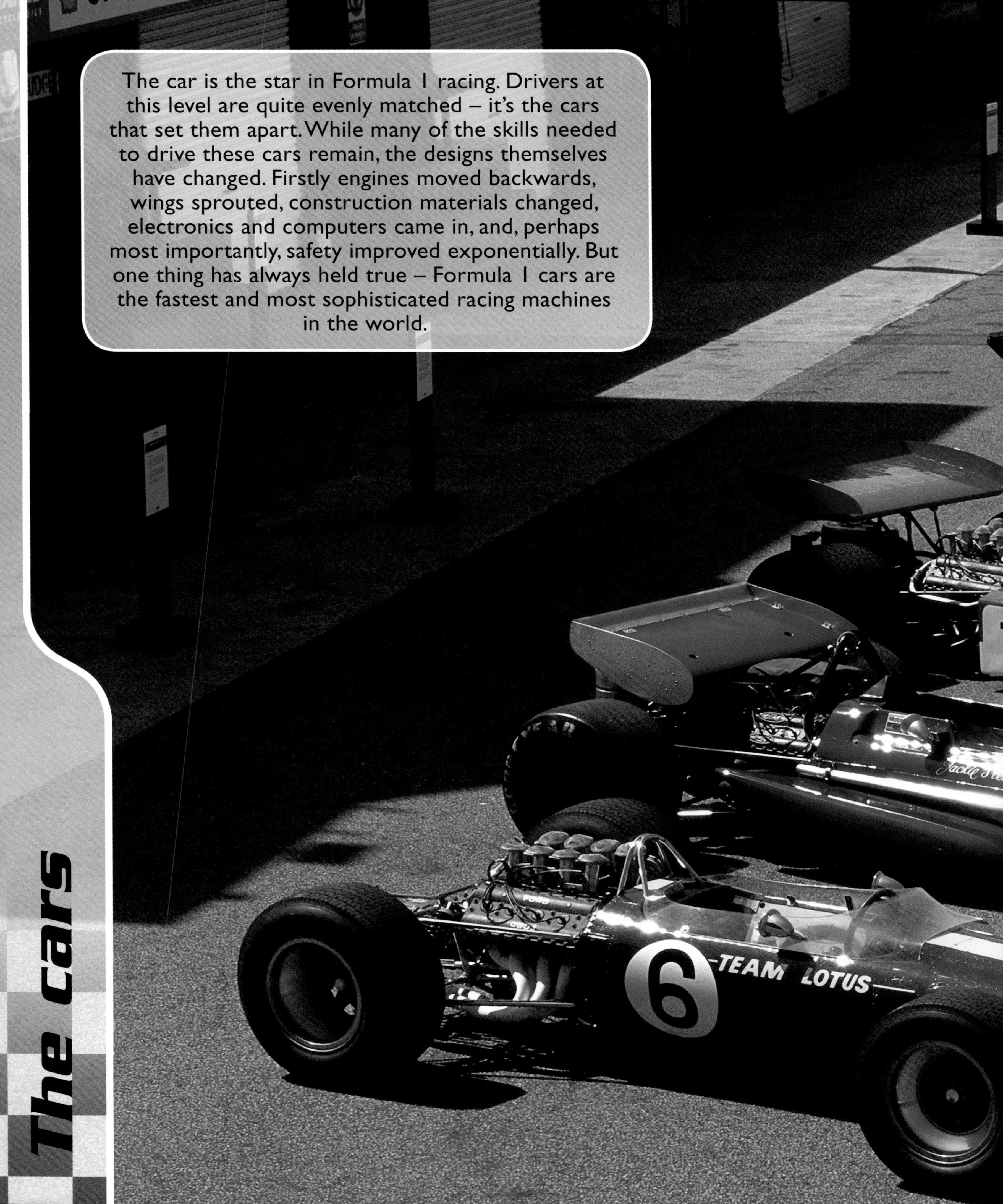

The cars lined up here, from the 1967 Lotus 49 at the front to the 1997 Stewart at the back, were all powered by Cosworth engines. The Northampton-based company supplied engines to Formula 1 teams for over 40 years, but has been away from the sport since 2006. It has plans to return in 2010.

In 1948, Grand Prix racing established a new 'formula' of technical regulations for manufacturers to abide by. The regulations were known as 'Formula 1', and in 1950 a formal world championship was created for these cars. Technological progress was slow compared to the modern era, and safety was a non-issue. There was no weight limit. In 1950, engines were set at 1,500 cc for compressed engines and 4,500 cc for normally aspirated engines. From 1952, these levels were reduced to 750 cc and 2,000 cc respectively.

1950 FERRARI 125

Ferrari's first Formula 1 car shared its engine with the 125S, the company's first road car which debuted in 1947. The compact, high-revving 1.5-litre V12 was supercharged to produce 280 hp. The torpedo-shaped body was beautiful, sitting on a steel tube frame, with a large egg-crate grille and long nose. It was particularly noted for its four-speed gearbox. The 125 had already taken Grand Prix wins before the new F1 world championship was launched, and though it raced in the inaugural series this car never actually won an F1 race.

1954 MERCEDES-BENZ W196

The W196 was the one and only Formula 1 car Mercedes-Benz built as a constructor. It dominated the 1954 and 1955 seasons, with Juan Manuel Fangio and Stirling Moss claiming nine wins from 12 races. Remarkable firsts included a spaceframe chassis rather than the traditional ladder chassis, and the use of desmodromic valves and fuel injection developed by Mercedes engineers through experience gained on the Messerschmitt BF109 fighter during World War II.

STAR CAR

1957 MASERATI 250F

This was the car in which Juan Manuel Fangio achieved his most impressive victory. At the 1957 German Grand Prix, he overcame a 50-second deficit in just 20 laps, passing the leader on the final lap to take the win – his last in F1 racing – and his record fifth world drivers' championship. Having first appeared in 1954, the 250F was a hit with privateers. In 46 official Grands Prix, 277 250Fs were entered.

1952 FERRARI 500

For 1952, the rules were switched, and that required a new four-cylinder 2-litre engine. Four-cylinder engines are rare in the Scuderia's history, but Enzo Ferrari was convinced it would be more competitive and fuel efficient than a V12. Ferrari's Tipo 500 engine produced 180 hp, which was enough to keep the car at the front of the pack. Alberto Ascari took six race wins with the Ferrari 500, storming to championship glory. It was the first Ferrari to win a world title.

DID YOU KNOW?

Between 1952 and 1953, Ferrari's Alberto Ascari won a record nine Grands Prix in a row. He won two consecutive drivers' titles in those years and is one of just two Italians to have held the Formula 1 title.

The last front-engined car to win a Grand Prix was the Ferrari D246 at Monza in 1960. A breed of innovative and forward-thinking engineers, led by Lotus boss Colin Chapman, moved the engine to the back. As drivers lobbied for greater safety, roll bars, seat belts, fire resistant clothing, and shatterproof visors all became mandatory, and the flag signalling code was established.

1960 COOPER T51

The T51 was the first rear-engined car to win the title, doing so in 1959 in the hands of Jack Brabham. It was the most popular car of the 1960s, with 38 drivers racing it until 1963. The rear-mounted Coventry Climax engine afforded better aerodynamics than its front-engined rivals. Also, with its fuel tanks either side of the cockpit, rather than at the rear, the car handled more consistently with different fuel loads.

1961 FERRARI 156

Designed by Carlo Chiti, the 156 gave Ferrari its first constructors' world title. It was known as 'the sharknose' for its arrow-shaped nose. Phil Hill and Wolfgang von Trips fought for the title in it, while Giancarlo Baghetti became the first driver to win his debut race in a 156. Von Trips lost the title to Hill when he was thrown from his car at the 1961 Italian Grand Prix, killing himself and 14 spectators.

1967 LOTUS 49

The Lotus 49 was the first car to be powered by the Cosworth DFV, which went on to win more races than any other engine to date. In fact, the DFV (which stood for 'Double Four-Valve') went on to achieve 12 drivers' world championships and ten constructors' world titles, plus ten Indy 500 wins. The 49 was the first successful car to feature its engine as a structural member, bolted to the monocoque at one end and the suspension and gearbox at the other. Since then, virtually all F1 cars have been built this way.

DID YOU KNOW?

Back in the '60s, The Beatles attended the Monaco Grand Prix. Guitarist George Harrison was a huge F1 fan and even invited Jackie Stewart to be in one of his music videos.

1962 LOTUS 25

The revolutionary Lotus 25 was first sketched by Colin Chapman on the back of a napkin. It used a monocoque chassis – something that had never been seen before. The single-shell monocoque made the car more rigid. It was three times stronger than the previous Lotus 21 and weighed half as much. The car was extremely low and narrow, reducing drag, and meant the driver had to recline, earning the 25 the nickname 'the bathtub'. It took Jim Clark to his first Grand Prix victory in 1962, and while BRM's Graham Hill took the title that year, Clark earned his first drivers' world championship in 1963 still driving a 25. He won seven races that year, and Lotus took the constructors' world title.

1968 FERRARI 312

The 1968 version of Ferrari's 312 featured something previously unseen in F1 racing. It was the first Grand Prix car to use a front wing, which of course boosted downforce and therefore cornering speeds. Ferrari's designer, Mauro Forghieri, had been inspired by the Can-Am series cars racing in the US. However, the three-litre V12 engine was heavy, and in 1968 the team registered just one victory.

The 1970s

The speed of F1 cars had risen dramatically since the 1950s, and that was to accelerate during the '70s, when designers began to consider aerodynamics and methods such as 'ground-effect'. But an increase in speed brought increased danger. Eleven drivers lost their lives in the 1970s, motivating drivers to campaign for greater safety standards. Hay bales were replaced by sturdy barriers and FIA inspections became mandatory. Six-point harnesses and on-board fire extinguishers became obligatory.

1975 FERRARI 312T

The 312T was raced in various versions from 1975 until 1980, winning 27 races, four constructors' titles, and three drivers' world championships. The 'T' in the name stood for 'transverse' as the gearbox was mounted this way, improving the car's handling. It was powered by a reliable flat-12 engine, which generated 510 bhp.

Swede Ronnie Peterson in a Lotus 79 during the 1978 Dutch Grand Prix. He finished second in the race and that year's drivers' world championship went to team mate Mario Andretti.

1976 TYRRELL P34

One of the most unusual-looking F1 cars ever, Tyrrell's six-wheeled P34 used four 25-cm (10-inch) wheels at the front and two ordinary sized wheels at the rear. The idea of the small front tyres was to increase air penetration and reduce drag. Smaller tyres resulted in a loss of contact area between the rubber and the tarmac, so the P34 was fitted with four wheels up front. It won the 1976 Swedish Grand Prix.

1977 RENAULT RS01

Nicknamed the 'yellow steam kettle', Renault's RS01 was the future. Appearing for the first time at the 1977 British Grand Prix, the car had an exotic turbocharged engine. The rules allowed for three-litre normally aspirated cars or 1.5-litre turbos, and Renault was the first team to go this route. The RS01 was cumbersome, but essentially an experimental test car. The engine block was made of cast iron to withstand the pressures of turbocharging, and the car was chronically unreliable. But slowly it improved, and five years later all the other teams would copy it.

STAR CAR

1978 LOTUS 79

The 79 is considered by many to be the most significant racing car design of all time. It took full advantage of ground-effect aerodynamics. Lotus discovered that by shaping the underside of the car, they could accelerate the air passing under it, thereby reducing the air pressure under the car relative to that over it and pushing the tyres down harder to the track. The need for smooth airflow meant that the car had clean lines, and as a result the handsome machine was nicknamed 'Black Beauty'. The car was near unbeatable, earning six wins and 10 poles in 1978.

1978 BRABHAM BT46B

The 'B' variant Brabham generated a huge amount of downforce by means of a fan, claimed to be for increased cooling, but which also extracted air from beneath the car. When the drivers blipped the throttle, the car was seen to squat down on its suspension. Mario Andretti described it as being "like a great big vacuum cleaner". It was introduced at the 1978 Swedish Grand Prix, where Niki Lauda steered it to victory. Shortly afterwards, the fan was outlawed by the FIA, and it is the only car in history with a 100 per cent winning record!

The 1980s

Formula 1 racing went power-crazy in the '80s, with turbocharged cars producing up to 1,500 hp! Safety had improved with the advent of carbon fibre, replacing aluminium as the material of choice for chassis construction, and the invention of the safety cell. Nevertheless, the sheer speeds of which F1 cars were capable needed to be reined in. In 1981 flexible skirts were banned, in 1983 ground-effect was outlawed completely, cars were not allowed to run on more than four wheels, and in 1988 turbos were banned altogether.

1980 WILLIAMS FW07B

The small, simple and extremely lightweight Williams FW07 was inspired by the Lotus 79. Designers Patrick Head and Neil Oatley had perfected ground-effect. It was so effective that a front wing was unnecessary. Powered by a trusty Ford Cosworth DFV, the FW07 gave Williams its first constructors' world title, with six wins in 1980.

1981 McLAREN MP4/1

The McLaren MP4 was the first car to be built following the merger of McLaren and Ron Dennis' Project 4 team. Engineer John Barnard created a revolutionary design. It was the first F1 car to use a carbon-fibre composite monocoque, a concept which has been used by all F1 teams since. Powered first by Ford and later Porsche, the MP4/1 raced for three seasons and won six Grands Prix.

1983 BRABHAM-BMW BT52

Powered by a 1,300 hp BMW M12/13 engine, the Brabham BT52 was the first turbocharged car to win the drivers' world championship. With ground-effect banned, the BT52 had short, angular sidepods to keep lift to a minimum. The car had a dart-like profile and an oversized rear wing to claw back as much downforce as possible. It scored four wins and gave Nelson Piquet his second world title.

1987 LOTUS-HONDA 99T

The Lotus 99T was the first car to use computer-controlled active suspension. The system's benefits of a consistent ride height with no pitch or roll in the chassis came at a cost, as it added significant weight. To compensate, designer Gerard Ducarouge spent many hours in the wind tunnel. Powered by Honda's 1,494 cc turbo, it proved competitive in the hands of Ayrton Senna who took it to two wins and six other podium finishes.

DID YOU KNOW?

In 1985, Nigel Mansell raced with a red number '5' on the nose of his Williams. He believed it brought him good luck, and used it again when he won the drivers' world championship seven years later during his second stint with Williams.

STAR CAR

1988 McLAREN MP4/4

The Honda-powered McLaren MP4/4 was the most dominant car in Formula 1 history. It was designed by Gordon Murray, as an evolution of his lowline Brabham BT55. A low car proved more aerodynamically efficient and allowed more air to pass over the rear wing, causing downforce without much drag. The small Honda engine, with its low centre of gravity, was ideal for this layout. The MP4/4 won 15 out of 16 races in 1988, including ten 1-2 finishes, as Ayrton Senna took his first drivers' world championship.

With electronic aids threatening to make the driver just a passenger, active suspension, traction control, launch control, and anti-lock brakes were all banned for the 1994 season. With the deaths of Roland Ratzenberger and Ayrton Senna, all attention returned to safety. Crash tests became much more stringent, wheels were tethered to the car, and circuits were reviewed. In 1995, engine capacity was reduced from 3,500 cc to 3,000 cc, and in a further bid to slow down escalating speeds, car width was reduced and grooved tyres were introduced in 1998.

"As of '94 the cars aren't too complicated. They have no traction control, for example, which means you can spin if you try too hard and damage your tyres if you're not careful with your driving style."

NIGEL MANSELL

STAR CAR

1992 WILLIAMS FW14B

The Adrian Newey-designed FW14, powered by a Renault V10, was the most technically sophisticated car on the grid, with active suspension, a semi-automatic gearbox, traction control, and superior aerodynamics. In 1991, the car suffered too many retirements to win the title, despite seven wins to its name. In 1992, the FW14B was unbeatable, and Nigel Mansell took a then record nine wins in the season to earn his only title. The FW14B and the FW15C are still considered among the most advanced racing cars ever built.

1994 BENETTON B194

Driver aids were banned for 1994, and there was some controversy as to whether the Benetton B194 was playing by the rules. Powered by a Ford V8, it was a well-designed car, light and nimble, but relatively underpowered. So how was it so fast? The FIA launched an investigation and found banned software in the computer systems. However, it couldn't prove that these systems had been used so the complaint was dropped. In the end, the Rory Byrne-designed B194 took Michael Schumacher to his first world title.

1996 WILLIAMS FW18

Aerodynamically, the Adrian Newey-designed FW18 was way ahead of the competition from Ferrari and Benetton, the drivers sitting lower than in the previous FW17. The car won 12 out of 16 races in 1996. It was developed by Damon Hill and it responded well to his smooth driving style. It was also extremely reliable, completing 1,778 laps of a possible 2,028. Hill beat team mate Jacques Villeneuve to the title, also earning Williams the constructors' prize.

1998 McLAREN MP4/13

For 1998, designer Adrian Newey left Williams for McLaren. With car width reduced from 2 m (6.6 ft) to 1.8 m (5.9 ft) for 1998, and grooved tyres, Newey capitalized on the new rules and the MP4/13 scored a 1-2 on its debut in Australia, leaving the whole field a lap behind. The Mercedes-powered car scored nine wins and handed Mika Häkkinen his first world championship, and McLaren their first since 1991.

DID YOU KNOW?
In 1992, Italian driver Giovanna Amati attempted to qualify for a Grand Prix three times for Brabham, before her seat was given to rookie Damon Hill. This is the last time a woman has attempted to qualify for a Formula 1 race. Amati went on to have a successful career racing sportscars.

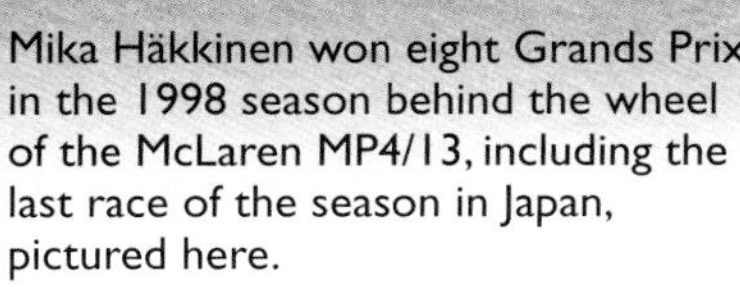

Mika Häkkinen won eight Grands Prix in the 1998 season behind the wheel of the McLaren MP4/13, including the last race of the season in Japan, pictured here.

1999 FERRARI 399

This car clinched Ferrari's first constructors' crown since 1983. For Michael Schumacher, it was the one that got away. He had to sit out over a third of the season due to leg fractures he sustained at the British Grand Prix. But the car was a match for the McLaren and used its Bridgestone tyres particularly well. Eddie Irvine led into the final round in Japan, where he was pipped to the drivers' world title by McLaren's Mika Häkkinen.

The influx of car manufacturers entering the sport at the turn of the century brought about a spending spree. With costs spiralling out of control, the FIA sought to clamp down on development. Since the 2009 season, aerodynamic development has been curtailed, car design completely renewed and there has been an imperative to develop environmentally friendly technologies.

2000 FERRARI F1-2000

The F1-2000 took Michael Schumacher to his first drivers' world title with Ferrari. It featured improved aerodynamics on the previous year's F399 and was on a par with the McLaren MP4/15. It scored ten wins and ten poles. Schumacher was the first Ferrari driver to win the championship in 21 years.

2002 FERRARI F2002

One of the most successful and fastest cars of all time, the F2002 won 16 Grands Prix from a possible 20 between 2002 and 2003. It was much lighter than its predecessor, with a lower centre of gravity, and as a result handled better. Other advancements included clutchless direct shift technology within the gearbox, and periscopic exhaust outlets at the rear.

2004 FERRARI F2004

Extremely fast and reliable, the F2004 is considered the pinnacle of the modern V10-era Formula 1 car. It was based on the same design principles as the F2002, and honed even further. It was kinder to its tyres than the intervening F2003-GA, and the engine was designed to last a full race weekend in accordance with FIA rules. It took Michael Schumacher to a record seventh world drivers' championship, and notched up 15 wins, and many lap records that still stand to this day.

STAR CAR

2006 RENAULT R26

Not only was the Renault R26 aerodynamically advanced, with fluid bodywork and gills at the rear of the engine cover, it was also extremely reliable. Powered by the new-spec 2.4-litre V8, Fernando Alonso was able to use the same chassis throughout 2006 en route to his second consecutive world drivers' championship, taking seven wins along the way. Renault also took the world constructors' title for the second year running.

2008 McLAREN MP4/23

Throughout 2008, McLaren pushed the MP4/23 as hard as possible, constantly refining the aerodynamics. By the end of the season, the car was littered with turning vanes and other devices to give it as much downforce as possible. Lewis Hamilton drove the MP4/23 to world championship victory at the last race of the year. Following that success, at the launch of the MP4/24, McLaren conceded that aerodynamic development of its '08 car had gone as far as it was possible to go.

McLaren took aerodynamics to extremes with the MP4/23, but rule changes in 2009 meant that they had to abandon many of their innovations.

DID YOU KNOW?

The Ferrari F2002 scored more points than any other car in Formula 1 history. The car was designed by a team led by technical director Ross Brawn and chief designer Rory Byrne, who, with team principal Jean Todt and driver Michael Schumacher, were known as the 'Ferrari dream team'.

The diffuser is longer and set further back to reduce 'dirty air'.
The 2009 rear wing is higher and narrower than in '08. It's intended to create less air turbulence, and allow cars to run closer to each other, thus improving overtaking.
Simpler, cleaner bodywork marks a return to the car shape of the early '90s. Now cars are less reliant on airflow to provide performance. A new rule limiting hours spent wind tunnel testing means there is less chance to fix errors made at the design stage.
Bargeboards have been banned as these affect transverse airflow when following another car.
Winglets have been banned, along with turning vanes and sidepod exhaust chimneys.
Slick tyres boost mechanical grip by 15 per cent. Tyre manufacturer Bridgestone brings two dry compounds to every race – soft and hard.
2009
The elements of the front wing can be moved up and down electronically by six degrees, twice per lap. This increases front-end grip and enables the driver to get close up to the car in front through a corner, before overtaking down the straight. The wing itself is lower and wider than in 2008.
PETRONAS
T··Systems·
bmw-sauber-f1.com
5
SYNTIUM

A new look

In 2009, Formula 1 racing underwent a radical re-design, primarily to make overtaking easier by making cars less dependant on aerodynamics. The difference between 2008 and 2009 is striking – Formula 1 cars now look a bit like they did 20 years ago.

The rear wing sat low and wide behind the rear wheels, producing as much downforce as possible.

These chimneys sprouting out from the sidepods provided cooling while also acting as mini-wings.

The car was covered with aerodynamic devices such as winglets, chimneys, and turning vanes. These parts helped to push the car down onto the track, but also created a wake of turbulent air, making it harder for another car to overtake.

Bargeboards, which were developed in the mid '90s, added around 15 per cent to the car's total downforce.

Grooved tyres were brought in from 1998 to increase braking distances and reduce cornering grip, in an effort to bring down the escalating speed of Formula 1 cars.

Narrow and deep, the 2008 front wing was designed to scoop up as much air as possible at speed, dispersing the airflow towards the wings and winglets behind and gaining maximum downforce.

2008

Creating a Formula 1 car is a long, methodical, and above all highly secretive process. It starts about 12 months before the car is raced for the first time. Following the FIA's technical regulations, the design team starts work on next year's car while still developing the present season's model. Once the first design is finalized and simulated via computers, the parts are moulded and machined by expert craftsmen and engineers.

THE FACTORY

Everybody calls them factories, but Formula 1 workshops aren't conveyor-belt style industrial operations. No, these factories are state-of-the-art offices and laboratories. Some, such as BMW Sauber's Hinwil headquarters, seem nondescript. Others, like the architecturally amazing McLaren Technology Centre, hint at the level of innovation that goes on inside. On site, between 400 and 1,000 staff work to push the team up the grid. Many of those staff will never attend a race, as the actual 'race team' consists of just 70 people.

BUILDING PARTS

When designing a Formula 1 car, the team has to think about the entire machine. However, invariably it's all about the detail, so individual parts will be changed and tested thousands of times throughout the process. Engineers work around the clock so, if a new part is needed over the race weekend, it can be put straight on a plane and dispatched. When Renault raced to get their double-diffuser ready for the 2009 FORMULA 1 CHINESE GRAND PRIX, the team tore the seats out of team boss Flavio Briatore's private jet to send Fernando Alonso a new chassis just hours before first practice.

The clean inside of the Williams factory floor (left) and the unimposing exterior of BMW Sauber's Hinwil headquarters (below).

THE BIG RIG

The term 'shaker' might sound more at home in a cocktail bar, but this is a fundamental tool for engineers – the seven-post 'shaker' test rig. This instrument, on which the car sits, accurately simulates the stresses and strains the car will encounter on the track. Putting the chassis and suspension to the test, the team can simulate a whole race on any specific circuit, recreating the car's behaviour in a controlled environment using computerized hydraulic plungers and rams.

The shaker rig uses seven hydraulic actuators – one for each wheel plus three additional units (two front and one rear) simulating aerodynamic loads.

WIND TUNNEL

Teams experiment with their car designs in wind tunnels, usually with 60 per cent scale models. Here, they can measure and analyze the different forces on the car in a bid to make it as fast as possible both around corners and in a straight line. This is the compromise that is at the heart of car design. Teams are restricted in their wind tunnel usage. They can only run them for a maximum of 40 hours per week. Here (left), we can see the wind tunnel inside Toyota's Cologne facility.

If you turned a Formula 1 car upside down, it could drive on the ceiling. F1 cars have more in common with fighter jets than regular cars, but their wings are designed to push them down rather than lift them up. Aerodynamicists have two primary concerns: to create downforce to improve cornering speeds, and to minimize drag, which acts to slow the car down. It's a fine balance, and must be got right because not only do aerodynamics influence outright speed, they also impact on the balance of the whole car and the way it uses its tyres.

"Aero is king. The car with the best aerodynamics is the car that will win."

DAVID COULTHARD

COMPUTATIONAL FLUID DYNAMICS

Designers are constantly looking for new ways to improve their cars, and once they've had a brainwave, the first step is to test it out on a computational fluid dynamics (CFD) simulation. CFD software simulates the interaction of air over the car's surface, displaying flow and temperature. The millions of calculations required to do this are made by a supercomputer, and many teams have these high-tech facilities on-site. It's a fast and fairly reliable way of judging if a new aerodynamic part will work before making it and testing it in a wind tunnel or on the track.

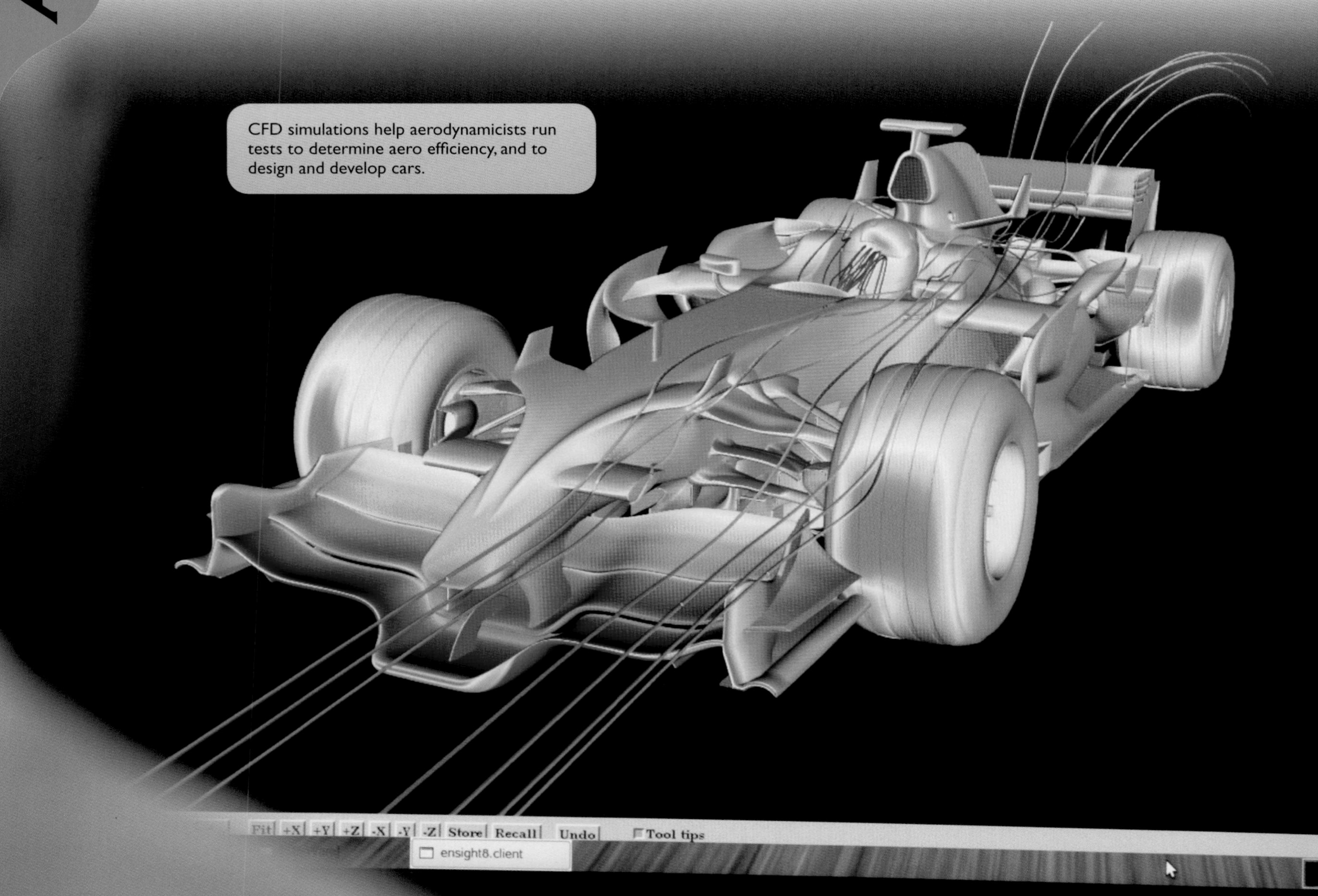

CFD simulations help aerodynamicists run tests to determine aero efficiency, and to design and develop cars.

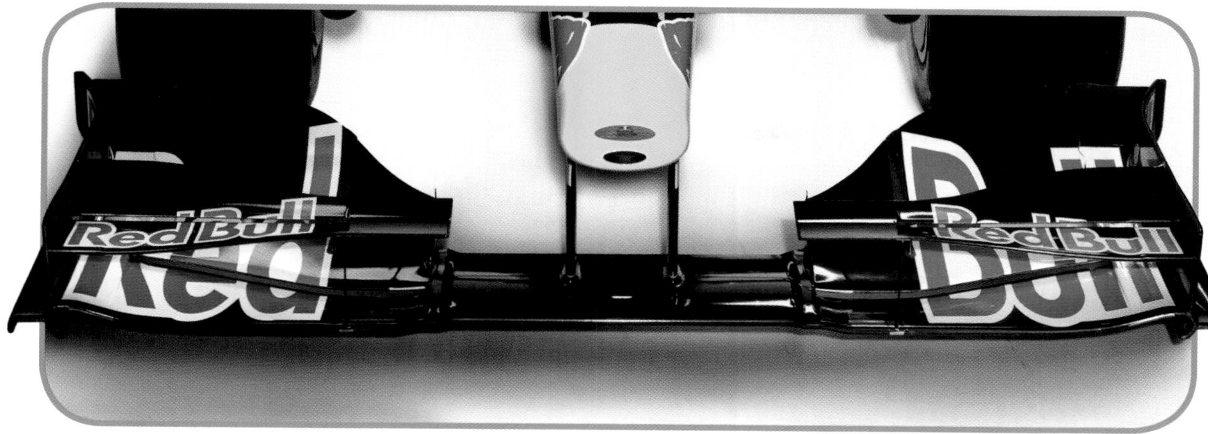

FRONT WING

The front wing is the first part of the car to cut through the air, so is therefore designed to disperse the flow of air behind it in order to maximize downforce and cooling. The front wing has a huge effect on the car's handling. Also, the driver can move the elements electronically by up to six degrees twice per lap. This is specially designed to aid overtaking.

REAR WING

Air flows at different speeds above and below the wing because it has to travel different distances over the wing's contours. This creates a difference in pressure, and as it tries to balance, the wing wants to move in the direction of low pressure. This is what creates downforce. Formula 1 cars are allowed to run a maximum of two separate elements on the rear wings, and these can be adjusted in the pits to suit individual circuits.

SIDEPODS

The sidepods cover the car's oil and water radiators, and taper to the rear. It's most efficient if the rear of the car is as low and as narrow as possible. This reduces drag and maximizes the amount of air available to the rear wing.

DIFFUSER

The diffuser is an extension of the floor at the back end of the car, between the rear wheels. Its purpose is to gather and organize high-speed air rushing under the car to reduce drag and increase downforce, thus increasing the speed and agility of the car.

WING MIRRORS

Mirrors on an F1 car are tiny. That's because the bigger they are, the more drag they create. At Monza, where top speed is key, cars are fitted with mirrors even smaller than normal.

The powertrain of a Formula 1 car is a stressed component, bolted to the carbon-fibre monocoque along with the rear suspension. Therefore it is designed to be strong as well as light, and positioned low to reduce the centre of gravity and enable the height of the rear bodywork to be minimized. Regulations dictate that engines must be 2.4-litre V8s, and as each driver is entitled to only eight engines for an entire season, they also need to be durable.

THE GEARBOX

Drivers will typically change gear 2,800 times during a race, and at a twisty circuit, such as Monaco, this can increase to 4,000 times. Every F1 car is now fitted with a seamless shift gearbox – a very clever device that eliminates the brief power interruption during a gear change. (Changes take just 0.004 seconds – it takes 50 times longer to bat an eyelid.) Forty working hours go into assembling a new gearbox, which is made from around 1,500 parts.

DID YOU KNOW?

New engine rules will be introduced in 2013, and the concept is likely to be a low-cost, lightweight powertrain. Small capacity turbo-charged engines could be reintroduced for the first time since 1988.

THE ENGINE

The engine weighs just 95 kg (209 lb) and revs to a limited 18,000 rpm, which equates to an accelerative force on the pistons of nearly 9,000 times gravity. The engine is built from around 5,000 parts. Over the course of a race, eight million ignitions will occur. It will accelerate the car from 0–100 km/h (0–60 mph) in 2.3 seconds, and 0–160 km/h (0–100 mph) in 3.8 seconds. Horsepower is a closely guarded secret, but it's around 800 bhp.

COOLING

F1 engines run very hot, and teams have to compromise between aerodynamic efficiency and getting enough air into the engine. At high speed, the engine will consume a phenomenal 650 litres (143 gallons) of air every second.

BLOW-UPS

When part of a Formula 1 engine cracks under stress, the fluids inside react and smoke is released like steam from a kettle. These days, this dramatic sight is fairly rare because engine-makers have focused less on tuning and more on reliability and durability.

MOST SUCCESSFUL ENGINE

The Cosworth DFV (Double Four Valve) was specifically built for Formula 1 racing in 1967, and went on to win more races than any other engine in the history of the sport – 155 from 262 races. It powered its drivers to 12 world championships. Not dissimilar to the modern engines you see in F1 racing today, it was a 90-degree, three-litre V8 that produced 530 bhp by the end of its remarkable career.

ENGINES FOR SALE

CUSTOMER TEAMS

Several manufacturers supply engines to independent teams. Mercedes-Benz supplies Force India and Brawn GP, Renault supplies Red Bull Racing, Ferrari supplies Toro Rosso, and Toyota supplies Williams. It's good for the manufacturers, of course, because they get twice the technical feedback and testing, and also some profit. But keeping costs down is important in current times, and there are moves afoot to offer 'indys' engines and gearboxes for around €5 million per season. Bargain!

Ordinary offices require a desk with a photo of the family in the corner and a yukka plant by the door. But a Formula 1 driver's office is more cramped and more high-tech, and there are no tea or coffee making facilities! To enter, he needs to remove the steering wheel and slide down inside the cockpit. Then a mechanic will affix his six-point harness so he's strapped in. The steering wheel is re-fixed and the car is lowered off its jacks, ignition is started, the driver awaits a radio call from his engineer, blips the throttle, and finally emerges out of the garage. Time to go to work.

THE PIT WALL

Like the bridge on a ship, the pit wall is where a team's captain and commanders sit and give orders. Up here you'll find the team principal and team manager, the race engineers, the chief mechanic, the chief strategist or data engineer, and the team's third driver. These guys work together to make quick decisions based on what they hear from their drivers and crew, and what they see on the screens in front of them. TVs show what's happening out on track, monitors show times and positions, and there are GPS devices, instant telemetry read-outs, and satellite weather information.

THE STEERING WHEEL

There's a huge gulf between the steering wheel of a road car and that of a Formula 1 car. In a Formula 1 car there is no horn and no airbag. Instead, you have paddle-shift gears, fingertip clutch-levers, shift-lights, a multi-function LED display, and a myriad of buttons and rotary switches that control, among other things, differential, KERS, and the movement of the front wing. During the race, the driver can make changes to his car's behaviour with the flick of a switch.

ONBOARD CAMERAS

Since 1985, Formula 1 cars have used onboard cameras to give TV viewers an impression of speed, to put them in the cockpit with the driver. Each car has at least three cameras capturing different angles.

Main onboard camera

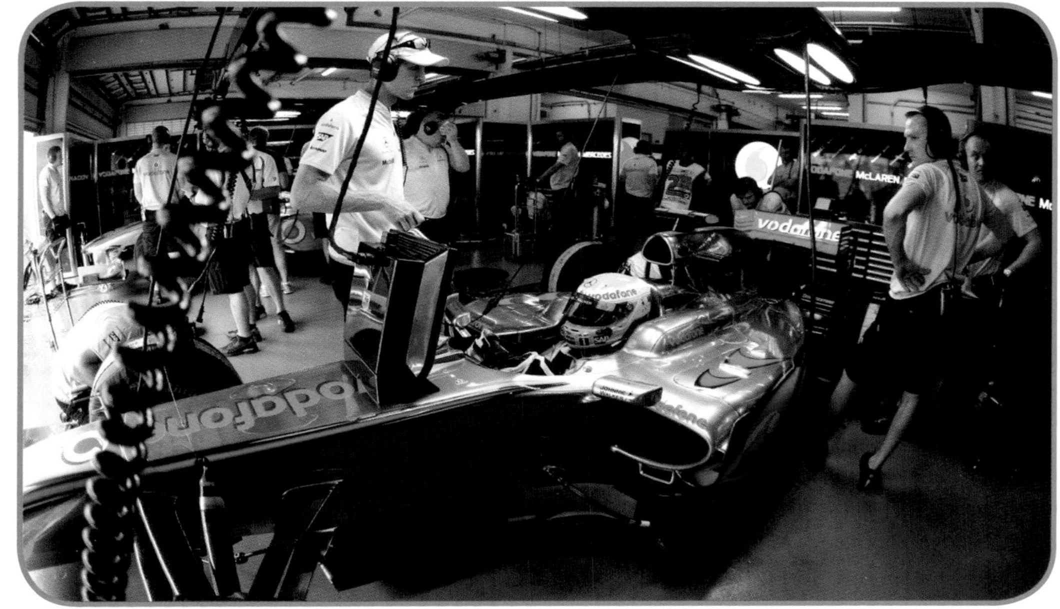

INFORMATION AT THE TOUCH OF A BUTTON

The race takes up 90 minutes on a Sunday, but for the teams there are two days of on-track build-up, made up of three practice sessions and qualifying. In order to set the cars up, the teams might only run a few laps at a time before returning to the garage and working on the car. Here (left) Lewis Hamilton keeps an eye on a TV and information screen. He can watch what's happening with his rivals, where he is in the timing order, and look at his telemetry graphs. This information shows his speed and revs throughout the lap, and he can compare these with his team mate's to ascertain where he could be quicker.

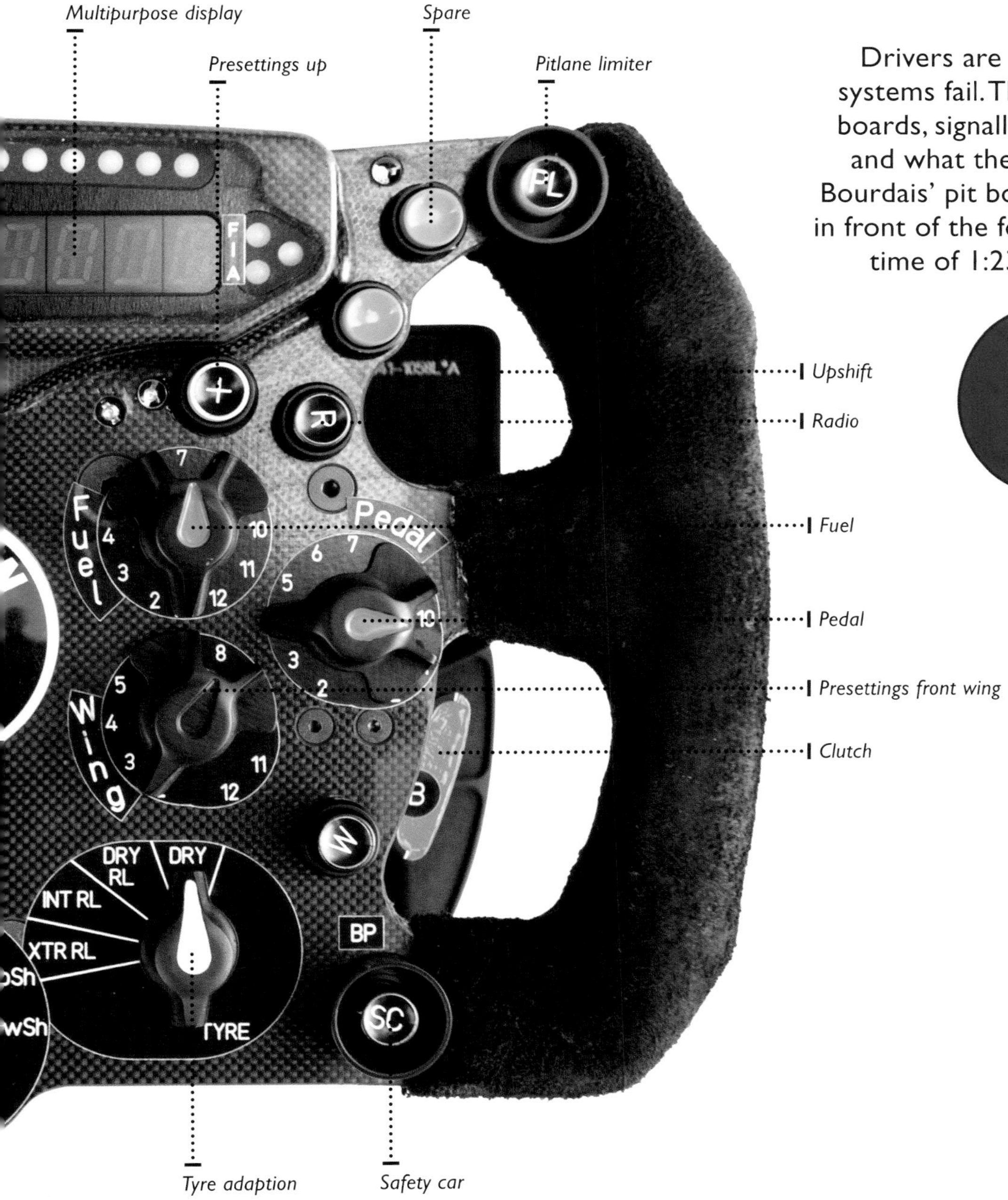
Multipurpose display
Presettings up
Spare
Pitlane limiter
Upshift
Radio
Fuel
Pedal
Presettings front wing
Clutch
Tyre adaption
Safety car
Fuel
Pedal
Wing
TYRE
DRY
DRY RL
INT RL
XTR RL
BP
SC

PIT BOARD

Drivers are in radio contact with their crews, but sometimes systems fail. Therefore, you'll always see mechanics wielding pit boards, signalling to their drivers on each lap how fast they are and what the gap is to the next car. Here (below) is Sebastien Bourdais' pit board. The '+19 1' means Sebastien is 19.1 seconds in front of the following car; the '23 8' means he's just done a lap time of 1:23.8 seconds; 'L8' means there are eight laps to go.

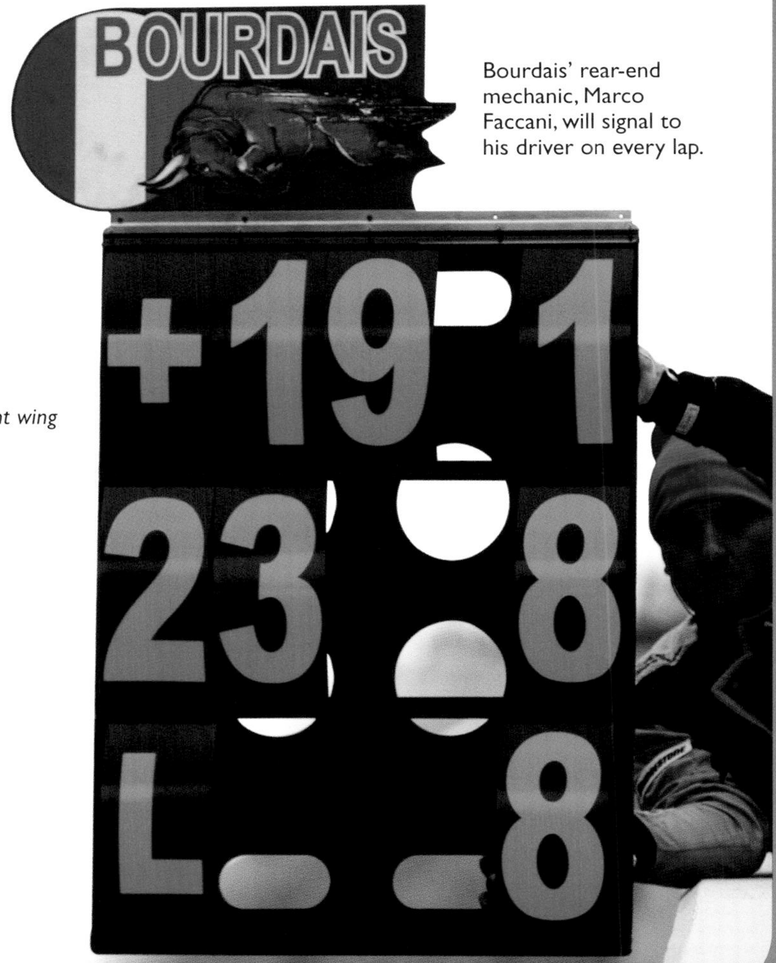
BOURDAIS
+19 1
23 8
L 8

Bourdais' rear-end mechanic, Marco Faccani, will signal to his driver on every lap.

Brakes, KERS

If you're ever lucky enough to drive a Formula 1 car, it is the brakes – even more than the rocket-like acceleration – that will leave you astounded. The force of deceleration is much higher. How a driver uses his brakes is critical to a quick laptime, and essential for overtaking, taking care to time his braking point just right and not lock the wheels up. The energy generated under braking can then be stored and used to provide an extra boost during the lap.

GLOWING BRAKES

Formula 1 cars use disc brakes just like most road cars, but these are made from a carbon-fibre composite that's able to withstand the enormous stresses and strains of a race. Rotating discs attached to the wheels are squeezed between two brake pads by a hydraulic caliper. The car is then slowed down, and the energy converted into heat which makes the brake discs glow red hot. The temperatures can be extreme – up to 1,000°C (1,832°F). Some circuits are more demanding on brakes than others. Monza, for instance, sees cars slowing from huge speeds and mechanics will fit thicker-than-normal discs and pads so that they last the entire race distance.

The discs on Heikki Kovalainen's McLaren (below) glow like the hob on an oven. However, the temperatures exerted by the brakes are much hotter than anything you'll find in a domestic kitchen.

LOCKING BRAKES

If the driver presses his brake pedal too hard, the brakes will overpower the available levels of grip and the wheel will lock. This is a real test of a driver's skill, as it can be costly. The car will be in danger of missing the apex of the upcoming corner because it will want to keep going straight. And the tyre will 'flat spot', which is when rubber is shaved off the contact point. A big lock-up will leave the driver with tyre vibration so bad it may impair his vision as well as the car's handling.

Storage battery

ELECTRICAL KERS

For the 2009 season, teams have the option of harnessing the waste energy generated by the car's brakes and reusing it via a Kinetic Energy Recovery System (KERS). This energy can then be released to boost acceleration for up to 6.67 seconds per lap, by pushing a button on the steering wheel. This can aid overtaking. Most KERS-fitted cars use an electrical system, like here in this BMW Sauber. It uses a motor-generator incorporated in the car's transmission that converts mechanical energy into electrical energy and vice versa. Once up to 400 kilojoules of energy has been harnessed, it is stored in a battery and released when required.

Flywheel casing

MECHANICAL KERS

The Williams team has gone a different route with their development of KERS. They are also developing a mechanical system which captures braking energy and uses it to turn a small flywheel at up to 80,000 rpm. When extra power is required, the flywheel is connected to the car's rear wheels. In contrast to the electrical KERS, the mechanical energy doesn't change state and is therefore more efficient.

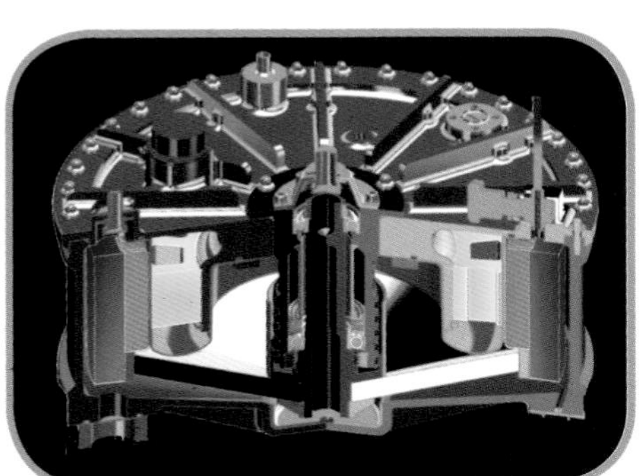

For all the technology involved in making a Formula 1 car fast, it is entirely reliant on the strip of rubber that sits between it and the tarmac. Tyres are the single biggest performance variable – use the wrong tyre in the wrong conditions and the car will be undriveable. It is also very important that the driver protects his tyres by preventing his car from sliding and the tyres graining.

RUBBER COMPOUNDS

Slick tyres provide optimum grip because the surface area of rubber in contact with the track is maximized. There are two compounds: 'soft' and 'hard', and the compound levels alter from circuit to circuit. The pace and durability of each compound depends on track conditions, but the driver must use at least one of each compound during the race. For damp conditions there is the 'intermediate' tyre with a shallow tread pattern, and a full 'wet' tyre with deeper tread designed to disperse heavy water and prevent the car from aquaplaning.

GREEN TRIM

With the wheels moving at speed, it can be difficult to tell which tyres are fitted. That's why Bridgestone paints the sidewalls of the softer compound tyres green, and one of the grooves of the full wets, so that they can be distinguished from 'hards' and 'inters'. The green colour was chosen to help promote the FIA's Make Cars Green environmental campaign.

A slick tyre will have zero grip in the wet and, likewise, a wet tyre will be utterly useless in the dry and be destroyed before the car has left the pitlane. On the right we see a stack of hard-compound slick tyres next to intermediates, and left of the 'inters' a stack of wet-weather tyres. The green groove in the tread shows that they are indeed 'full wets'.

ROAD AND RACE

A typical radial road car tyre will last 16,100 km (10,000 miles) or more. Formula 1 tyres are made to last just 200 km (124 miles) and are designed to be as light and as strong as possible. They are filled with a nitrogen-rich air mixture, which minimizes variations in tyre pressure with temperature.

TYRE BLANKETS

A road car doesn't need its tyres to be warmed before it can perform. In Formula 1 racing, however, tyres have a very distinct operating temperature of between 70–120°C (158–248°F), depending on the compound. That's why teams use electrical blankets that warm the tyres while the car sits on the grid. These blankets make sure that the tyres are at the correct operating temperature from the start. Only at the very last second, before the formation lap, will the team take those blankets off. However, from 2010 onwards, tyre blankets are to be banned.

Life in the fast lane

The best job in the world? Probably. But driving a Formula 1 car is also an opportunity no driver can afford to squander. The pressure to succeed in Formula 1 racing is intense. Success brings fame and riches, but it is essential for the driver to remain single-minded in his approach to winning. The greatest drivers are totally dedicated, ruthless, and have huge self-belief. Talent is just part of it. No one said becoming a legend was easy.

Brawn GP's Jenson Button celebrates winning the 2009 FORMULA 1 ING TURKISH GRAND PRIX, after finishing ahead of Mark Webber and Sebastian Vettel of Red Bull.

Fangio

Considered by many to be the greatest driver ever born, Juan Manuel Fangio held the record for the most drivers' championship victories for 46 long years, before Michael Schumacher overtook him. If anything, though, the old man's stats are even more impressive: in his 51 championship races, he started on the front row 48 times and took 35 podiums, 24 of them victories. His results were achieved with daring, skill, and grace.

HISTORY

The son of an Italian plasterer who emigrated to Argentina, Fangio started work as a mechanic aged 11 before learning to race in a primitive South American series aged 18, driving what had originally been a taxi. He was 38 before he came to Europe. His car control was the stuff of legend, as was his concentration, and he became the dominant driver of the 1950s. He won five world titles with four different teams, and his ratio of starts-to-wins was 47.06 per cent, the highest in history.

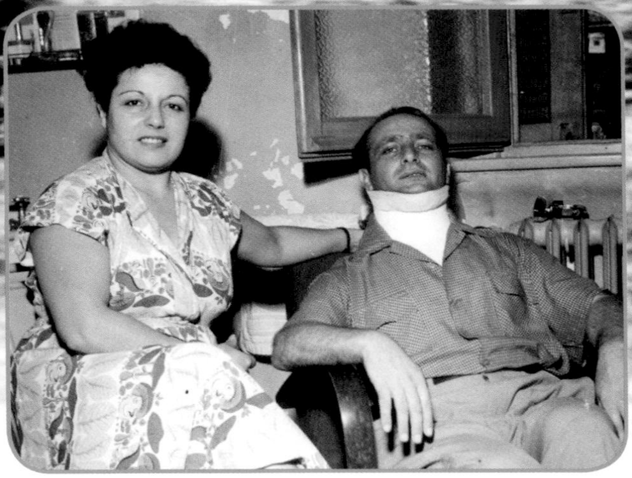

CRASH

Fangio suffered few accidents, but a crash at Monza in 1952 left him with a broken neck. He'd been in Belfast the day before and missed a flight connection, so he had driven through the night from Paris to Monza – and arrived just half an hour before the race. A lapse in concentration was nearly fatal – his Maserati slid wide on the second lap, hit an earthen bank, and somersaulted in the air. He was thrown from the cockpit. His injuries left him on the sidelines for a season. Here he is seen recovering in Argentina alongside his wife.

THE LAST WIN

Fangio's last win was arguably his greatest. After a botched pit stop at the 1957 German Grand Prix, 'El Maestro' fought to make up the minutes he'd lost around the Nürburgring's unforgiving bends to snatch the lead from Peter Collins and take victory, smashing the lap record to smithereens. He was a full 11 seconds faster than the Ferraris. Even Fangio admitted afterwards that he had never driven so hard. On that day, he took his fifth and final title.

"You must always strive to be the best, but you must never believe that you are."

JUAN MANUEL FANGIO

Here, the Argentinian races an Alfa Romeo at the 1950 British Grand Prix at Silverstone. In subsequent years he would race for Maserati, Mercedes, and Ferrari. His friend and rival, Stirling Moss, once said: "The cheapest method of becoming a successful Grand Prix team was to sign up Fangio."

KIDNAPPED

In 1958, ahead of a Grand Prix in Havana, Cuba, Fangio was kidnapped by members of Fidel Castro's revolutionary movement in a bid to publicize their cause. In the end, his captors were charmed by Fangio and he was released unharmed. He kept in touch with his kidnappers afterwards, saying they had become friends. Fangio's easy charm made him a popular member of the racing community, not to mention with the fairer sex.

La Domenica del Corriere

FACT FILE: FANGIO

NATIONALITY: Argentinian

DATE OF BIRTH: 24 June 1911 – Balcarce, Argentina

DATE OF DEATH: 17 July 1995 – Buenos Aires, Argentina

YEARS ACTIVE IN F1: 1950 to 1958

TEAMS: Alfa Romeo, Maserati, Mercedes-Benz, Ferrari

RACES COMPETED: 51

DRIVERS' CHAMPIONSHIPS: 1951, 1954, 1955, 1956, 1957

RACE VICTORIES: 24

POLE POSITIONS: 28

FASTEST LAPS: 23

FIRST RACE: 1950 British Grand Prix

LAST RACE: 1958 French Grand Prix

CAREER POINTS: 245

MEMORIES

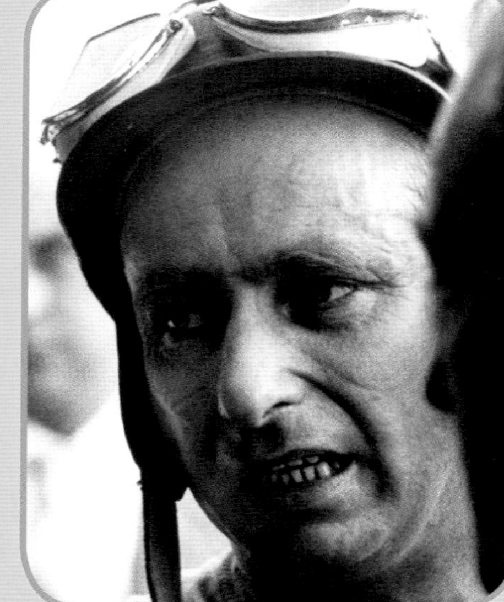

THE FINAL RACE

After his series of back-to-back championship victories, Fangio chose to retire following the 1958 French Grand Prix, aged 47. Such was the respect for the great man, Mike Hawthorn – who was leading the race and had lapped Fangio – braked before the finish line and allowed Fangio to pass so that he could complete the 50-lap distance of his final race. When he got out of the car, he said simply: "It's finished."

They were rivals, but Stirling Moss and Juan Manuel Fangio had so much respect for one another that there was never any foul play. Quite the opposite – as team mates at Mercedes-Benz they would help one another win. Putting them together was a risky strategy – like pairing Ayrton Senna with Michael Schumacher. But they found a way to work together that made each of them better drivers. Today, Sir Stirling maintains his greatest honour was racing Fangio, "because he was the best bloody driver!"

MUTUAL RESPECT

It is fair to say that they were like master and pupil. Moss and Fangio were friends and, more than that, role models. "I can't think of any facets of Juan's character which one wouldn't like to have in one's own," said Moss. As team mates, the duo became known as 'The Train' as they would allow each other to race so closely. Here (below) Fangio congratulates Moss on winning the Italian Grand Prix, as Stirling's wife Susie looks on. However, Fangio didn't speak English. The pair could communicate with Stirling's moderate grasp of Italian, but they had an understanding and respect that was beyond language.

RACE IN THE PITS

Shortly before half distance at the 1956 Italian Grand Prix, Fangio was forced to pit with a broken steering arm. His team mate, Peter Collins, was running second behind Stirling Moss and in a position to win the world championship, but when he pitted for a tyre check with 15 laps to go he made the remarkable decision to hand his car over to Fangio. The Argentine rejoined and went after Moss. With five laps to go, Moss ran out of fuel. As this happened, Fangio had another steering arm break on his Lancia-Ferrari and came to a stop. Both cars were pushed into the pits and they scrambled to get the necessary work done in time to take victory. In the end, Moss won the race by six seconds, but Fangio took the title.

DID YOU KNOW?

Today, two supercars have been named in honour of these great racers: The McLaren-Mercedes SLR Stirling Moss, which has a top speed of 350 km/h (217 mph); and the Pagani Zonda F (for Fangio), with a top speed of 344 km/h (214 mph).

AN ENGLISH GENT

Like Fangio, Moss was famous for his sense of fair play and good manners. When Mike Hawthorn was disqualified from the 1958 Portuguese Grand Prix, Stirling persuaded the organizers to reinstate his countryman. Hawthorn won the title that year from Moss by one point. Stirling finished runner-up in the championship four times and is considered the greatest driver never to have won a championship.

FANGIO'S FAVOUR?

At the 1955 British Grand Prix, Moss and Fangio raced nose-to-tail. Team mates for Mercedes, at the final corner the Englishman passed Fangio to take victory – his first in F1 racing – in front of an ecstatic home crowd. It is often speculated that Fangio slowed and gave the win to his friend, something he always denied. Moss himself would ask frequently, but the Argentine would reply, "No, you were better than me that day."

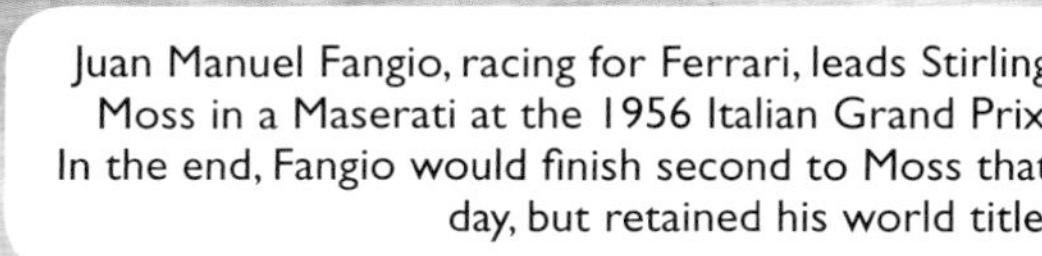

Juan Manuel Fangio, racing for Ferrari, leads Stirling Moss in a Maserati at the 1956 Italian Grand Prix. In the end, Fangio would finish second to Moss that day, but retained his world title.

Few champions are remembered as fondly as Jim Clark. He was a reluctant racer, shy of the attention his success brought him, but he was one of the most naturally gifted drivers the sport has ever seen. When he was killed at the age of 32, motor racing was rocked to its core. If it could happen to Jimmy, they said, it could happen to anyone.

"Clark came through at the end of the first lap of the race so far ahead that we in the pits were convinced that the rest of the field must have been wiped out in an accident."

EDDIE DENNIS

HISTORY

Jim Clark was brought up on a Scottish farm, and learned to drive aboard a tractor. When he passed his test he started to race a Sunbeam Talbot in local rallies, but he felt guilty about racing against his family's wishes. His friends, though, encouraged him to continue. Racing at Brands Hatch on Boxing Day 1958, he impressed Lotus boss Colin Chapman. Theirs would be the closest bond in motor racing, and they went on to win 25 Grands Prix and two world championships.

LOTUS

Clark was promoted to F1 racing with Lotus at the end of the 1960 season. Although haunted by a collision with Wolfgang von Trips in 1961 at Monza, in which von Trips and 14 spectators were killed, success swiftly followed. In 1963, he took seven wins from ten races and won his first championship. In 1965, he won six more races and his second title. His 25th victory, at the 1968 South African Grand Prix, eclipsed Fangio's record.

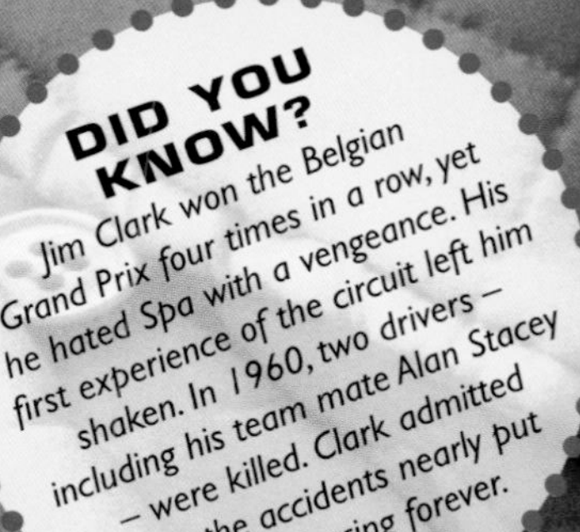

INDY 500

Clark competed in the legendary Indianapolis 500 five times, winning in 1965 with the Lotus 38. He had to miss the Monaco Grand Prix to compete, but in doing so, he became the first driver to win in a mid-engined car. With an average speed of 240 km/h (150 mph), he was the first non-American in almost half a century to win Indy. He also became the only driver to date to win Indianapolis and the Formula 1 world championship in the same year.

MEMORIES

ITALY 1967

This race is considered by many to be the greatest performance of all time. Clark led from pole in his Lotus 49, but suffered a puncture and lost an entire lap in the pits. He rejoined in 16th place and, astonishingly, fought his way back into the lead – setting record-breaking lap times. To everyone's dismay, on the last lap, the Lotus started to splutter – it was out of fuel. Finally, he coasted over the finish line in third place.

FATAL CRASH

Driving a Formula 2 Lotus at Hockenheim on 7 April 1968, Jim Clark suddenly veered off the track and crashed into the trees. It is thought a rear tyre deflated. He suffered a broken neck and skull fracture, and died before reaching the hospital. A devastated Colin Chapman declared that he'd lost his best friend, and ordered that the traditional green and yellow badge on the nose of all Lotus road cars be replaced with a black one for a month following Clark's untimely death.

FACT FILE: JIM CLARK

NATIONALITY: British

DATE OF BIRTH: 4 March 1936 – Fife, Scotland

DATE OF DEATH: 7 April 1968 – Hockenheim, Germany

YEARS ACTIVE IN F1: 1960 to 1968

TEAMS: Lotus

RACES COMPETED: 72

DRIVERS' CHAMPIONSHIPS: 1963, 1965

RACE VICTORIES: 25

POLE POSITIONS: 33

FASTEST LAPS: 28

FIRST RACE: 1960 Dutch Grand Prix

LAST RACE: 1968 South African Grand Prix

CAREER POINTS: 255

Intense and intelligent, charismatic and eloquent, spiritual and committed, Ayrton Senna will be remembered by everyone who met him, and millions who never did. He was gifted with a god-like driving talent, and has inspired every generation of racer who followed him with his passion and bravery. Over one lap, there was no one faster. He scored 65 pole positions in his Formula 1 career – a record that would stand until 12 years after his death. He drove like a man possessed, but his ruthlessness on track was tempered by his warm, gentle nature off it. Senna's appeal was magnetic, and F1 racing still bears the scars of his loss.

HISTORY

Senna was infatuated with a go-kart he received as a young boy. He started racing at 13 and won immediately. Eight years later he arrived in Britain and won four single-seater titles in three years. In 1984, he stepped up to F1 racing with the Toleman team. In Monaco that year – a race he would go on to win a record six times – he finished a superb second to Alain Prost. He then went to Lotus for three seasons, where he took 16 poles and six wins. At McLaren, between 1988 and 1993, he won 35 races and three world titles. The following year, he was taken from the sport at the height of his powers.

"Racing, competing, is in my blood. It's part of me, it's part of my life; I've been doing it all my life. And it stands up before anything else."

AYRTON SENNA

WET WEATHER WONDER

Senna was a genius in the wet. His performance at Donington at the 1993 European Grand Prix was mesmerizing to such an extent that Alain Prost, his greatest rival, was speechless. He passed four cars on the first lap to take the lead. On the next lap he pulled a seven-second advantage. Thereafter, the rain was intermittent, but Senna made all the right tyre calls and ended up lapping third place finisher Prost.

MEMORIES

FIRM FRIENDS

Senna was a very serious individual, but when Gerhard Berger joined him at McLaren in the early 1990s, he started to see the lighter side of life. Gerhard was a notorious prankster. Legend has it that he once replaced Senna's passport photo with a picture of a gorilla, threw his brand new briefcase out of a helicopter, and filled his hotel room with live frogs. When Senna called him in a panic, Berger replied: "Have you found the snakes yet?" They became great friends. "He taught me a lot about our sport," said Berger. "I taught him how to laugh."

CHARITABLE GIVING

During his life, Senna was deeply concerned by the poverty faced by young people from less privileged backgrounds than himself. He donated large sums of money anonymously to various causes and, months before his death, began to set up a foundation with his sister Viviane. Today, the Instituto Ayrton Senna donates tens of millions of pounds a year, generated by Senna's image rights, to poor children who are threatened by life on the streets in Brazil.

FATAL CRASH

On 1 May 1994, Formula 1 racing was changed forever. While leading the San Marino Grand Prix at Imola, Senna left the track and hit an unprotected concrete wall at Tamborello at 218 km/h (135 mph). As the Williams came to a halt, Senna remained motionless in the car. Medical teams arrived at the scene and the race was stopped. He was airlifted to a hospital in Bologna and pronounced dead. Millions of mourners turned out for his funeral as he was driven through the streets of Sao Paulo.

FACT FILE: AYRTON SENNA

NATIONALITY: Brazilian

DATE OF BIRTH: 21 March 1960 – Sao Paulo, Brazil

DATE OF DEATH: 1 May 1994 – Bologna, Italy

YEARS ACTIVE IN F1: 1984 to 1994

TEAMS: Toleman, Lotus, McLaren, Williams

RACES COMPETED: 161

DRIVERS' CHAMPIONSHIPS: 1988, 1990, 1991

RACE VICTORIES: 41

POLE POSITIONS: 65

FASTEST LAPS: 19

FIRST RACE: 1984 Brazilian Grand Prix

LAST RACE: 1994 San Marino Grand Prix

CAREER POINTS: 614

He was known as The Professor due to his studious, considered approach to racing and the high level of technical feedback he gave to his engineers. Professorships take many years to acquire, but it took Prost just six years to claim the first of his four world titles. His style was as smooth as they come, and his consistency was unequalled – he could always be relied upon to bring the car home. What marked him out from his great rival, Ayrton Senna, was that Prost would only ever drive as fast as he had to. "I always say that my ideal is to win the race at the slowest speed possible," he once said. But Prost was just playing with his prey and nursing his tyres. He still recorded 41 fastest laps.

HISTORY

But for a twist of fate, Alain Prost could have been a professional footballer. But a trip to a go-kart track aged 14 inspired him to take up motor racing. He went on to dominate French karting, and won the French and European F3 titles before entering F1 racing with McLaren in 1980. The following year he joined Renault and took his first victory at the French Grand Prix. It was the first of 51 victories. He finished his career at Williams in 1993, bowing out at the top by taking his fourth title.

RED AND WHITE TEAM

Prost re-joined McLaren just as the Woking-based team was getting into its stride. He took his first world championship in 1985 – the first for a Frenchman. In 1987, his 28th victory beat Jackie Stewart's 14-year record, and in 1988 Prost contributed seven wins to McLaren's total of 15 victories from 16 rounds. His team mate Ayrton Senna scored eight wins. And so began the fiercest rivalry in racing.

"A big part of my success is that I hated not to finish a race."

ALAIN PROST

Alain Prost steers his TAG-McLaren around Brands Hatch at the 1985 European Grand Prix, en route to his first championship victory.

FRUSTRATIONS AT FERRARI

Prost raced for four teams, and managed to fall out with all of them when he came to leave. The most acrimonious split was with Ferrari. He won five races with them in 1990, but 1991 was winless. Prost said his uncompetitive Ferrari handled "like a truck" and criticized the team publicly. The Scuderia responded by firing him.

MEMORIES

THE LAST HURRAH

Prost went on a sabbatical in 1992, but came back with Williams-Renault when Nigel Mansell went off to Indy Car. Aged 38, he found himself back in a super-competitive car, and took his fourth title. At his final race, in Australia, Ayrton Senna embraced him on the podium. They were no longer rivals, so there was no more reason for hostility.

MANAGEMENT

Alain Prost had harboured ambitions of team ownership for years and in 1997 purchased the Ligier team. Prost Grand Prix scored two points on its debut, but the following year could only score one point during the entire season. In 2001, Prost mended his relationship with Ferrari and agreed an engine supply, but it was too late. In early 2002, Prost Grand Prix went bankrupt.

DID YOU KNOW?

Prost is known for his slightly crooked Gallic nose, a gift for satirical artists. He broke it several times playing sports as a young boy. The young Alain played many different sports before he discovered karting, including football and wrestling.

FACT FILE: ALAIN PROST

NATIONALITY: French

DATE OF BIRTH: 24 February 1955 – Lorette, France

YEARS ACTIVE IN F1: 1980 to 1991, 1993

TEAMS: McLaren, Renault, Ferrari, Williams

RACES COMPETED: 199

DRIVERS' CHAMPIONSHIPS: 1985, 1986, 1989, 1993

RACE VICTORIES: 51

POLE POSITIONS: 33

FASTEST LAPS: 41

FIRST RACE: 1980 Argentine Grand Prix

LAST RACE: 1993 Australian Grand Prix

CAREER POINTS: 768.5

For McLaren, Alain Prost and Ayrton Senna were a dream team – the two most talented drivers of their generation at the very top of their game. But they were also a nightmare. Prost had actually campaigned for Senna to come to McLaren for 1988. But when Senna pulled a dangerous manoeuvre on Prost at the Portuguese Grand Prix that year, the goodwill dried up. The following year, feeling that McLaren was favouring the Brazilian, Prost announced that he was off to Ferrari. And that's when the gloves really came off. Dominance turned into destruction.

DRAMA IN JAPAN

The embittered 1989 season ended as many had feared – in a shower of carbon fibre. On lap 46 of the Japanese Grand Prix, Senna went to pass Prost at the chicane. Prost turned into his team mate and the two interlocked McLarens slid off the track. Prost, thinking the championship was his, climbed out of the car. Senna had other ideas, and, with the help of some marshals, bump-started his car and went on to win. However, the FIA disqualified Senna and handed him a US$100,000 fine. Thus, Prost claimed his third title in the most controversial of circumstances. Senna swore revenge...

OPPOSITES REPEL

Senna and Prost were very different characters. A passionate man whose emotions frequently rose to the surface, Senna raced with his heart, whereas Prost always raced with his head. The Frenchman was a quiet, calculating individual who needed all his brainpower and driving skill to take on the formidable Brazilian. Prost's driving style was conservative – starting cautiously, preserving the brakes and tyres, and pushing hard when necessary, but only ever driving as fast as he needed to. He knew how to pace himself. Senna, meanwhile, liked to extract the maximum from the car on every lap – a tactic that would sometimes cost him, and hand victory to Prost. His need for speed, and brilliance in the rain – something Prost was never keen on – made Senna the people's favourite, which was yet another factor in their feud.

Ayrton embraces Alain on the podium of the 1988 Australian Grand Prix. Prost had just won the race, while Senna had secured the first of three world titles.

PAYBACK

... and revenge he delivered. One British tabloid ran the headline 'Malice in Hondaland'. At the Suzuka circuit where, 12 months earlier, Prost had taken the title that Senna felt was his, the Brazilian intentionally rammed Prost's Ferrari at the start, taking both cars out at 260 km/h (160 mph) and sealing the title in his favour. Such a desperate and dangerous tactic bore out Prost's opinion that the Brazilian was reckless. "What he did was disgusting," cried Prost afterwards. "He is a man without value!"

"Ayrton has a small problem. He thinks he can't kill himself because he believes in God and I think that is very dangerous for the other drivers."

ALAIN PROST

ALL MADE UP

Once Prost retired in 1993, he and Senna patched up their differences. With no races left to run, there was no rivalry and therefore no bitterness. Their relationship returned to mutual respect. Prost was at Imola on that ill-fated weekend in 1994. Speaking on the radio as he went around the track, knowing the Frenchman was in the pit, Senna said, "I'd like to welcome back my old friend Alain – we all miss you." Prost was touched. When Senna was killed, he flew to Sao Paulo to be a pallbearer. Because their careers had been so tightly bound, Prost commented that a part of him had died also.

From left to right: Emerson Fittipaldi, Alain Prost, Christian Fittipaldi, Jackie Stewart, and Gerard Berger carry the coffin of their colleague Ayrton Senna during his funeral in Sao Paulo, Brazil, on 5 May 1994.

MOMENTS

Niki Lauda bought his way into Formula 1 racing and nearly paid for it with his life. This straight-talking Austrian was fighting to retain his title when a crash at the Nürburgring left him dreadfully scarred. His astonishingly quick return to the cockpit was arguably the bravest comeback in sporting history. He would win a total of three world championships.

HISTORY

Lauda bought his first F1 drives at March and BRM with a loan secured against his life insurance policy. Impressed by his confidence, Enzo Ferrari signed the young Austrian in 1974. The following year, five victories took him to his first title. In 1976, the championship seemed to be a formality, until his crash at the Nürburgring. He took another title in 1977, before joining Brabham and then bowing out of the sport to concentrate on his business. He returned in 1982 with McLaren, and won his final title in 1984.

DID YOU KNOW?

Now a pundit for German TV, Niki is one of the most outspoken characters in the pitlane. Back in 1982, when negotiating his lucrative contract with McLaren, he said: "You'll be paying only one dollar for my driving ability – all the rest is for my personality."

THE RAT AND THE PRANCING HORSE

Lauda was known as 'The Rat' due to his prominent front teeth. Enzo Ferrari was quite amazed by The Rat's brutal honesty. Driving a Ferrari for the first time, Lauda announced it was "a piece of crap". The following year he became the Scuderia's first champion in over a decade. The rain at the 1976 Japanese Grand Prix was atrocious and, with his eyes still healing after his horrific crash, Lauda couldn't see. He pulled out of the race, and Ferrari slated him for it. In 1977, after securing the drivers' title with two races left, Lauda walked away from Ferrari.

CRASH

Niki Lauda was on lap 2 of the 1976 German Grand Prix when his Ferrari hit an embankment and skewed into the path of another car and burst into flames. Other drivers stopped to pull him from his car, but he had already sustained severe burns. Against the odds, Lauda survived and incredibly, with blood still seeping from the bandages on his head, he returned to racing six weeks later. Jackie Stewart called it "the most courageous comeback in the history of sport".

NIKI'S BIGGEST FAN

By taking the Brabham BT46B to victory at the 1978 Swedish Grand Prix, Niki Lauda created a legend. With a fan on the rear to create extra downforce, Lauda won the race by over half a minute. The other drivers, however, were not happy as the fan kept flicking stones and muck at them. The result stood, but the car was banned. It remains the only F1 car to have a 100 per cent success record.

MOMENTS

TAKING TO THE SKIES

Tired of "driving round in circles", Lauda quit F1 racing in 1980 to run his own airline. A passionate pilot, he found he needed more money to keep it going, which is why he returned with McLaren in 1982 and continued winning like he'd never been away. Lauda Air was sold to Austrian Airlines in 1999 and, in 2003, he set up a new charter airline, Fly Niki.

FACT FILE: NIKI LAUDA

NATIONALITY: Austrian

DATE OF BIRTH: 2 February 1949 – Vienna, Austria

YEARS ACTIVE IN F1: 1971 to 1979, 1982 to 1985

TEAMS: March, BRM, Ferrari, Brabham, McLaren

RACES COMPETED: 171

DRIVERS' CHAMPIONSHIPS: 1975, 1977, 1984

RACE VICTORIES: 25

POLE POSITIONS: 24

FASTEST LAPS: 25

FIRST RACE: 1971 Austrian Grand Prix

LAST RACE: 1985 Australian Grand Prix

CAREER POINTS: 420.5

The records that Michael Schumacher has set may never be broken. He is, by almost every measure, the most successful driver in the history of Grand Prix racing. A man driven to win at all costs: although his ethics were sometimes questionable, his skill behind the wheel was never in dispute.

"Michael Schumacher is the most unsporting driver in the history of Formula 1. That doesn't mean he hasn't been the best driver, and fighting against him has been an honour and a pleasure."

FERNANDO ALONSO

ONE TIME ONLY

Michael Schumacher's first race was with the Jordan team. Schumacher had been racing sportscars for Mercedes, and in 1991 the German marque paid team boss Eddie Jordan to run him for one weekend. He qualified for the Belgian Grand Prix in seventh place, a fantastic result for the team. In the race, clutch problems forced him into retirement, but he had done enough to get the experts excited. Within a week he had been signed to the Benetton team, where he would win his first two titles.

Schumacher celebrates breaking Ayrton Senna's record for pole positions at the 2006 San Marino Grand Prix.

REVIVING THE REDS

Ferrari hadn't won a drivers' title since Jody Scheckter's in 1979, but in 1996 Schumacher joined the famous Italian marque intent on returning it to greatness. A year later, he was joined by his former Benetton technical team of Rory Byrne and Ross Brawn. That year he finished second to Jacques Villeneuve, and to Mika Häkkinen in 1998 and 1999. But the Ferrari package was fast improving and between 2000–2004 Schumacher was simply unbeatable. In those five seasons, he won 48 Grands Prix from 85 races. In his final two seasons he was still in his element, but he had always promised that when someone faster came along he would hang up his helmet with dignity. That man was Fernando Alonso. In 2006, the championship went down to the wire, and Schumacher retired from the sport after an electric final performance in Brazil.

CONTROVERSY

Schumacher was the most divisive of drivers. Some loved his obsession with winning. Others questioned whether he was a true sportsman. It is certainly true he was never far from controversy. In 1994, he won the world championship after driving into Damon Hill, writing off both cars and winning by a single point. In 1997, he tried to do the same thing to Jacques Villeneuve, but failed. At the 2002 race in Austria, he was booed by the crowds after team orders forced his team mate, Rubens Barrichello, to yield victory to the German. And in 2006, to prevent Fernando Alonso completing his qualifying lap, he parked in the middle of the track, faking a technical problem.

INJURY

During his long career, Schumacher had relatively few accidents, but at the 1999 British Grand Prix his title hopes were ruined. Racing towards Stowe Corner at Silverstone, his rear brake failed and he slammed into a tyre wall, breaking a leg. It put him out for six races.

"It was not a race. It was a demonstration of brilliance."

STIRLING MOSS

FACT FILE: SCHUMACHER

NATIONALITY: German

DATE OF BIRTH: 3 January 1969 – Hurth-Hermulheim, Germany

YEARS ACTIVE IN F1: 1991 to 2006

TEAMS: Jordan, Benetton, Ferrari

RACES COMPETED: 249

DRIVERS' CHAMPIONSHIPS: 1994, 1995, 2000, 2001, 2002, 2003, 2004

RACE VICTORIES: 91

POLE POSITIONS: 68

FASTEST LAPS: 76

FIRST RACE: 1991 Belgian Grand Prix

LAST RACE: 2006 Brazilian Grand Prix

CAREER POINTS: 1,369

MOMENTS

TAXI DRIVER

Michael is always in a hurry, and when he and his family were running late for an aeroplane, Schumi asked a taxi driver if he could take the wheel. "He drove at full throttle around the corners," said the Bavarian cab driver, "and overtook in some unbelievable places!"

Following the death of his team mate Ayrton Senna, Damon Hill assumed the mantle of Williams' number one driver. But he had Michael Schumacher to beat. Hill responded brilliantly, winning six races that summer, and developing his car to be a match for the Benetton B194 of Schumacher. But the season finale ended in tears, and stoked a bitter rivalry that would dog the two men for years.

TITLE WINNER

The British media played up the nationalistic aspect of seeing an Englishman fighting a German. While Hill might have struggled to match Schumacher's natural abilities, he had steely resolve in his veins, and it would reward him in 1996 – his championship year. That season he won eight races and never qualified off the front row. He sealed the championship by winning the final race at Suzuka. Afterwards, the teams crammed into the circuit's karaoke log cabin, and Hill serenaded his old foe with the *Dad's Army* theme song, changing the words to, "Who do you think you are kidding Michael Schumacher?"

BAD BLOOD

Damon could do nothing in the Adelaide pitlane but shake his head, his car forced into retirement. Schumacher had had a problem, Hill had gone to pass, but the German turned in and broke the Williams' front suspension. In doing so, he won the title by a single point. Hill vowed to take the title off Michael in 1995. Schumi fouled again in the Belgian Grand Prix and incurred a suspended one-race ban. In frustration, Hill tried some risky moves himself at the British Grand Prix and Monza, but both backfired. Schumacher won the title again, this time with two races to spare, and added insult to injury by calling Hill "not a top driver".

HILL SHOOTS HIS ARROWS

Williams dumped Hill unceremoniously for 1997, and the world champion chose to join the Arrows team – who hadn't won a race in its 20-year history. At the first race, he could only qualify at the back of the grid. The car's Yamaha engine was hopelessly weak. But, in Hungary, Damon performed a miracle. He qualified third and then astounded everyone by passing Schumacher for the lead. In the closing laps, though, an electrical problem slowed the Arrows, and Damon coasted to a heroic second place behind Villeneuve.

"The difference between the rivalry between Ayrton Senna and Alain Prost and mine with Michael is that I was never held in esteem by Michael."

DAMON HILL

Michael Schumacher, on slick tyres, passes Damon Hill on wets for first place at Spa in 1995, and squeezes the Williams onto the grass for good measure. Neither Hill nor the authorities were impressed.

DID YOU KNOW?

Damon desperately wanted to win in Monaco – a race his father Graham had won five times. In 1996, Damon led until his engine blew on lap 40. Michael suffered bad luck that day, too, careering into the barriers on the opening lap.

Stewart

Jackie Stewart was Formula 1 racing's first superstar. Wearing long hair, sideburns like pork chops, and big sunglasses, the Scotsman looked like a Rolling Stone. He dominated the sport in the late 1960s and early 1970s, and bowed out at the top. But his legacy is much more than his three world championships. Stewart's tireless commitment shaped F1 racing's future and saved countless lives.

HISTORY

Stewart left school at 15 with no qualifications. He was diagnosed with severe dyslexia, which made his subsequent achievements quite remarkable. Team boss Ken Tyrrell spotted his talent early, and together they destroyed the competition in F3. He turned down many offers from F1 teams before agreeing to race for BRM between 1965 and 1967, taking his first win at Monza in his debut year. When Tyrrell entered F1 racing, initially running a Matra chassis, the Scot joined them. It was a wonderful pairing. Together they achieved 25 wins.

SAFETY

At a time when drivers who raced for five years had a two in three chance of being killed, Stewart defied opposition and campaigned for stronger cars, safety barriers, and proper medical facilities. This followed the 1966 Belgian Grand Prix, when he was trapped in a ditch, fuel spilling from his BRM. He was dragged out and loaded into an old ambulance, which then got lost en route to the hospital.

"I would have been a much more popular world champion if I had always said what people wanted to hear. I might have been dead, but definitely more popular."

JACKIE STEWART

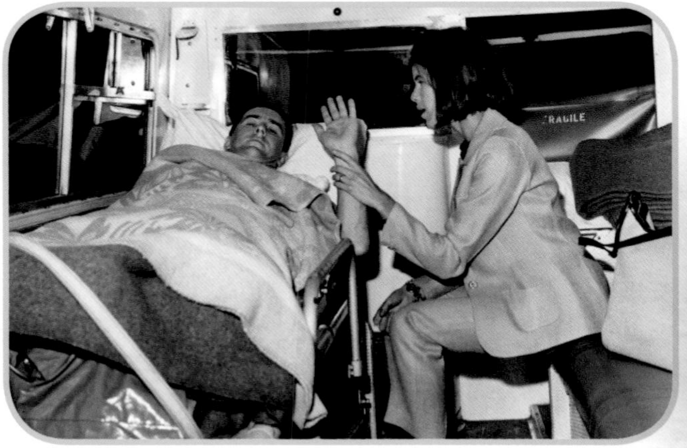

THE FLYING SCOTSMAN

Stewart's first win came at the end of his debut season at the Italian Grand Prix, racing his illustrious team mate Graham Hill to the flag. His finest-ever win came at the Nürburgring – which Jackie christened 'The Green Hell' – in 1968. It was a track he admitted finding terrifying, but in perilous rain and fog his Matra won four minutes ahead of the competition. The following year he became the only driver in F1 history to win a title in a French-built car. In addition, he busied himself racing in many other championships, including Can-Am, the European Touring Car Championship, the Tasman series, Formula 2, and the Indianapolis 500, racking up more air miles than any other driver. In one year he travelled 724,000 km (450,000 miles).

MOMENTS

FRANÇOIS CEVERT

In early 1973 at the relatively youthful age of 34, Jackie Stewart decided it was time to retire while he was still at the top of his game. He'd already won the world championship when the teams arrived at Watkins Glen for the US Grand Prix. But the year was to end in tragedy. Stewart's team mate, the charismatic François Cevert, was killed during qualifying. Jackie was very close to the 29-year-old – he was his mentor and felt that the Frenchman was destined for greatness. Indeed, Cevert would have become team leader once Stewart retired. As a mark of respect, Stewart didn't race that weekend, foregoing his 100th and final Grand Prix.

TEAM BOSS

Sir Jackie was much more than a talented driver. He had a very successful business career, and even founded his own team. In 1997, Stewart Grand Prix arrived on the grid, covered in tartan, and won the 1999 European Grand Prix. It was then sold to Ford, who branded it Jaguar Racing, and was later bought by Red Bull.

Jackie Stewart steered this Matra-Ford MS10 to a dominant victory at the United States Grand Prix at Watkins Glen in 1968.

FACT FILE: JACKIE STEWART

NATIONALITY: British

DATE OF BIRTH: 11 June 1939 – Milton, Scotland

YEARS ACTIVE IN F1: 1965 to 1973

TEAMS: BRM, Tyrrell

RACES COMPETED: 99

DRIVERS' CHAMPIONSHIPS: 1969, 1971, 1973

RACE VICTORIES: 27

POLE POSITIONS: 17

FASTEST LAPS: 15

FIRST RACE: 1965 South African Grand Prix

LAST RACE: 1973 Canadian Grand Prix

CAREER POINTS: 360

"I had my fair share of heartaches and disappointments, but I got a lot of satisfaction. I only ever drove as hard as I knew how."

NIGEL MANSELL

Nobody fought harder to get into Formula 1 racing than Nigel Mansell, and few fought harder when they got there. He was so aggressive it was practically grievous, and his talent for racing was matched by his tenacity. His bushy moustache and Midlands accent belied his courageous attitude. He might have looked like a geography teacher, but he was the king of overtaking.

MANSELL MANIA

Mansell's heroic performances and everyman persona endeared him to millions of fans. When his first win came at Brands Hatch in 1985 he wept on the podium – he had been through so much to get there. The British Grand Prix was a sea of Union Jacks, all with his name on. Playing to the crowds, 'Our Nige' claimed people power made him a second per lap quicker.

HISTORY

Following great success in kart racing, Mansell became 1977's British Formula Ford champion, despite breaking his neck. He sold his house to finance an F3 drive, and in 1979 had a huge crash that broke vertebrae. Loaded with painkillers, he tested for Lotus and landed his F1 racing debut. Williams brought him his first victories, then he took three wins for Ferrari before returning to Williams to take the title in '92. He is the most successful British driver ever, and was loved for his win-or-bust approach – 31 wins and 32 crashes to be precise.

BEST OF ENEMIES

Motivated by adversarial situations, Mansell found his greatest nemesis in Nelson Piquet. They were team mates in 1986–87, and they hated each other. Piquet once called the Englishman 'an uneducated blockhead' and regularly insulted his wife, Rosanne. Mansell's response came at Silverstone in '86. He passed Piquet flat-out at Stowe corner to win on home soil in dramatic style. After the race, he returned to where he'd made the pass and kissed the tarmac.

IL LEONE

Known as *Il Leone* (The Lion) by the *tifosi*, Mansell was the last driver to be personally signed by Enzo Ferrari, an honour he described as "one of the greatest of my entire career". On his debut in Brazil in 1989, Mansell joked that he'd booked his plane ticket for halfway through the race because the gearbox was so unreliable. However, against the odds, he won the race and remained the last man to win on his Ferrari debut until Kimi Räikkönen in 2007.

MOMENTS

TITLE WINNER

At the 1990 British Grand Prix, Mansell threw his gloves into the crowd and announced that he was going to retire. However, Frank Williams stepped in with an offer he couldn't refuse – number one status. In 1991 he won five races, but lost out on reliability to Ayrton Senna. The following year, though, was a stormer. Mansell won nine out of 16 races in the superb Williams-Renault FW14B, taking 14 poles along the way. Finally, he was world champion. He subsequently left and returned to Williams, eventually ending his Formula 1 career after a brief stint with McLaren.

Nigel was 39 when he won the world championship. Here he lifts the second place trophy at the 1992 Hungarian Grand Prix, having just set a points score that was mathematically unbeatable.

FACT FILE: NIGEL MANSELL

NATIONALITY: British

DATE OF BIRTH: 8 August 1953 – Upton-upon-Severn, England

YEARS ACTIVE IN F1: 1980 to 1992, 1994 to 1995

TEAMS: Lotus, Williams, Ferrari, McLaren

RACES COMPETED: 187

DRIVERS' CHAMPIONSHIPS: 1992

RACE VICTORIES: 31

POLE POSITIONS: 32

FASTEST LAPS: 30

FIRST RACE: 1980 Austrian Grand Prix

LAST RACE: 1995 Spanish Grand Prix

CAREER POINTS: 482

The physical endurance required to run a race distance is similar to that required of running a marathon. But as much as stamina, drivers need strong muscles, unflinching concentration, and a careful diet. Each driver has his own trainer and physiotherapist to monitor his fitness and keep him motivated.

DRIVER TRAINING

Drivers tend to focus their training on intensive gym work, running, cycling, and swimming. The more varied the training, the better their cardiovascular conditioning will be. Driving is hardest on the neck and arms, and drivers use specially designed rigs to develop the muscles they will need to withstand cornering forces.

RED HOT HEAT

Races are sometimes extremely hot and cockpit temperatures can reach 60°C (140°F). That means drivers need to drink lots of water before the start of a race. They usually lose 2 kg (4.5 lb) of body water during each race, but it can be more. At the 2009 FORMULA 1 PETRONAS MALAYSIAN GRAND PRIX Fernando Alonso lost 5 kg (11 lb). This was because his drinks bottle broke. To train for this heat, drivers sometimes play tennis in their race suits or take a gym bike into the sauna.

"You're bracing yourself so hard, it sends your heart rate soaring, and yet you're so focused, you don't realize. There is also a phenomenal amount of adrenaline going round your system for two hours."

MARK WEBBER

"Drivers need the speed of a sprinter, the endurance of a marathon runner, the agility of a racket sports player, the flexibility of a gymnast, and the power of a rugby player. Therefore the training has to be multi-levelled. And we have to prepare for the worst, because if the power steering fails, or the drinks bottle fails, or the driver flat spots a tyre, it can make the race ten times tougher physically. Before the race, I'll warm up the driver's spine and neck muscles with a massage. I'll also have him do some mental agility tests... You don't want any delay between the brain and your hands and feet, otherwise you could spin or crash."

FEELING THE FORCE

Drivers need to be able to sustain loads of 3–5G around fast corners, and much higher still in the event of a crash. Therefore, a lot of training is focused on the neck muscles. Using special rigs, drivers will train with helmets attached to weights by a cord. You'll notice that most drivers have necks like tree trunks.

DID YOU KNOW?

Drivers have a supply of isotonic water in the car that they can drink via a straw in their helmet chin-guard. The liquid, available in different flavours, is released by pressing a button on the steering wheel. As this can get warm during the race, Damon Hill flavoured his liquid with tea.

SIMULATOR

Because testing is restricted, simulators are now more important than ever. Drivers spend around 30 days a year sitting in what is essentially a very expensive games console – a full-size car with a wrap-around screen, and a computer system that is loaded with every track. It is highly realistic, and with this tool, drivers can learn the circuits and how to get the most out of their cars.

Williams' German driver Nico Rosberg shows off his driving skills on a Formula 1 driving simulator.

Car safety

Drivers crash just as they always have, yet we haven't witnessed a fatal accident in Formula 1 racing since 1994, which is a testament to how far the safety of the cars has come. The quote below, from Robert Kubica, came just days after one of the most dramatic accidents ever seen. At the 2007 Canadian Grand Prix, Kubica lost control of his car and slammed head-on into a concrete wall at 227.5 km/h (141.4 mph). The car then barrel-rolled across the track before hitting a second wall. The BMW Sauber driver was saved by the car's survival cell, the restraint system, and the front and side impact structures, not forgetting his helmet and HANS device.

"When the car finally stopped, I realized I was not in bad shape. Probably ten years ago we would not be speaking here, and this time I'm like nothing has happened."

ROBERT KUBICA

CRASHES

Drivers sit in a safety cell or 'tub' that is made from 12 layers of carbon-fibre mats and weighs less than 60 kg (132 lb). Crash tests were first introduced in 1985. Now each car must pass 15 impact and endurance tests before it is approved. The safety cell must always remain intact.

Quick-release steering-wheel thread

Fire extinguisher button on steering wheel

Driver's water bottle

Six-point harness release

Digital read-out screen

Side-impact safety cell structure

Carbon-fibre helmet

Detachable upper cockpit sides

Headrest made from foam and carbon fibre

COCKPIT

Even under normal braking, the 5G load means a driver weighing 75 kg (165 lb) is pushing against his seatbelt with a weight of 375 kg (827 lb). The driver is strapped into the car by a six-point harness that has no give whatsoever, and that he can undo with one hand. In an emergency, he must be able to get out of the car within five seconds, and is tested on this before being given a 'superlicence' to race. On the sides of the cockpit are two pins that can be pulled to remove the upper cockpit for an easier exit. Under the driver's knees are two fire extinguisher chambers. If he pushes a button on the steering wheel, one-third goes into the cockpit, the rest into the engine. There is also an external handle for the marshals or pit crew to operate.

BLACK BOX

Since 1999, every Formula 1 car has been fitted with an accident recorder. Rather like the black box that can be found on an aircraft, it records all the speed and deceleration data of the car, and provides the information needed for making further safety improvements. It can also be used to reconstruct a driver's actions in the event of an accident. In addition, a warning light system located at the top of the cockpit provides an immediate indication of the severity of the accident.

ARE YOU SITTING COMFORTABLY?

Seats are tailor-made for each driver. The mould is cast by the driver sitting in the correct position on a bag of foam, which forms around his body. The mould is scanned and then produced in carbon fibre, with a softer external material to provide comfort. The seat is designed to be removed from the car with the driver still in it to reduce the risk of spinal injury in the event of an accident.

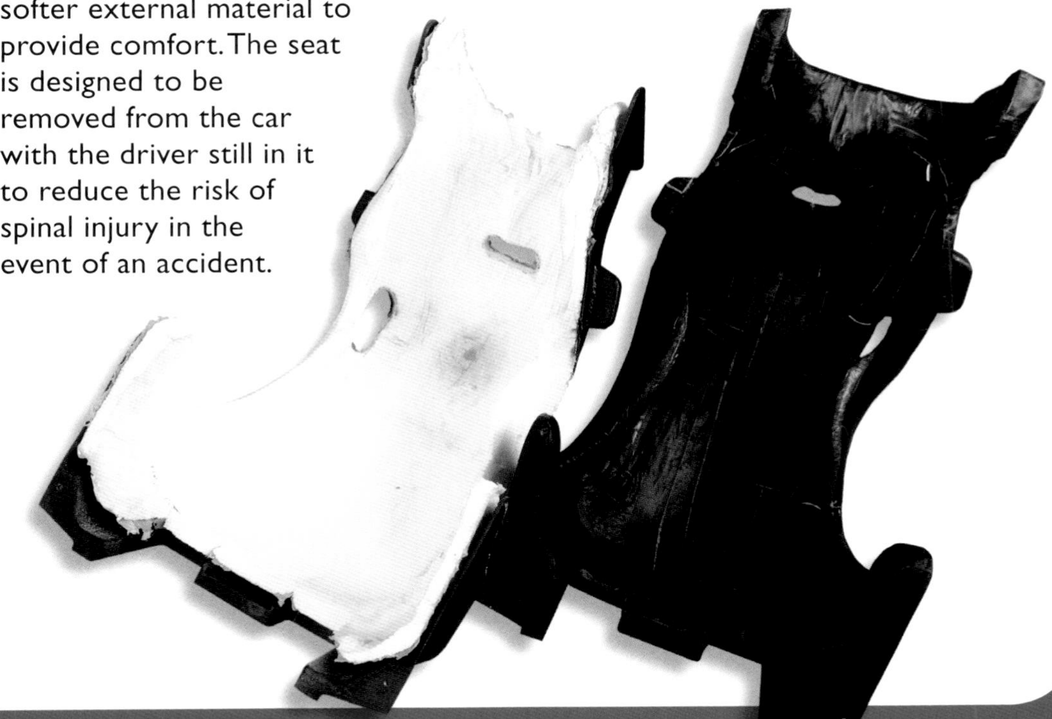

"There is no doubt that Formula 1 has the best risk management of any sport and any industry in the world."

SIR JACKIE STEWART

Helmets weren't compulsory when the world championship started. Now a driver's wardrobe is a serious business. The clothing and helmets the drivers wear are both fireproof and lightweight. Looking good is important too, so often they customize their kit, adding decorative touches in the colours of their country.

VINTAGE FASHION

Back in the 1950s, drivers such as Stirling Moss (above) turned up for races wearing pretty much whatever they felt like. Most wore white cotton overalls, which obviously offered no protection in the event of a fire. In the mid-1970s, drivers started to wear fire-resistant overalls similar to the ones you see today, but much heavier. The garment consisted of five thick layers of a material used by NASA for its spacesuits.

UNDERWEAR

Drivers wear fireproof socks, long-john stockings, roll-neck t-shirts, and balaclavas under their race suits for extra protection. At one time the material these garments were made from was very itchy, but now they are made from a fabric called Nomex®, they are much more comfortable. Nomex® is naturally a yellow colour, but often the garments made from it will be dyed white or black, depending on the driver's preference.

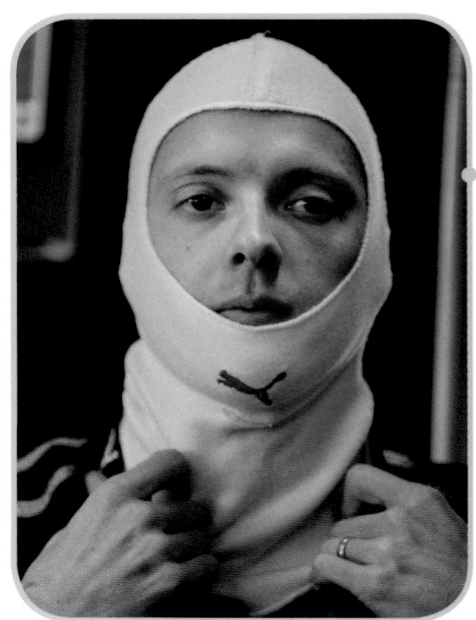

RACE SUIT

The correct attire for driving the fastest cars in the world is modelled here by Nico Rosberg (right). Unlike the bulky suits of the 1970s, this one is made from just two layers of Nomex®, and is tested to survive temperatures of 840°C (1,544°F) for 11 seconds. It's designed to be light and breathable, allowing sweat to escape. Note the two large 'handles' on the driver's shoulders. These are intended for marshals to lift him from his car, and they are designed to support the weight of his seat too.

HELMET

Helmets are designed to be lightweight (or else the drivers will get whiplash in the corners), aerodynamic, and strong. They weigh 1.25 kg (2.76 lb) and are made from carbon fibre, so are, essentially, bulletproof. Inside, there is a softer deformable layer coated in fireproof material. The visor is made of a clear polycarbonate that is shatterproof, flame resistant, and coated with anti-fogging chemicals. Several transparent tear-off strips are attached to the outside, so if the driver has dirt or oil obscuring his vision, he can remove it by tearing off a strip. Also, his helmet is strapped to a HANS (head and neck support) system, which rests on the shoulders. This helps to avoid overstretching the spinal vertebrae.

SPEEDING HEART

Kimi Räikkönen is sometimes accused of being robotic, and it's hard to argue when he unzips his race suit and a load of wires spill out. In fact, these wires are linked to a heart monitor, which both Ferrari drivers use during races to give their trainers feedback on their responses to the physical stresses and strains of high-speed driving under the most demanding conditions. During a Grand Prix, a driver's heart rate ranges between 160 and 190 beats per minute. He also burns approximately 600 calories over a race distance.

GLOVES

Fireproof gloves are made as thin as possible in order to give the driver maximum sensitivity to the steering wheel. It's quite normal for a driver to get through a set of gloves each weekend, and for hot races he'll wear slightly bigger ones to allow for his hands swelling.

BOOTS

The soles of a driver's boots are far thinner than those of ordinary shoes so that he can get an accurate feel for the pedals. Those on the right, belonging to Jarno Trulli, have been customized in his national colours.

Welcome to the Class of 2009. There are several well-known champions here, a few old veterans, and one fresh-faced rookie. What they have in common is a single goal – winning.

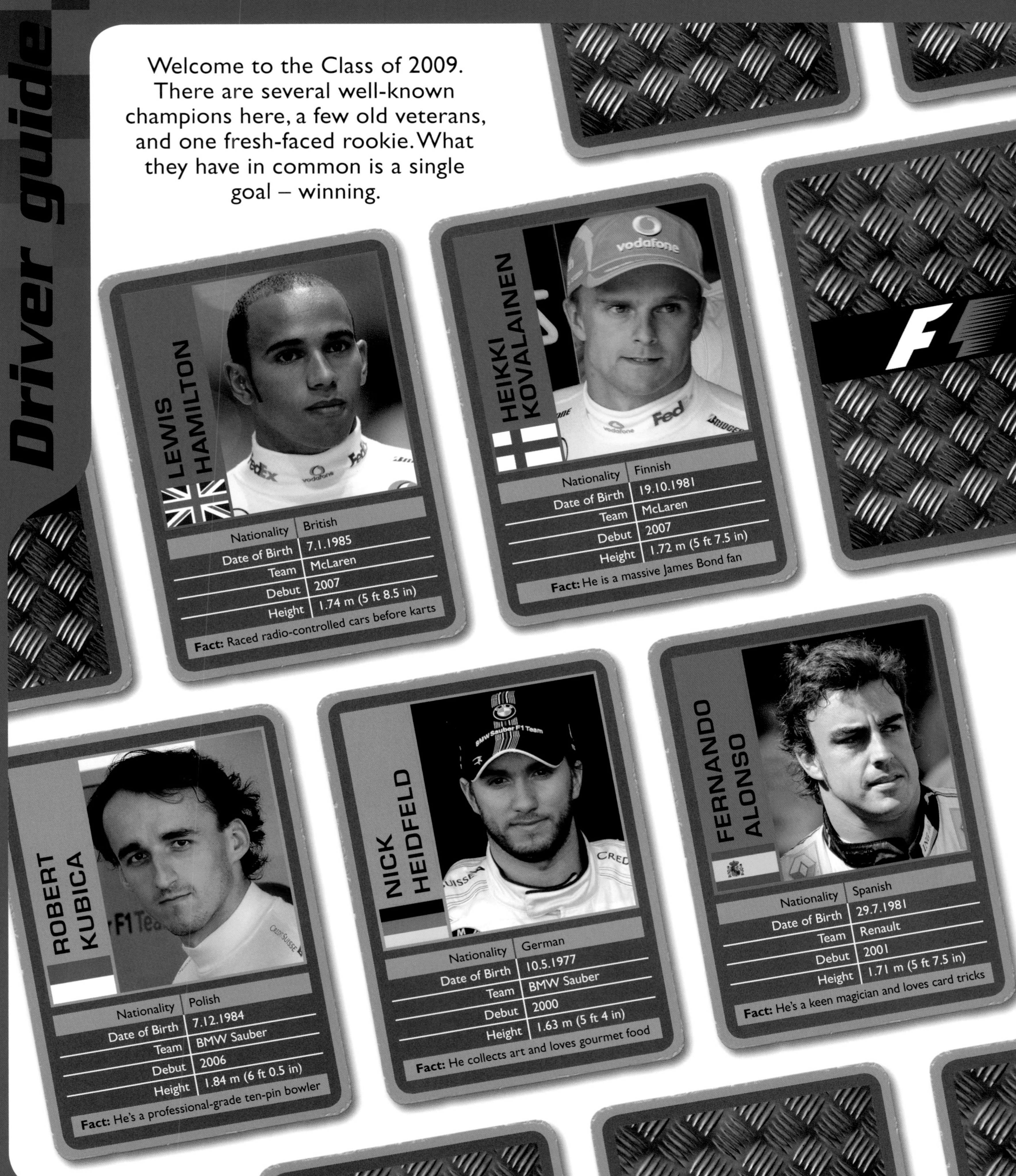

KIMI RÄIKKÖNEN

Nationality	Finnish
Date of Birth	17.10.1979
Team	Ferrari
Debut	2001
Height	1.75 m (5 ft 9 in)

Fact: His first car was a Lada

FELIPE MASSA

Nationality	Brazilian
Date of Birth	25.4.1981
Team	Ferrari
Debut	2002
Height	1.66 m (5 ft 5.5 in)

Fact: First visited a Grand Prix as a delivery boy

NELSON PIQUET JR

Nationality	Brazilian
Date of Birth	25.7.1985
Team	Renault
Debut	2008
Height	1.73 m (5 ft 8 in)

Fact: Scar on his cheek after attack by a dog

JARNO TRULLI

Nationality	Italian
Date of Birth	13.7.1974
Team	Toyota
Debut	1997
Height	1.73 m (5 ft 8 in)

Fact: He collects 1950s jukeboxes

TIMO GLOCK

Nationality	German
Date of Birth	18.3.1982
Team	Toyota
Debut	2004
Height	1.69 m (5 ft 6.5 in)

Fact: His first job was as a scaffolder

SEBASTIEN BUEMI

Nationality	Swiss
Date of Birth	31.10.1988
Team	Toro Rosso
Debut	2009
Height	1.76 m (5 ft 9.5 in)

Fact: He used to drive the FIA medical car

SEBASTIEN BOURDAIS

Nationality	French
Date of Birth	28.2.1979
Team	Toro Rosso
Debut	2008
Height	1.79 m (5 ft 10.5 in)

Fact: He has to wear glasses in the car

NICO ROSBERG

Nationality	German
Date of Birth	27.6.1985
Team	Williams
Debut	2006
Height	1.78 m (5 ft 10 in)

Fact: His mechanics call him 'Britney'

KAZUKI NAKAJIMA

Nationality	Japanese
Date of Birth	11.1.1985
Team	Williams
Debut	2007
Height	1.73 m (5 ft 8 in)

Fact: Kazuki's dad was also an F1 driver

JENSON BUTTON

Nationality	British
Date of Birth	19.1.1980
Team	Brawn
Debut	2000
Height	1.83 m (6 ft 0 in)

Fact: He has a pub named after him

MARK WEBBER
Nationality Australian
Date of Birth 27.8.1976
Team Red Bull Racing
Debut 2002
Height 1.84 m (6 ft 0.5 in)
Fact: He owns two donkeys

SEBASTIAN VETTEL
Nationality German
Date of Birth 3.7.1987
Team Red Bull Racing
Debut 2007
Height 1.76 m (5 ft 10.5 in)
Fact: He absolutely loves British TV comedy

RUBENS BARRICHELLO
Nationality Brazilian
Date of Birth 23.5.1972
Team Brawn
Debut 1993
Height 1.72 m (5 ft 7.5 in)
Fact: The only current driver to have raced Senna

GIANCARLO FISICHELLA
Nationality Italian
Date of Birth 14.1.1973
Team Force India
Debut 1997
Height 1.72 m (5 ft 7.5 in)
Fact: A football fanatic, he supports Roma

ADRIAN SUTIL
Nationality German
Date of Birth 11.1.1983
Team Force India
Debut 2007
Height 1.83 m (6 ft 0 in)
Fact: He's a talented pianist

When McLaren fielded the reigning world champion alongside a rookie in 2007, no one foresaw the power struggle that would bring the team to its knees. Politics, mind games, and paranoia were all served up with some truly aggressive racing. And although Alonso tore up his contract and returned to Renault the following year, the rivalry continues – there is little love lost.

HISTORY

It was an all-new line up for McLaren in 2007. The team had enticed Fernando Alonso – the most successful driver of his generation – from Renault and matched him with the prodigy Lewis Hamilton, whom the team had supported since he was 13. Hamilton, however, refused to play number two, taking nine podiums from his first nine races. It came to a head in Monaco. Alonso was leading and Hamilton, in second, was ordered to hold position. He complained publicly about this, which Fernando viewed as disrespectful. And it was about to get more acrimonious.

"I am easy to get on with, I don't hold grudges. I'm still leading the world championship and I haven't lost my respect for Fernando. If he doesn't want to speak to me that's up to him, I'm open."

LEWIS HAMILTON

CIVIL WAR

Team boss Ron Dennis was a father figure to Lewis, and Fernando found it hard to compete for that affection. Nonetheless, publicly, Hamilton and Alonso seemed to get on... until the 2007 Hungarian Grand Prix. The team's strategy demanded that Lewis let Fernando past during qualifying. He did not. Alonso, feeling he'd been compromised, then deliberately loitered in the pit ahead of the waiting Hamilton. Alonso drove off and got pole while Hamilton failed to get new tyres in time and lost out. At the final race of the year, in Brazil, Alonso's third place gave him 109 points, while Hamilton suffered a series of mishaps to finish seventh – also bringing his total to 109. However, Kimi Räikkönen won the race, claiming the title by a single point. As Hamilton had more second places that season, he took the runner-up spot.

PODIUM FINISH

Fernando Alonso tried to improve relations with Hamilton, stating that his problem was with McLaren's management and not with Lewis himself. However, when Lewis's title hopes went down to the wire again in 2008, Alonso said he hoped Felipe Massa would be victorious. Whenever Fernando beats Lewis, he can't hide his delight, and vice versa.

"When you hear the declarations of your boss saying that he feels a paternal sentiment for your team mate and rival, then you know that you can never have much trust in what that person will do."

FERNANDO ALONSO

A year on from their title clash in 2007, Lewis Hamilton keeps Fernando Alonso in his mirrors at the Brazilian Grand Prix, en route to becoming the sport's youngest champion.

DID YOU KNOW?

Hamilton and Alonso starred in a TV advertisement for Mercedes that played on their rivalry. Racing each other through hotel corridors, they burst into a sauna only to find Mika Häkkinen had got there first.

The race weekend

Roughly every fortnight, over the course of nine months, 20 F1 cars and tonnes of spares are dispatched to different race circuits around the world. They come with a legion of technical and commercial personnel, some of whom will be changing a transmission while another pours the perfect cappuccino for a VIP guest. In front of the pits sit thousands of fans, decked out in team shirts and caps, who have travelled to see their heroes race to victory.

Drivers line up in the rain at the start of the 2009 FORMULA 1 CHINESE GRAND PRIX at the Shanghai International Circuit.

The FIA Formula One World Championship is a massive logistical operation, and the biggest challenges of the weekend are often before the cars have turned a wheel. There are motorhomes, workstations, and garages to set up first, and the amount of kit needed to run two Formula 1 cars is incredible.

LONG HAUL

Outside Europe, the teams load their cars onto specially chartered cargo planes, along with the equipment they need. They'll send around 30–35 tonnes of gear each to the 'flyaway' races. Some equipment – such as office and catering items – are sent by sea freight to save money. Tyres, fuel, and certain other equipment are brought separately by technical partners, such as Bridgestone.

ON THE ROAD

Within Europe, a team's cargo always travels by road – each truck driver racking up around 30,000 km (18,650 miles). Teams bring around six trucks to each race, with three cars, a spare chassis, engines, gearboxes, bodywork, thousands of spare parts, tools, and other items. Transporting the motorhomes can be an even bigger exercise. BMW Sauber, for instance, takes eight trucks to load up its motorhome. And Red Bull takes over 30 for its Energy Station, along with 40 riggers.

AT THE RACE

The garage is the focus of work for the mechanics and engineers, but behind sit the trucks, which can be used like little factories. Here the technicians can machine parts and make new composites. The telescopic trucks are raised to create extra office space where engineers can work. Nearby are the motorhomes, which include management offices, drivers' changing rooms, and the canteen. Above the garages is the Paddock Club, which provides VIP hospitality and a great view of everything going on.

ON BOARD

IN-TOUCH

Communication is very important. Teams will take 70 radios with them so that all key personnel know everything that's going on all the time, and that's true of the people back at base too. Secure data links enable telemetry and other data to be sent back to the factory, even when the race is running.

DID YOU KNOW?
For the Monaco Grand Prix, Red Bull floats its massive Energy Station in the harbour, which can be accessed from the paddock by a jetty. It takes 7,000 man-hours to build and is constructed down the coast and then tugged across the Mediterranean Sea, buoyed by big polystyrene blocks.

The trucks in the F1 paddock are parked with military precision. Each one has to line up perfectly with the next. And trucks with personalized number plates will even be parked in numerical order!

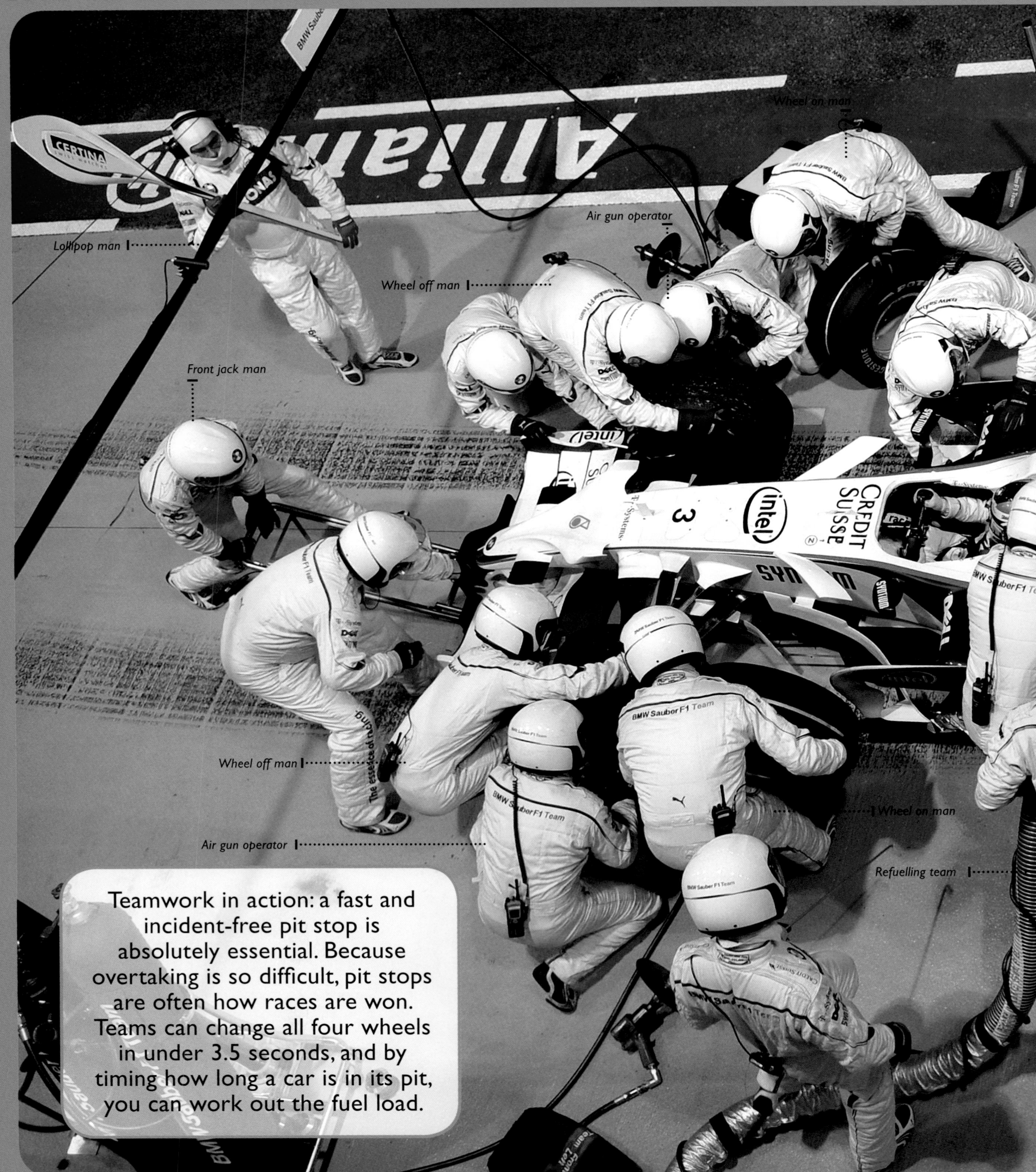

Teamwork in action: a fast and incident-free pit stop is absolutely essential. Because overtaking is so difficult, pit stops are often how races are won. Teams can change all four wheels in under 3.5 seconds, and by timing how long a car is in its pit, you can work out the fuel load.

DID YOU KNOW?

The fastest-ever pit stop was achieved in 1993 at the Belgian Grand Prix. Benetton's Riccardo Patrese had all four wheels changed in 3.2 seconds.

Members of the pit crew for BMW Sauber get to grips with Nick Heidfeld's car during the 2008 Singapore Grand Prix.

Pit stop

Twenty-two crew members work to replace the tyres, refuel, check the air intakes, maybe make a wing adjustment, and replace any broken parts – all under the watchful eye of the team manager. And don't forget to clean the driver's visor. Practice makes perfect. Teams will practise stops 1,000 times over the course of a season. Here the BMW Sauber team shows us how it's done.

❶ STAND BY

Provided it's a scheduled stop, the pit crew will emerge from the garage and get ready to receive a driver one lap ahead of the stop. The blankets will remain fixed to the tyres until the last possible second.

❷ CAR IN

Some pitlanes are longer than others, but the race engineer keeps everything closely timed. When the car comes into view, he'll order the blankets off. The lollipop man signals the driver into the box, and two men by the front wheels indicate when the car is in position.

❸ JACK UP

It's essential the car stops precisely on the line. The front jack man is already waiting and will slide his rake-like device onto jack points located under the front wing. Meanwhile, the rear jack man gets into position and elevates the rear.

❹ CAR RAISED

Even before the car is raised, the kneeling wheel men will be undoing the nuts with powerful pneumatic air guns. Once jacked, there is a clearance of just a few centimetres.

❺ TYRES OFF

There's a switch on the wheel gun: flick left to undo the nut, flick right to put it back on the thread. The nut is removed with the 'spinner' – a round piece of carbon designed to aid aerodynamics. To the left of the air gun man crouches one crew member to yank the wheel off, and to the right another to slide a fresh wheel on. The gun makes a growling noise when the nuts are tight enough.

❻ REFUELLING

With the car in the air, the fuel hose goes in. The hose plus its nozzle weighs 65 kg (143 lb), so it requires two men to hold it. The fuel itself is not allowed to contain any power-boosting chemical compounds, and the amount going into the fuel cell is controlled by a computer in the garage. The fuelling rig is standardized for all teams.

❽ EXIT

Once the hose is out, the lollipop flips round and the driver engages first gear. Once the rear is down, everyone leans back, the front man checks the coast is clear, and the lollipop is raised. The driver lights the rear tyres and exits.

❼ HANDS UP

The lollipop man is looking for a show of hands from the wheel men to indicate they've finished. They wear red gloves, while the others wear blue. With four hands in the air, the front jack can come down. Attention turns to the refueller. When the hose is clear, the rear goes down.

MISTAKES

Fires occasionally occur when fuel spits onto the hot exhaust and ignites, so extinguishers are always to hand. Raising the lollipop too early is also very dangerous. At the 2008 Singapore Grand Prix, Ferrari used a traffic light system, which mistakenly signalled Felipe Massa to drive when the hose was still attached. He launched down the pitlane, trailing the hose and a poor mechanic with him.

Robert Kubica gets a fright during qualifying for the 2009 FORMULA 1 GULF AIR BAHRAIN GRAND PRIX, with flames erupting from the car.

From moments of frantic labour and high pressure to periods where the mechanics aren't allowed to touch the cars at all, working in the pitlane is a very regimented business. But it also gets you as close to the action as it's possible to get without actually driving the car.

INSPECTIONS

The FIA conducts random technical inspections during the race weekend to ensure the cars comply fully with the regulations. After qualifying, the mechanics wheel their cars down to the FIA garage for weighing and inspection. Between qualifying and the race, they are not allowed to make changes. If they do, they have to start the race from the pitlane.

HOW MUCH FUEL?

The FIA designates a litres-per-second rate for the fuel rigs, so you can work out the fuel load by timing how long the nozzle is on the car. The rigs refuel at 12 litres (2.6 gallons) per second, and the car tanks have a capacity of between 115–125 litres (25–27.5 gallons). The maximum refuelling time is ten seconds. The amount of fuel is computer-controlled. Over a weekend, each team will get through around 1,200 litres (264 gallons).

Ferrari pit crew refuel Kimi Räikkönen during the 2008 Japanese Grand Prix.

SETTING UP THE SPARE CAR

There is a third car in the garage at each race, which is set up for one particular driver, usually alternating from race to race. But if the spare car is needed by the driver that the car isn't set up for, the team will scramble to get it altered. What they do depends on how much time is available. If they have only five minutes, they'll change the pedals, seat belts, and name stickers. If they have an hour, they'll transfer the entire set-up of the car. And if they have longer, they'll go further and change the gearbox ratios.

WET WEATHER SET-UP

Teams cannot make any changes once qualifying has started, so few gamble on a full wet set-up – if the race turns out to be dry, the car will be slow. In case of rain, the mechanics soften the dampers, springs, and roll bars, and put a lot of wing on the car, all of which make it less skittish. They can also change the cooling exits to allow for any change in the weather.

PENALTIES

Pitlane speed limits weren't introduced until 1994 – imagine how dangerous it must have been to work in the pitlane before then! Now there is a strict speed limit of 80 km/h (50 mph) in practice and 100 km/h (62 mph) in qualifying and the race. The driver needs to hit a button on his steering wheel as he crosses a line at the start of the pitlane to activate the car's speed limiter. If caught speeding, he'll be fined US$250 for every km/h he drives over the limit.

WHERE DO MECHANICS DO THEIR LAUNDRY?

The race team is sent off with enough gear for a fresh change of clothes every day, but if they're on back-to-back flyaways, they'll use the hotel laundry, simple as that. They don't tend to get covered in oil, but if a shirt gets really dirty, it's thrown away.

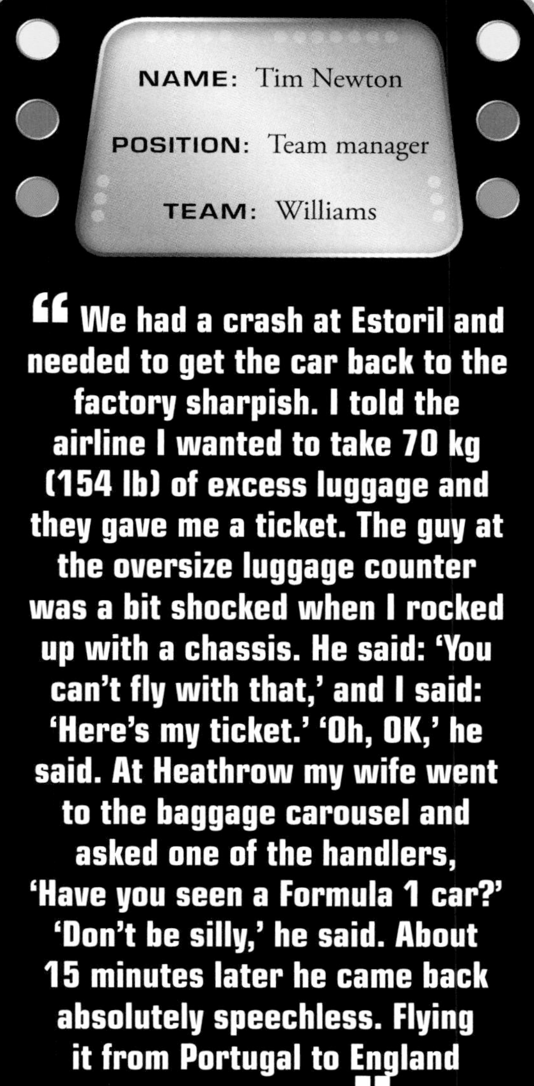

NAME: Tim Newton

POSITION: Team manager

TEAM: Williams

"We had a crash at Estoril and needed to get the car back to the factory sharpish. I told the airline I wanted to take 70 kg (154 lb) of excess luggage and they gave me a ticket. The guy at the oversize luggage counter was a bit shocked when I rocked up with a chassis. He said: 'You can't fly with that,' and I said: 'Here's my ticket.' 'Oh, OK,' he said. At Heathrow my wife went to the baggage carousel and asked one of the handlers, 'Have you seen a Formula 1 car?' 'Don't be silly,' he said. About 15 minutes later he came back absolutely speechless. Flying it from Portugal to England only cost £70."

"And suddenly I realized that I was no longer driving the car consciously. I was driving it by a kind of instinct, only I was in a different dimension. It was like I was in a tunnel. I was way over the limit but still able to find even more."

AYRTON SENNA

The starting grid for a Grand Prix is determined by qualifying – a one-hour event held the day before the race, where every driver aims to set the quickest possible time. The drivers are under huge pressure not to make any mistakes. Traffic can be a problem, so it's essential the teams send their drivers out at the right time. The man with the fastest time earns the coveted pole position.

2009 RULES

Qualifying is split into three distinct parts. 'Q1' comes first – a 20-minute free-for-all, where drivers try to beat each other's times. The five slowest cars drop out at the end of the session, taking the final five grid places. After a seven-minute break, there's the 15-minute 'Q2'. Again, the five slowest drop out and take grid spots 11–15. After a further eight-minute break to turn the cars around, there is the ten-minute 'Q3' shoot-out. Here strategy must be considered, as cars qualify with their race fuel on board. The driver with the fastest time gets the number one slot.

EYE ON THE TIMES

Circuits are fitted with sophisticated timing systems that are accurate to 1,000th of a second. There are three timing sectors, and monitors allow teams to see all three split-times to judge a driver's speed in each section. Almost incredibly, at the 1997 European Grand Prix three drivers shared the fastest time – right down to 1,000th of a second! Jacques Villeneuve, Michael Schumacher, and Heinz-Harald Frentzen lined up for the race in the order of when they posted the lap.

QUALIFYING KING

Considered the greatest ever qualifying lap, Ayrton Senna's pole position at the 1988 Monaco Grand Prix was a full 1.4 seconds faster than P2 man Alain Prost – in an identical McLaren – and 2.7 seconds quicker than the P3 Ferrari of Gerhard Berger. Senna later confessed he had felt a strange out-of-body experience while he was doing it. It scared him so much that he drove back to the pits slowly.

HAS QUALIFYING CHANGED?

Traditionally, qualifying was a one-hour shoot-out between cars, all on the lightest-possible fuel loads. But drivers would delay going out, wanting other drivers to lay grippy rubber down on the track before them. The watching fans got bored waiting for something to happen, so a one-shot system was introduced. Every driver had one flying lap to do his best, and if he made a mistake he paid the price. The current knock-out system was adopted in 2006, and it means there are usually always cars on track, and drivers have an unlimited number of laps.

DEALING WITH PRESSURE

Some drivers thrive on qualifying, some don't. Back when qualifying was a one flying-lap affair, the pressure was immense, as a single mistake in that lap would wreck an entire weekend – maybe even an entire season. David Coulthard (above) found that hard to deal with, and, along with other drivers, sought advice from a sports psychologist to get the best out of himself.

Ayrton Senna flies around the track during qualifying for the Monaco Grand Prix.

DID YOU KNOW?

The fastest-ever qualifying performance was recorded by Juan Pablo Montoya at the 2002 Italian Grand Prix. The Colombian's time of 1 min 20.264 secs over the 5.793 km (3.600 miles) Monza course gave his BMW Williams an average speed of 259.827 km/h (161.449 mph).

"In Hungary in 1998 I had to push really hard to win. Ross [Brawn] came on the radio and said 'We're in some trouble and we need 20 qualifying laps from you'. I said 'OK, let's try!'"

MICHAEL SCHUMACHER

Racing is like playing chess in a washing machine. It's a tactical game of wits played out in an extreme environment, and it can get turned upside down without warning. The trick is to second-guess what the other drivers are doing and react accordingly. As the race pans out, drivers might need to drive defensively, or they might get the opportunity to attack.

TAKING A CORNER

In order to take a corner at the fastest possible speed, you must approach it at the widest angle, turning in from the opposite side (outside) of the track, kissing the apex (the middle part of the inside corner), then reapply the power and use the full width of the track before straightening up the steering. So there are three stages to taking a single-apex corner. A 90-degree corner, like the one shown below, is relatively straightforward, but some corners may demand a late or earlier apex. A double-apex corner requires greater concentration and strong neck muscles.

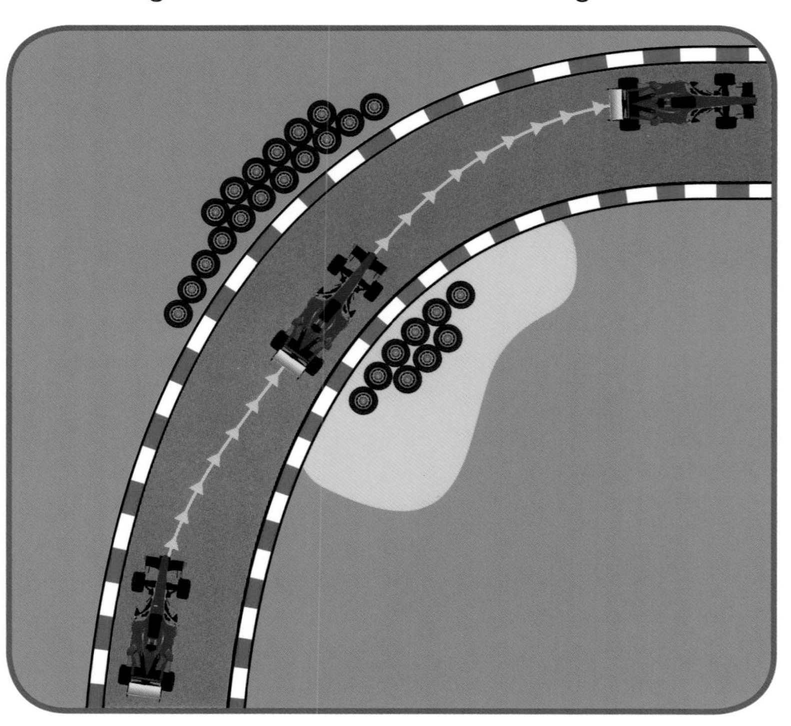

SLIPSTREAMING

To overtake you need to catapult yourself past the driver in front, and to do that you need to get a better exit out of a corner that leads onto a straight. If you can get close, you can slipstream behind the car you're chasing. The car ahead is cutting into the air, creating a space about 60 m (197 ft) behind it that is largely free from turbulence or wind resistance. Once in the slipstream, your car will begin to accelerate faster than your opponent's. You need to judge the correct moment to pull out of the slipstream. Do so too early and you'll lose your advantage. Too late, and the bend ahead will be too near to make the move stick. And if you get too close directly behind the other driver's gearbox, his 'dirty air' will play havoc with your aerodynamics. Another thing to be aware of is that you have less downforce when you're slipstreaming, so if you follow another car through a fast corner, you might need to reduce your speed.

OVERTAKING

Having got the speed to pass another car, it is important that you pull far enough alongside him before committing to the approaching corner. If you are on the inside but are not fully alongside as you turn, it's his corner – his right of way. You need to brake and swerve out of the way before your race ends with a huge crunch. If you can squeeze down the inside in time for the approaching corner, and are a nose ahead, the other driver should give you enough room and then the position is yours.

Kimi Räikkönen lines up Timo Glock for a pass, his Ferrari closing up in the Toyota's wake.

STRATEGY

IT'S THE PITS

Unless your strategy is sound, you won't win. Most strategic decisions revolve around the tyres and fuel loads. For some circuits – such as Monza, which has a very long start/finish straight – the best strategy is to one-stop. For others, a three-stop can work. When considering the length of your stints, you also need to consider tyre compounds. Soft compounds are generally faster but last fewer laps. Teams will plan their strategies ahead of the race, but if it rains or there's a safety car period, everything needs to be recalculated. Those who make the right call will profit. It's what makes motor racing so unpredictable.

USING KERS

Having KERS on board means you have a boost button at your fingertips, and that can make overtaking much easier, and being overtaken much more difficult. For 6.7 seconds per lap you have an extra 80 hp at your disposal, which will increase top speed by around 8 km/h (5 mph) and could give you as much as a 10 m (33 ft) advantage in the run down to the first corner. Also, should a non-KERS car pull alongside you, a quick squirt of your boost button should send him back to where he came from. The slight disadvantage with KERS, though, is that it increases the car's centre of gravity, which does nothing for its handling.

Night race

The Singapore Grand Prix is the only Formula 1 race to be held at night. Laid out on a street circuit that curls around the island's Marina Bay area, it looks totally different from any other. With some beautiful floodlit architecture – modern and old – rising above and beyond the artificially lit track, the drivers find it brighter than daylight!

A BRIGHT IDEA

Holding a night race in Singapore makes perfect sense because, as well as being unique and exciting, the sport's European audience can tune in at a normal lunchtime hour, six or seven time zones behind. The circuit is lit by 1,500 2,000-watt halide light projectors, which are spaced 4 m (13 ft) apart and situated 10 m (33 ft) above the ground. It's four times brighter than a normal sports stadium, and at the inaugural race in 2008 the drivers encountered no vision problems. However, if it were to rain, there are fears that it could create some lens glare on the drivers' visors.

DID YOU KNOW?

In the first Singapore Grand Prix, Mark Webber was running in second place when his gearbox selected two gears simultaneously and the Red Bull driver was forced to retire. An investigation suggested static, caused by a subway train passing under the track, may have been responsible.

ADAPTING TO THE NIGHT

When F1 personnel arrive in Singapore they stick rigidly to European time and resist going to bed before 5 a.m. To ensure they can sleep in the daytime drivers have their hotel bedroom windows blacked out, and ask that cleaning staff stay away from their floors before lunchtime so that the clatter of service trolleys does not wake them. It turns the Singapore Grand Prix into a truly unique experience, where F1 drivers are almost encouraged to club the night away before a race.

Felipe Massa leaves the Supreme Court building in his wake during the 2008 Singapore Grand Prix. Despite starting on pole, the Brazilian was unable to record a podium finish.

Not only are the cars much safer now than previously, but the whole infrastructure of the Grand Prix is geared towards minimizing risk and acting promptly. Motor racing will always be dangerous, but the drivers and spectators are protected as much as they can be, and marshals and medical help are never far away. In the event of an incident, the safety car sweeps out and keeps the drivers treading water until the race can get under way again.

SAFETY CAR

The safety car helps to keep a race going even when there has been an accident. The F1 cars gather behind it in formation until the problem has been cleared away. It needs to be a fast car, though – if the speed of the cars following it falls too low, the tyres go cold and the engines can overheat. Safety car periods can provide a tactical advantage for drivers who wish to refuel without losing too much time. However, in order to preserve safety and prevent cars rushing to the pits, the drivers are given a speed limit while they are out on track.

MARSHALS

Every circuit has track marshals with fire extinguishers posted along both sides of the track every 300 m (985 ft). These people are volunteers – motor racing fans themselves – and undergo intensive training in the run-up to the Grand Prix, learning what to do in the event of an accident. Sometimes they have to put themselves in quite hazardous situations, so everyone is very grateful for their work.

DID YOU KNOW?

A safety car was first used in Formula 1 racing at the 1973 Canadian Grand Prix. However, the safety car ran in front of the wrong driver, which incorrectly placed part of the field a lap down. After the race ended, it took several hours to sort out who the winner was.

EMERGENCY RESPONSE

There are approximately 130 medics and doctors on stand-by, and a high-performance medical car capable of reaching the scene of any accident within two minutes. Also on hand are six ambulances and two helicopters, and all the hospitals in the area will be on alert. In addition, every track has a fully equipped medical centre with an operating theatre.

WARNING FLAGS

Yellow means there is danger on or near the track, so drivers must slow and not overtake. Blue means you are about to be lapped and should yield to the following car. Red means the race has been stopped – drivers must immediately slow down and return to the start line. Black means you must stop within one lap and report to the race director – this usually relates to dangerous driving.

The safety car is a Mercedes-Benz SL63 AMG, a 525-bhp supercar driven by former DTM racer Bernd Maylander. He's had this role since 2000.

NAME: Bernd Maylander

POSITION: Safety car driver

"When I'm leading the pack, I'm setting lap times that are probably no more than a tenth or two slower than the very quickest I could go. The F1 cars need to go quickly to keep heat in their tyres – without heat, they'll have no grip – and the engines need to get enough air into them to keep cool or else they'll blow up. If I can't keep up the speed, I'd have a lot of broken cars behind me. It's a balancing act – if I ended up in the gravel, we'd have to red flag the race. Believe me, if that happened you wouldn't see me again. But it's my job to drive on the limit – and besides, this is a sweet car to drive quickly."

The finish

A wise man once said, "To finish first, first you must finish." This is the end goal for every driver – seeing the chequered flag at the end of the afternoon. Finishing a Grand Prix is a great achievement because, regardless of your ultimate position, it shows you have kept your head and not made many mistakes. With cars worth millions and points worth even more, bringing the car home is important. And if you can do so before everyone else, then it's been a very good day at the office.

CHEQUERED FLAG

Passing the finish line, the driver will dart towards the pit wall where his team has converged, leaning over the wall and cheering him on. The driver, at this stage, has usually got both hands off the wheel and is waving them wildly in the air while screaming down the radio to his team, thanking everyone for all their hard work.

Sebastian Vettel survives the rain to snatch victory for Red Bull Racing – the team's first win – at the 2009 FORMULA 1 CHINESE GRAND PRIX.

PARC FERME

Parc ferme is the FIA's holding pen for cars. The top three drivers get their own little VIP parking spots with '1', '2', and '3' marked out for them. Around the outside of the pen crowd the team personnel of those podium finishers. The winning driver will usually stand up in his seat and let the photographers get a triumphant picture. Then all three go into the FIA garage and are weighed with their helmets.

DID YOU KNOW?

When James Hunt won his title in Japan in 1976, finishing third at Fuji, he never made it onto the podium. Due to torrential rain, the race had run late and Hunt had a plane to catch.

PODIUM

There are three steps on the winner's podium. The actual race winner gets to stand on the highest step, the second-place man a level down to the winner's right, and the third-place finisher to the winner's left. The protocol on this is very clear and any deviation is punished. In 2002, after Rubens Barrichello was ordered to slow down to hand victory to his team mate Michael Schumacher in Austria, Schumacher felt embarrassed and let Rubens take the top step. As punishment, Ferrari was given a US$1 million fine for this infringement.

PRESENTATION

After the drivers take their positions on the podium, the national anthem of the winner is played, followed, if different, by that of the constructor. The drivers and a representative of the winning team are then handed their trophies, usually by a senior politician from the host country and by the title sponsor.

CHAMPAGNE

The bubbling finale is provided by three magnums of Mumm champagne, handily uncorked and ready to spray by the celebrating drivers. Champagne first appeared on a motor racing podium at the Vanderbilt Cup in New York in 1936 – a race won by Tazio Nuvolari – and was first sprayed by mistake at Le Mans in 1967. The heat that day caused the bottles to pop prematurely. Dan Gurney grabbed one bottle and tried to put his hand over the flow. Everyone got drenched in bubbly and a tradition was born.

Dry ice swirls around BMW Sauber's new model at its press launch.

The future

Formula 1 racing never stays the same for long – it's constantly evolving. Everyone looks forward to the new year, when the covers are taken off the new cars. But who will be the new teams? And where will they (and we) be going? Pack your bags for the following itinerary…

As Formula I racing becomes more and more popular, the events themselves are in demand. Cities and governments are vying for the rights to host a Grand Prix. And while the focus of development is in Asia at the moment, some hot new venues in Europe are also under discussion.

INDIA

A country of over one billion people represents a market of tremendous growth potential for Formula I racing. India already has its own FI team, but what it really wants is a home-grown driver. Meanwhile, what better way to promote racing there than by staging what promises to be one of the most exciting and colourful of races. A circuit is being built in Greater Noida, 50 km (30 miles) from Delhi, and will host its first Grand Prix in 2011.

LONDON

In 2004, London's famous Regent Street and Piccadilly Circus hosted a demonstration of Formula I cars that drew half a million spectators. So just imagine the attention it would get if the cars were racing flat out! The city gave consideration to hosting a Grand Prix, but instead chose to invest £6 billion in holding the 2012 Olympic Games. Still, a London Grand Prix might well happen in the future.

ROME

Formula I racing could be returning to its chariot-racing roots if the mayor of Rome gets his way. The city has marked out a street circuit in its financial district and set aside €150 million to host the event from 2012. A Grand Prix on the cobbles of the ancient city was a dream Enzo Ferrari held dear. Shame the circuit won't pass landmarks like the Colosseum (right) or St Peter's Basilica.

PARIS

Paris was the scene of the world's first-ever motor race, so it would be fantastic to introduce Formula I racing to the 'city of lights'. Since the Magny-Cours circuit let the French Grand Prix go in 2008, the sport has been searching for a suitable venue close to the capital. Disneyland was a leading contender, but ran into opposition from environmental campaigners. The front-running venue now is Flins-Les Mureaux, northwest of Paris, which hopes to host the race from 2011. The €112 million project is already under way.

KOREA

The Korean Grand Prix is set to be held from 2010 at a circuit 400 km (250 miles) south of Seoul. Located in Yeongam County, it will race along a harbour and through the town. As at Monaco, spectators will be able to watch the action from luxury yachts. Work should be completed in late 2009.

MOSCOW

Talks about hosting a Russian Grand Prix have been going on since 1982. Work has begun on a new Hermann Tilke-designed track, 'Moscow Raceway', about 80 km (50 miles) from the capital in the town of Fedyukino. The circuit has said its goal is to host Formula 1 racing as soon as possible. David Coulthard attended the ground breaking ceremony in October 2008.

DID YOU KNOW?

In 2007, Shell produced a TV advertisement with Ferrari that took Formula 1 cars from six different decades and raced them in a series of exciting locations: Rome, New York City, Hong Kong, Rio de Janeiro, and Monaco. It was breathtaking.

As we have seen before in Formula 1 racing, founding a completely new team and being competitive is an almighty task. Some have been successful, others not. In 2010, the grid will expand to welcome six more cars and three new teams. For Campos Meta Team, Team US F1, and Manor Grand Prix, the winter will be a very busy one – building the team, developing a fast and reliable F1 car from scratch, and raising the money necessary to compete at the top level.

CAMPOS META TEAM

Country: Spain
Engine: Cosworth
Team principal: Adrian Campos

The Campos Racing team was launched in 1998 by former F1 driver Adrian Campos, who competed in 21 Grands Prix for Minardi between 1987 and 1988, but failed to finished better than 14th place. The results of his own teams have been better. He also gave Fernando Alonso his first-ever car test, and the Spaniard went on to win the Euro Open MovieStar Series by Nissan with Campos. The team has also enjoyed success in other formulae, including F3 and GP2, and with the Mexico A1GP team.

DID YOU KNOW?

US F1 co-founder and sporting director Peter Windsor is a journalist and former Williams team manager. He was a passenger in the car when Sir Frank Williams had his crippling accident in 1986.

Former F1 driver driver Giorgio Pantano raced for Campos in 2007. Here he is in action during the GP2 race at Monza.

MANOR GRAND PRIX

Country: United Kingdom
Engine: Cosworth
Team principal: John Booth

Based in Sheffield, in the north of England, Manor has been active in the lower motor racing formulae ever since former racer John Booth turned to management. The team quickly won in Formula Ford, the entry level single-seater series, and then dominated Formula Renault between 1997 and 2000. Kimi Räikkönen took his first title with Manor. In 2003, Lewis Hamilton raced for it and won the British F3 championship. The team's technical director is Nick Wirth, who was previously technical director at Benetton and founded the Simtek F1 team, which raced between 1994 and 1995. In total, Manor has won 171 races and 19 championships in other formulae.

Under the guidance of John Booth, Manor has taken part in Formula Ford, Formula Renault, and F3 races. They also engineered the car for Ireland's A1 GP team.

TEAM US F1

Country: USA
Engine: Cosworth
Team principal: Ken Anderson

Running under the slogan 'Made in America', US F1 is an entirely new racing operation, but its directors have been involved in F1 racing for many years. Ken Anderson who was previously technical director of the Ligier and Onyx F1 teams, has designed and constructed multiple Indy 500 and Indy Car Series winning cars, and created the state-of-the-art Windshear wind tunnel in North Carolina. It is in this American state – the epicentre for NASCAR racing teams – that US F1 will be based, and the team plans to field American drivers. It will be the first time a modern F1 team has been based outside of Europe.

Team principal Ken Anderson (left) and sporting director Peter Windsor (right) announce the launch of the US F1 team.

Win the Formula 1 World Championship and you may as well kiss your private life goodbye. Lewis Hamilton, Kimi Räikkönen, and Fernando Alonso are all household names. But who else has got what it takes to attain megastar status? Here we introduce the next big things to hit the racetrack...

DID YOU KNOW?
'Bobby K', aka Robert Kubica, is a titan of the bowling lanes, regularly competing in prestigious European Championship games. But he doesn't appreciate Big Lebowski jokes. "[It's not] a party game – where you go drinking beer and have fun."

ROBERT KUBICA

Poland's Robert Kubica put himself on the map when he topped qualifying in Bahrain in 2008 (giving journalists a field day with their 'Pole on pole' headlines). He then went all the way in Canada, with victory at the circuit where he'd had a breathtaking accident 12 months earlier. Overall, the 24-year-old has proved he is not only quick, but error free and utterly ruthless. If BMW Sauber give him a car that can fight at the front, Kubica will be a good tip for the championship.

TIMO GLOCK

Not many drivers get a second bite of the cherry, but Timo is the exception. The 27-year-old got his break in F1 racing in 2004 with Jordan, but found himself in Champ Car shortly afterwards. However, after winning the GP2 title in 2007 (following in the tyre tracks of Nico Rosberg and Lewis Hamilton), he was back, and with the promising Toyota team. At the 2008 Hungarian Grand Prix, he finished a superb second – equalling the team's best-ever result. A level-headed character, the German's easy relationship with team and press is a complete contrast to that of his predecessor, Ralf Schumacher.

Timo Glock celebrates his podium finish at the 2009 FORMULA 1 PETRONAS MALAYSIAN GRAND PRIX, where he finished behind Nick Heidfeld and Jenson Button.

SEBASTIEN BUEMI

With Red Bull-sponsored drivers including Sebastien Loeb, Sebastian Vettel, Sebastien Bourdais, and now Sebastien Buemi, it's clear there's a pattern developing. This 20-year-old comes from Switzerland, where motor racing is banned. Still, he didn't let that stop him, coming second in the 2007 Formula 3 Euroseries and the 2008 GP2 Asia Series. So he's used to coming second. But with his relative inexperience, he has immediately confounded expectations in F1 racing, regularly beating his team mate and picking up points.

SEBASTIAN VETTEL

Sebastian Vettel is never usually short of words. However, when he passed the finish line at Monza in 2008, he was rendered speechless. The 21-year-old became the youngest Grand Prix winner ever, after dominating in the wet from pole. It was clear throughout the year that the Toro Rosso team had found a rather special driver, but that first win came even sooner than expected. At the 2009 FORMULA 1 CHINESE GRAND PRIX, he added Red Bull Racing's first win to his list of achievements. Now it seems just a matter of time before he adds 'world champion' to his CV. In his German homeland he's known as 'Baby Schumi'. He hates being called that.

Only one or two seats become available in F1 racing each year, and there are many young drivers in the junior categories hoping they'll be picked. Here are a few hotshots who might just make the grade.

ROMAIN GROSJEAN

Frenchman Grosjean is the favourite son of Renault, for whom he is F1 reserve driver. He beat Sebastien Buemi to the 2007 F3 Euroseries title and dominated the 2008 GP2 Asia Series. Last year he won two main GP2 Series races for ART, but was beaten overall by Giorgio Pantano and Bruno Senna. In 2009, the 23-year-old set the pace again. He knows how to lead a race, but there are some doubts as to whether he can race in the pack.

BRUNO SENNA

Bruno came close to competing in F1 racing in 2009. He tried to persuade Honda to give him a seat, but the Japanese manufacturer pulled out of the sport. The team, then rebranded as Brawn, decided it needed a driver with more experience. Bruno got into racing late in life, but was runner-up in the 2008 GP2 series. In 2009, he raced at Le Mans but was largely at a loose end, having missed out on a competitive GP2 ride due to his focus on F1 racing. Of course, it's hard to ignore the surname, Bruno is the nephew of the legendary Ayrton Senna.

"If you think I'm good, just wait until you see my nephew."

AYRTON SENNA

MARCO ANDRETTI

Racing royalty, 22-year-old Marco is the son of Michael Andretti and grandson of 1978 F1 world champion Mario. He came second in the 2006 Indy 500, a race his granddad won in 1969. He successfully tested for the Honda F1 team in 2007, but his recent Indy Car performances have been disappointing. His immediate goal is to win the Indy 500, and then his attention may return to F1 racing.

NICO HULKENBERG

Managed by Willi Weber, the man who guided Michael Schumacher's career, 22-year-old Hulkenberg is Germany's latest *wunderkind* and has the CV to prove it. He won a highly competitive F3 Euroseries title in 2008 and was crowned world champion by the A1GP series in 2007. He competed in four GP2 Asia Series races for the ART team earlier this year, taking one win and two pole positions. For the main series he's sticking with ART – the team who previously took both Nico Rosberg and Lewis Hamilton to the title. He also has an air of Kimi Räikkönen about him.

LUCAS DI GRASSI

Having finished runner up to Timo Glock in GP2 in 2007, this 25-year-old Brazilian was appointed reserve driver to Renault F1. Although he missed the first six GP2 races of 2008, he rejoined to take three wins and finished third in the championship – overall he had the highest points-to-starts ratio. He has a permanent drive in GP2 this year and is winning once again. A strong contender for an F1 seat in 2010.

WILDCARDS

A female driver, such as Danica Patrick, could help increase Formula 1 racing's global audience still further.

YOU NEVER KNOW...

If F1 racing could pick anyone in motorsport, it would be the three shown here. Eight-times MotoGP champion Valentino Rossi set competitive times in a series of F1 tests and says "the potential is definitely there". Sebastien Loeb, the most successful rally driver of all time, successfully tested a Red Bull F1 car, but admits that at 35 he may be too old. And of course, the sport would love to have US racing sensation Danica Patrick.

Formula 1 racing always welcomes characters, and Valentino Rossi is as engaging as they come.

Sebastien Loeb is multi-skilled and can easily adapt from a WRC Citroën to an F1 car.

Rubens Barrichello puts his car through its paces during practice for the 2009 FORMULA 1 PETRONAS MALAYSIAN GRAND PRIX. Team mate Jenson Button went on to win in a race cut short by torrential rain.

Statistics

TOTAL CHAMPIONSHIP WINS

Michael Schumacher (Germany) ... 7
Juan Manuel Fangio (Argentina) ... 5
Alain Prost (France) ... 4
Jack Brabham (Australia) ... 3
Jackie Stewart (UK) ... 3
Niki Lauda (Austria) ... 3
Ayrton Senna (Brazil) ... 3
Nelson Piquet (Brazil) ... 3
Alberto Ascari (Italy) ... 2
Jim Clark (UK) ... 2
Graham Hill (UK) ... 2
Emerson Fittipaldi (Brazil) ... 2
Mika Häkkinen (Finland) ... 2
Fernando Alonso (Spain) ... 2

TOTAL GRAND PRIX WINS

Michael Schumacher (Germany) ... 91
Alain Prost (France) ... 51
Ayrton Senna (Brazil) ... 41
Nigel Mansell (UK) ... 31
Jackie Stewart (UK) ... 27
Jim Clark (UK) ... 25
Niki Lauda (Austria) ... 25
Juan Manuel Fangio (Argentina) ... 24
Nelson Piquet (Brazil) ... 23
Damon Hill (UK) ... 22

CAREER POINTS

Michael Schumacher (Germany) ... 1369
Alain Prost (France) ... 768.5
Ayrton Senna (Brazil) ... 614
Fernando Alonso (Spain) ... 551
David Coulthard (UK) ... 535
Kimi Räikkönen (Finland) ... 531
Rubens Barrichello (Brazil) ... 530
Nelson Piquet (Brazil) ... 485.5
Nigel Mansell (UK) ... 482
Niki Lauda (Austria) ... 420.5

TOTAL PODIUM FINISHES

Michael Schumacher (Germany) ... 154
Alain Prost (France) ... 106
Ayrton Senna (Brazil) ... 80
David Coulthard (UK) ... 62
Rubens Barrichello (Brazil) ... 62
Nelson Piquet (Brazil) ... 60
Nigel Mansell (UK) ... 59
Kimi Räikkönen (Finland) ... 57
Niki Lauda (Austria) ... 54
Fernando Alonso (Spain) ... 52

F1 CHAMPIONSHIP WINNERS

Nino Farina (Italy) ... 1950
Alberto Ascari (Italy) ... 1952–1953
Juan Manuel Fangio (Argentina) ... 1951, 1954–1957
Mike Hawthorn (UK) ... 1958
Phil Hill (US) ... 1961
John Surtees (UK) ... 1964
Jim Clark (UK) ... 1963, 1965
Jack Brabham (Australia) ... 1959-1960, 1966
Denny Hulme (Australia) ... 1967
Graham Hill (UK) ... 1962, 1968
Jochen Rindt (Austria) ... 1970
Jackie Stewart (UK) ... 1969, 1971, 1973
Emerson Fittipaldi (Brazil) ... 1972, 1974
James Hunt (UK) ... 1976
Mario Andretti (US) ... 1978
Jody Scheckter (South Africa) ... 1979
Alan Jones (Australia) ... 1980
Keke Rosberg (Finland) ... 1982
Niki Lauda (Austria) ... 1975, 1977, 1984
Nelson Piquet (Brazil) ... 1981, 1983,1987
Ayrton Senna (Brazil) ... 1988, 1990–1991
Nigel Mansell (UK) ... 1992
Alain Prost (France) ... 1985-1986, 1989, 1993
Damon Hill (UK) ... 1996
Jacques Villeneuve (Canada) ... 1997
Mika Häkkinen (Finland) ... 1998–1999
Michael Schumacher (Germany) ... 1994–1995, 2000–2004
Fernando Alonso (Spain) ... 2005–2006
Kimi Räikkönen (Finland) ... 2007
Lewis Hamilton (UK) ... 2008

Information correct as of end of the 2008 season

TOTAL POLE POSITIONS

Michael Schumacher (Germany) ... 68
Ayrton Senna (Brazil) ... 65
Jim Clark (UK) ... 33
Alain Prost (France) ... 33
Nigel Mansell (UK) ... 32
Juan Manuel Fangio (Argentina) ... 29
Mika Häkkinen (Finland) ... 26
Niki Lauda (Austria) ... 24
Nelson Piquet (Brazil) ... 24
Damon Hill (UK) ... 20

TOTAL FASTEST LAPS

Michael Schumacher (Germany) ... 76
Alain Prost (France) ... 41
Kimi Räikkönen (Finland) ... 35
Nigel Mansell (UK) ... 30
Jim Clark (UK) ... 28
Mika Häkkinen (Finland) ... 25
Niki Lauda (Austria) ... 25
Juan Manuel Fangio (Argentina) ... 23
Nelson Piquet (Brazil) ... 23
Gerhard Berger (Austria) ... 21

NOTABLE CONSTRUCTORS AND THEIR SEASONS

Alfa Romeo (Italy) ... 1950–1951, 1979–1985
Arrows (UK) ... 1978–2002
BAR *British-American Racing* (UK) ... 1999–2005
Benetton (UK) ... 1986–1995; (Italy) ... 1996–2001
Brabham (UK) ... 1962-1987, 1989–1992
BRM *British Racing Motors* (UK) ... 1951, 1956–1977
Cooper (UK) ... 1950, 1952–1969
Ferrari (Italy) ... 1950–present
Jordan (UK) ... 1991–2005
Ligier (France) ... 1976–1996
Lola (UK) ... 1962-1963, 1967–1968, 1974–1975, 1985–1991, 1997
Lotus (UK) ... 1958–1994
March (UK) ... 1970-1978, 1981–1982, 1987–1989, 1992
Maserati (Italy) ... 1950–1960
Matra (France) ... 1967–1972
McLaren (UK) ... 1966–present
Minardi (Italy) ... 1985–2005
Renault (France) ... 1977–1985, 2002–present
Sauber (Switzerland) ... 1993–2005; BMW Sauber (Germany) ... 2006–present
Tyrrell (UK) ... 1970–1998
Vanwall (UK) ... 1954–1960
Williams (UK) ... 1978–present

TOTAL CHAMPIONSHIP WINS

Ferrari ... 16
Williams ... 9
McLaren ... 8
Lotus ... 7
Cooper ... 2
Brabham ... 2
Renault ... 2
Vanwall ... 1
BRM ... 1
Matra ... 1
Tyrrell ... 1
Benetton ... 1

TOTAL RACE ENTRIES

Ferrari ... 776
McLaren ... 649
Williams ... 568
Lotus ... 491
Tyrrell ... 463
Brabham ... 394
Arrows ... 382
Minardi ... 340
Ligier ... 326
Benetton ... 317

CONSTRUCTORS' CHAMPIONSHIP WINNERS

Vanwall ... 1958
Cooper ... 1959, 1960
Ferrari ... 1961, 1964, 1975–1977, 1979, 1982–1983, 1999-2004, 2007–2008
BRM ... 1962
Lotus ... 1963, 1965, 1968, 1970, 1972–1973, 1978
Brabham ... 1966–1967
Matra ... 1969
Tyrrell ... 1971
McLaren ... 1974, 1984–1985, 1988–1991, 1998
Williams ... 1980–1981, 1986–1987, 1992–1994, 1996–1997
Benetton ... 1995
Renault ... 2005–2006

CONSTRUCTOR TOTAL GRAND PRIX WINS

Ferrari ... 209
McLaren ... 162
Williams ... 113
Lotus ... 79
Brabham ... 35
Renault ... 35
Benetton ... 27
Tyrrell ... 23
BRM ... 17
Cooper ... 16

TOTAL POINTS

Ferrari ... 4021.5
McLaren ... 3302.5
Williams ... 2571.5
Lotus ... 1368
Renault ... 1056
Brabham ... 864
Benetton ... 851.5
Tyrrell ... 621
BRM ... 433
Ligier ... 388
Cooper ... 342
Jordan ... 291

TOTAL PODIUM FINISHES

Ferrari ... 623
McLaren ... 430
Williams ... 296
Lotus ... 172
Brabham ... 124
Benetton ... 105
Renault ... 94
Tyrrell ... 77
BRM ... 61
Cooper ... 58

TOTAL POLE POSITIONS

Ferrari ... 203
McLaren ... 141
Williams ... 125
Lotus ... 107
Renault ... 50

Brabham ... 39
Benetton ... 15
Tyrrell ... 14
Alfa Romeo ... 12
Cooper ... 11
BRM ... 11

TOTAL FASTEST LAPS

Ferrari ... 218
McLaren ... 137
Williams ... 129
Lotus ... 71
Brabham ... 40
Benetton ... 38
Renault ... 27
Tyrrell ... 20
BRM ... 15
Maserati ... 15

GRAND PRIX (IN ORDER OF FIRST APPEARANCE)

– Race, date, *winner*, team, laps, time

- Great Britain, 13 May 1950, *Nino Farina*, Alfa Romeo, 70, 2:13'23.6
- Monaco, 21 May 1950, *Juan Manuel Fangio*, Alfa Romeo, 100, 3:13'16.7
- Indianapolis 500, 30 May 1950, *Johnnie Parsons*, Kurtis Kraft-Offenhauser, 138, 2:46'55.97
- Switzerland, 4 June 1950, *Nino Farina*, Alfa Romeo, 42, 2:02'53.7
- Belgium, 18 June 1950, *Juan Manuel Fangio*, Alfa Romeo, 35, 2:47'26
- France, 2 July 1950, *Juan Manuel Fangio*, Alfa Romeo, 64, 2:57'52.8
- Italy, 3 September 1950, *Nino Farina*, Alfa Romeo, 80, 2:51'17.4

- Switzerland, 27 May 1951, *Juan Manuel Fangio*, Alfa Romeo, 42, 2:07'53.64
- Indianapolis 500, 30 May 1951, *Lee Wallard*, Kurtis Kraft-Offenhauser, 200, 3:57'38.05
- Belgium, 17 June 1951, *Nino Farina*, Alfa Romeo, 36, 2:45'66.2
- France, 1 July 1951, *Juan Manuel Fangio/Luigi Fagioli*, Alfa Romeo, 77, 3:22'11.0
- Great Britain, 14 July 1951, *Jose Froilan Gonzalez*, Ferrari, 90, 2:44'11
- Germany, 29 July 1951, *Alberto Ascari*, Ferrari, 20, 3:23'03.3
- Italy, 16 September 1951, *Alberto Ascari*, Ferrari, 80, 2:42'39.3
- Spain, 28 October 1951, *Juan Manuel Fangio*, Alfa Romeo, 70, 2:46'54.10

- Switzerland, 18 May 1952, *Piero Taruffi*, Ferrari, 62, 3.01'46.1
- Indianapolis 500, 30 May 1952, *Troy Ruttman*, Kuzma-Offenhauser, 200, 3:52'41.88
- Belgium, 22 June 1952, *Alberto Ascari*, Ferrari, 36, 3:03'46.3
- France, 6 July 1952, *Alberto Ascari*, Ferrari, 77, 3:00'00
- Great Britain, 19 July 1952, *Alberto Ascari*, Ferrari, 85, 2'46.11
- Germany, 3 August 1952, *Alberto Ascari*, Ferrari, 18, 3:06'13.3
- Netherlands, 17 August 1952, *Alberto Ascari*, Ferrari, 90, 2:53'28.5
- Italy, 7 September 1952, *Alberto Ascari*, Ferrari, 80, 2:50'45.6

- Argentina, 18 January 1953, *Alberto Ascari*, Ferrari, 97, 3:01'04.6
- Indianapolis 500, 30 May 1953, *Bill Vukovich*, Kurtis Kraft-Offenhauser, 200, 3:53'01.69
- Netherlands, 7 June 1953, *Alberto Ascari*, Ferrari, 90, 2:53'35.8
- Belgium, 21 June 1953, *Alberto Ascari*, Ferrari, 36, 2:48'30.3
- France, 5 July 1953, *Mike Hawthorn*, Ferrari, 60, 2:44'18.6
- Great Britain, 18 July 1953, *Alberto Ascari*, Ferrari, 90, 2:50'00
- Germany, 2 August 1953, *Nino Farina*, Ferrari, 18, 3:02'25.0
- Switzerland, 23 August 1953, *Alberto Ascari*, Ferrari, 65, 3:01'34.40
- Italy, 13 September 1953, *Juan Manuel Fangio*, Maserati, 80, 2:49'45.9

- Argentina, 17 January 1954, *Juan Manuel Fangio*, Maserati, 87, 3:00'55.8
- Indianapolis 500, 31 May 1954, *Bill Vukovich*, Kurtis Kraft-Offenhauser, 200, 3:49'17.27
- Belgium, 20 June 1954, *Juan Manuel Fangio*, Maserati, 36, 2:44'42.4
- France, 4 July 1954, *Juan Manuel Fangio*, Mercedes, 61, 2:42'47.9
- Great Britain, 17 July 1954, *Jose Froilan Gonzalez*, Ferrari, 90, 2:56'14
- Germany, 1 August 1954, *Juan Manuel Fangio*, Mercedes, 22, 3:45'45.8
- Switzerland, 22 August 1954, *Juan Manuel Fangio*, Mercedes, 66, 3:00'34.5
- Italy, 5 September 1954, *Juan Manuel Fangio*, Mercedes, 80, 2:47'47.9
- Spain, 24 October 1954, *Mike Hawthorn*, Ferrari, 80, 3:13'52.1

- Argentina, 16 January 1955, *Juan Manuel Fangio*, Mercedes, 96, 3:00'38.6
- Monaco, 22 May 1955, *Maurice Trintignant*, Ferrari, 100, 2:58'09.8
- Indianapolis 500, 30 May 1955, *Bob Sweikert*, Kurtis Kraft-Offenhauser, 200, 3:53'59.53
- Belgium, 5 June 1955, *Juan Manuel Fangio*, Mercedes, 36, 2:39'29.0
- Netherlands, 19 June 1955, *Juan Manuel Fangio*, Mercedes, 100, 2:54'23.8
- Great Britain, 16 July 1955, *Stirling Moss*, Mercedes, 90, 3:07'21.2
- Italy, 11 September 1955, *Juan Manuel Fangio*, Mercedes, 50, 2:25'04.4

- Argentina, 22 January 1956, *Luigi Musso/Juan Manuel Fangio*, Ferrari, 98, 3:00'03.7
- Monaco, 13 May 1956, *Stirling Moss*, Maserati, 100, 3:00'32.9
- Indianapolis 500, 30 May 1956, *Pat Flaherty*, Watson-Offenhauser, 200, 3:53'28.84
- Belgium, 3 June 1956, *Peter Collins*, Ferrari, 36, 2:40'00.3
- France, 1 July 1956, *Peter Collins*, Ferrari, 61, 2:34'23.4
- Great Britain, 14 July 1956, *Juan Manuel Fangio*, Ferrari, 101, 2:59'47.0
- Germany, 5 August 1956, *Juan Manuel Fangio*, Ferrari, 22, 3:38'43.7
- Italy, 2 September 1956, *Stirling Moss*, Maserati, 50, 2:23'41.3

- Argentina, 13 January 1957, *Juan Manuel Fangio*, Maserati, 100, 3:00'55.9
- Monaco, 19 May 1957, *Juan Manuel Fangio*, Maserati, 105, 3:10'12.8
- Indianapolis 500, 30 May 1957, *Sam Hanks*, Epperly- Offenhauser, 200, 3:41'14.25
- France, 7 July 1957, *Juan Manuel Fangio*, Maserati, 77, 3:07'46.4
- Great Britain, 20 July 1957, *Stirling Moss/Tony Brooks*, Vanwall, 90, 3:06'37.8
- Germany, 4 August 1957, *Juan Manuel Fangio*, Maserati, 22, 3:30'38.3
- Pescara, 18 August 1957, *Stirling Moss*, Vanwall, 18, 2:59'22.7
- Italy, 8 September 1957, *Stirling Moss*, Vanwall, 87, 2:35'03.9

- Argentina, 19 January 1958, *Stirling Moss*, Cooper-Climax, 80, 2:19'33.7
- Monaco, 18 May 1958, *Maurice Trintignant*, Cooper-Climax, 100, 2:52'27.9
- Netherlands, 26 May 1958, *Stirling Moss*, Vanwall, 75, 2:04'49.2
- Indianapolis 500, 30 May 1958, *Jimmy Bryan*, Epperly-Offenhauser, 200, 3:44'13.80
- Belgium, 15 June 1958, *Tony Brooks*, Vanwall, 24, 1:37'06.3
- France, 6 July 1958, *Mike Hawthorn*, Ferrari, 50, 2:03'21.3
- Great Britain, 19 July 1958, *Peter Collins*, Ferrari, 75, 2:09'04.2
- Germany, 3 August 1958, *Tony Brooks*, Vanwall, 15, 2:21'15.0
- Portugal, 24 August 1958, *Stirling Moss*, Vanwall, 50, 2:11'27.80
- Italy, 7 September 1958, *Tony Brooks*, Vanwall, 70, 2:03'47.8
- Morocco, 19 October 1958, *Stirling Moss*, Vanwall, 53, 2:09'15.1

- Monaco, 10 May 1959, *Jack Brabham*, Cooper-Climax, 100, 2:55'51.3
- Indianapolis 500, 30 May 1959, *Rodger Ward*, Watson-Offenhauser, 200, 3:40'49.20
- Netherlands, 31 May 1959, *Jo Bonnier*, BRM, 75, 2:05'26.8
- France, 5 July 1959, *Tony Brooks*, Ferrari, 50, 2:01'26.5
- Great Britain, 18 July 1959, *Jack Brabham*, Cooper-Climax, 75, 2:30'11.6
- Germany, 2 August 1959, *Tony Brooks*, Ferrari, 60, 2:09'31.6
- Portugal, 23 August 1959, *Stirling Moss*, Cooper-Climax, 62, 2:11'55.41
- Italy, 13 September 1959, *Stirling Moss*, Cooper-Climax, 72, 2:04'05.4
- United States, 12 December 1959, *Bruce McLaren*, Cooper-Climax, 42, 2:12'35.7

- Argentina, 7 February 1960, *Bruce McLaren*, Cooper-Climax, 80, 2:17'49.5
- Monaco, 29 May 1960, *Stirling Moss*, Lotus-Climax, 100, 2:53'45.5
- Indianapolis 500, 30 May 1960, *Jim Rathmann*, Watson-Offenhauser, 200, 3:36.11.36
- Netherlands, 6 June 1960, *Jack Brabham*, Cooper-Climax, 75, 2.01'47.2
- Belgium, 19 June 1960, *Jack Brabham*, Cooper-Climax, 36, 2:21'37.3
- France, 3 July 1960, *Jack Brabham*, Cooper-Climax, 50, 1:57'24.9
- Great Britain, 16 July 1960, *Jack Brabham*, Cooper-Climax, 77, 2:04'24.6
- Portugal, 14 August 1960, *Jack Brabham*, Cooper-Climax, 55, 2:19'00.03
- Italy, 4 September 1960, *Phil Hill*, Ferrari, 50, 2:21'09.2
- United States, 20 November 1960, *Stirling Moss*, Lotus-Climax, 75, 2:28'52.2

- Monaco, 14 May 1961, *Stirling Moss*, Lotus-Climax, 100, 2:45'50.1
- Netherlands, 22 May 1961, *Wolfgang von Trips*, Ferrari, 75, 2:01'52.1
- Belgium, 18 June 1961, *Phil Hill*, Ferrari, 30, 2:03'03.8
- France, 2 July 1961, *Giancarlo Baghetti*, Ferrari, 52, 2:14'17.5
- Great Britain, 15 July 1961, *Wolfgang von Trips*, Ferrari, 75, 2:40'53.6
- Germany, 6 August 1961, *Stirling Moss*, Lotus-Climax, 15, 2:18'12.4
- Italy, 10 September 1961, *Phil Hill*, Ferrari, 43, 2:03'13.0
- United States, 8 October 1961, *Innes Ireland*, Lotus-Climax, 100, 2:13'45.8

- Netherlands, 20 May 1962, *Graham Hill*, BRM, 80, 2:11'02.1
- Monaco, 3 June 1962, *Bruce McLaren*, Cooper-Climax, 100, 2:46'29.7
- Belgium, 17 June 1962, *Jim Clark*, Lotus-Climax, 32, 2:07'32.3
- France, 8 July 1962, *Dan Gurney*, Porsche, 54, 2:07'35.5
- Great Britain, 21 July 1962, *Jim Clark*, Lotus-Climax, 75, 2:26'20.8
- Germany, 5 August 1962, *Graham Hill*, BRM, 15, 2:38'45.3
- Italy, 16 September 1962, *Graham Hill*, BRM, 86, 2:29'08.4
- United States, 7 October 1962, *Jim Clark*, Lotus-Climax, 100, 2:07'13.0
- South Africa, 29 December 1962, *Graham Hill*, BRM, 82, 2:08'03.3

- Monaco, 26 May 1963, *Graham Hill*, BRM, 100, 2:41'49.7
- Belgium, 9 June 1963, *Jim Clark*, Lotus-Climax, 32, 2:27'47.6
- Netherlands, 23 June 1963, *Jim Clark*, Lotus-Climax, 80, 2:08'13.7
- France, 30 June 1963, *Jim Clark*, Lotus-Climax, 53, 2:10'54.3
- Great Britain, 20 July 1963, *Jim Clark*, Lotus-Climax, 82, 2:14'09.6
- Germany, 4 August 1963, *John Surtees*, Ferrari, 15, 2:13'06.8
- Italy, 8 September 1963, *Jim Clark*, Lotus-Climax, 86, 2:24'19.6
- United States, 6 October 1963, *Graham Hill*, BRM, 110, 2:19'22.1
- Mexico, 27 October 1963, *Jim Clark*, Lotus-Climax, 65, 2:09'52.1
- South Africa, 28 December 1963, *Jim Clark*, Lotus-Climax, 85, 2:10'36.9

- Monaco, 10 May 1964, *Graham Hill*, BRM, 100, 2:41'19.5
- Netherlands, 24 May 1964, *Jim Clark*, Lotus-Climax, 80, 2:07'35.4
- Belgium, 14 June 1964, *Jim Clark*, Lotus-Climax, 32, 2:06'40.5
- France, 28 June 1964, *Dan Gurney*, Brabham-Climax, 57, 2:07'49.1
- Great Britain, 11 July 1964, *Jim Clark*, Lotus-Climax, 80, 2:15'07.0
- Germany, 2 August 1964, *John Surtees*, Ferrari, 15, 2:12'04.8
- Austria, 23 August 1964, *Lorenzo Bandini*, Ferrari, 105, 2:06'18.23
- Italy, 6 September 1964, *John Surtees*, Ferrari, 78, 2:10'51.8
- United States, 4 October 1964, *Graham Hill*, BRM, 110, 2:16'38.0
- Mexico, 25 October 1964, *Dan Gurney*, Brabham-Climax, 65, 2:09'50.32

- South Africa, 1 January 1965, *Jim Clark*, Lotus-Climax, 85, 2.06'46.0
- Monaco, 30 May 1965, *Graham Hill*, BRM, 100, 2:37'39.6
- Belgium, 13 June 1965, *Jim Clark*, Lotus-Climax, 32, 2:23'34.8
- France, 27 June 1965, *Jim Clark*, Lotus-Climax, 40, 2:14'38.4
- Great Britain, 10 July 1965, *Jim Clark*, Lotus-Climax, 80, 2:05'25.4
- Netherlands, 18 July 1965, *Jim Clark*, Lotus-Climax, 80, 2:03'59.1
- Germany, 1 August 1965, *Jim Clark*, Lotus-Climax, 15, 2:07'52.4
- Italy, 12 September 1965, *Jackie Stewart*, BRM, 76, 2:04'52.8
- United States, 3 October 1965, *Graham Hill*, BRM, 110, 2:20'36.1
- Mexico, 24 October 1965, *Richie Ginther*, Honda, 65, 2:08'32.10

- Monaco, 22 May 1966, *Jackie Stewart*, BRM, 100, 2:33'10.5
- Belgium, 12 June 1966, *John Surtees*, Ferrari, 28, 2:09'11.3
- France, 3 July 1966, *Jack Brabham*, Brabham-Repco, 48, 1:48'31.3
- Great Britain, 16 July 1966, *Jack Brabham*, Brabham-Repco, 80, 2:13'13.4
- Netherlands, 24 July 1966, *Jack Brabham*, Brabham-Repco, 90, 2:20'32.5

- Germany, 7 August 1966, *Jack Brabham*, Brabham-Repco, 15, 2:27'03.0
- Italy, 4 September 1966, *Ludovico Scarfiotti*, Ferrari, 68, 1:47'14.8
- United States, 2 October 1966, *Jim Clark*, Lotus-BRM, 108, 2:09'40.11
- Mexico, 23 October 1966, *John Surtees*, Cooper-Maserati, 65, 2:06'35.34

- South Africa, 2 January 1967, *Pedro Rodriguez*, Cooper-Maserati, 80, 2:05'45.9
- Monaco, 7 May 1967, *Denny Hulme*, Brabham-Repco, 100, 2:34'34.3
- Netherlands, 4 June 1967, *Jim Clark*, Lotus-Ford, 90, 2:14'45.1
- Belgium, 18 June 1967, *Dan Gurney*, Eagle-Weslake, 28, 1:40'49.4
- France, 2 July 1967, *Jack Brabham*, Brabham-Repco, 80, 2:13'21.3
- Great Britain, 15July 1967, *Jim Clark*, Lotus-Ford, 80, 1:59'25.6
- Germany, 6 August 1967, *Denny Hulme*, Brabham-Repco, 15, 2:05'55.7
- Canada, 27 August 1967, *Jack Brabham*, Brabham-Repco, 90, 2:40'40.0
- Italy, 10 September 1967, *John Surtees*, Honda, 68, 1:43'45.0
- United States, 1 October 1967, *Jim Clark*, Lotus-Ford, 108, 2:03'13.2
- Mexico, 22 October 1967, *Jim Clark*, Lotus-Ford, 65, 1:59'28.70

- South Africa, 1 January 1968, *Jim Clark*, Lotus-Ford, 80, 1:53'56.6
- Spain, 12 May 1968, *Graham Hill*, Lotus-Ford, 90, 2:15'20.1
- Monaco, 26 May 1968, *Graham Hill*, Lotus-Ford, 80, 2:00'32.3
- Belgium, 9 June 1968, *Bruce McLaren*, McLaren-Ford, 28, 1:40'02.1
- Netherlands, 23 June 1968, *Jackie Stewart*, Matra-Ford, 90, 2:46'11.26
- France, 7 July 1968, *Jacky Ickx*, Ferrari, 60, 2:25'40.9
- Great Britain, 20 July 1968, *Jo Siffert*, Lotus-Ford, 80, 2:01'20.3
- Germany, 4 August 1968, *Jackie Stewart*, Matra-Ford, 14, 2:19'03.2
- Italy, 8 September 1968, *Denny Hulme*, McLaren-Ford, 68, 1:40'14.8
- Canada, 22 September 1968, *Denny Hulme*, McLaren-Ford, 90, 2:27'11.2
- United States, 6 October 1968, *Jackie Stewart*, Matra-Ford, 108, 1:59'20.29
- Mexico, 3 November 1968, *Graham Hill*, Lotus-Ford, 65, 1:56'43.95

- South Africa, 1 March 1969, *Jackie Stewart*, Matra-Ford, 80, 1:50'39.1
- Spain, 4 May 1969, *Jackie Stewart*, Matra-Ford, 90, 2:16'54.0
- Monaco, 18 May 1969, *Graham Hill*, Lotus-Ford, 80, 1:56'59.4
- Netherlands, 21 June 1969, *Jackie Stewart*, Matra-Ford, 90, 2:06'42.08
- France, 6 July 1969, *Jackie Stewart*, Matra-Ford, 38, 1:56'47.4
- Great Britain, 19 July 1969, *Jackie Stewart*, Matra-Ford, 84, 1:55'55.6
- Germany, 3 August 1969, *Jacky Ickx*, Brabham-Ford, 14, 1:49'55.4
- Italy, 7 September 1969, *Jackie Stewart*, Matra-Ford, 68, 1:39'11.26
- Canada, 20 September 1969, *Jacky Ickx*, Brabham-Ford, 90, 1:59'25.7
- United States, 5 October 1969, *Jochen Rindt*, Lotus-Ford, 108, 1:57'56.84
- Mexico, 19 October 1969, *Denny Hulme*, McLaren-Ford, 65, 1:54'08.80

- South Africa, 7 March 1970, *Jack Brabham*, Brabham-Ford, 80, 1:49'34.6
- Spain, 19 April 1970, *Jackie Stewart*, March-Ford, 90, 2:10'58.2
- Monaco, 10 May 1970, *Jochen Rindt*, Lotus-Ford, 80, 1:54'36.6
- Belgium, 7 June 1970, *Pedro Rodriguez*, BRM, 28, 1:38'09.9
- Netherlands, 21 June 1970, *Jochen Rindt*, Lotus-Ford, 80, 1:50'43.41
- France, 5 July 1970, *Jochen Rindt*, Lotus-Ford, 38, 1:55'57.00
- Great Britain, 18 July 1970, *Jochen Rindt*, Lotus-Ford, 80, 1:57'02.0
- Germany, 2 August 1970, *Jochen Rindt*, Lotus-Ford, 50, 1:42'00.3
- Austria, 16 August 1970, *Jacky Ickx*, Ferrari, 60, 1:42'17.32
- Italy, 6 September 1970, *Clay Regazzoni*, Ferrari, 68, 1:39'06.88
- Canada, 20 September 1970, *Jacky Ickx*, Ferrari, 90, 2:21'18.4
- United States, 4 October 1970, *Emerson Fittipaldi*, Lotus-Ford, 108, 1:57'32.79
- Mexico, 25 October 1970, *Jacky Ickx*, Ferrari, 65, 1:53'28.36

- South Africa, 6 March 1971, *Mario Andretti*, Ferrari, 79, 1:47'35.5
- Spain, 18 April 1971, *Jackie Stewart*, Tyrrell-Ford, 75, 1:49'03.4
- Monaco, 23 May 1971, *Jackie Stewart*, Tyrrell-Ford, 80, 1:52'21.3
- Netherlands, 20 June 1971, *Jacky Ickx*, Ferrari, 70, 1:56'20.09
- France, 4 July 1971, *Jackie Stewart*, Tyrrell-Ford, 55, 1:46'41.68
- Great Britain, 17 July 1971, *Jackie Stewart*, Tyrrell-Ford, 68, 1:31'31.5
- Germany, 1 August 1971, *Jackie Stewart*, Tyrrell-Ford, 12, 1:29'15.7
- Austria, 15 August 1971, *Jo Siffert*, BRM, 54, 1:30.23.91
- Italy, 5 September 1971, *Peter Gethin*, BRM, 55, 1:18'12.60
- Canada, 19 September 1971, *Jackie Stewart*, Tyrrell-Ford, 64, 1:55'12.9
- United States, 3 October 1971, *Francois Cevert*, Tyrrell-Ford, 59, 1:43'51.991

- Argentina, 23 January 1972, *Jackie Stewart*, Tyrrell-Ford, 95, 1:57'58.82
- South Africa, 4 March 1972, *Denny Hulme*, McLaren-Ford, 79, 1:45'49.1
- Spain, 1 May 1972, *Emerson Fittipaldi*, Lotus-Ford, 90, 2:03'41.23

- Monaco, 14 May 1972, *Jean Pierre Beltoise*, BRM, 80, 2:26'54.7
- Belgium, 4 June 1972, *Emerson Fittipaldi*, Lotus-Ford, 85, 1:44'06.7
- France, 2 July 1972, *Jackie Stewart*, Tyrrell-Ford, 38, 1:52'21.5
- Great Britain, 15 July 1972, *Emerson Fittipaldi*, Lotus-Ford, 76, 1:47'50.2
- Germany, 30 July 1972, *Jacky Ickx*, Ferrari, 14, 1:42'12.3
- Austria, 13 August 1972, *Emerson Fittipaldi*, Lotus-Ford, 54, 1:29'16.66
- Italy, 10 September 1972, *Emerson Fittipaldi*, Lotus-Ford, 55, 1:29'58.4
- Canada, 24 September 1972, *Jackie Stewart*, Tyrrell-Ford, 80, 1:43'16.9
- United States, 8 October 1972, *Jackie Stewart*, Tyrrell-Ford, 59, 1:41'45.354

- Argentina, 28 January 1973, *Emerson Fittipaldi*, Lotus-Ford, 96, 1:56'18.22
- Brazil, 11 February 1973, *Emerson Fittipaldi*, Lotus-Ford, 40, 1:43'55.6
- South Africa, 3 March 1973, *Jackie Stewart*, Tyrrell-Ford, 79, 1:43'11.07
- Spain, 29 March 1973, *Emerson Fittipaldi*, Lotus-Ford, 75, 1:48'18.7
- Belgium, 20 May 1973, *Jackie Stewart*, Tyrrell-Ford, 70, 1:42'13.43
- Monaco, 3 June 1973, *Jackie Stewart*, Tyrrell-Ford, 78, 1:57'44.3
- Sweden, 17 June 1973, *Denny Hulme*, McLaren-Ford, 80, 1:56'46.049
- France, 1 July 1973, *Ronnie Peterson*, Lotus-Ford, 54, 1:41'36.52
- Great Britain, 14 July 1973, *Peter Revson*, McLaren-Ford, 67, 1:29'18.5
- Netherlands, 29 July 1973, *Jackie Stewart*, Tyrrell-Ford, 72, 1:39'12.45
- Germany, 5 August 1973, *Jackie Stewart*, Tyrrell-Ford, 14, 1:42'03.0
- Austria, 19 August 1973, *Ronnie Peterson*, Lotus-Ford, 54, 1:28'48.78
- Italy, 9 September 1973, *Ronnie Peterson*, Lotus-Ford, 55, 1:29'17.0
- Canada, 23 September 1973, *Peter Revson*, McLaren-Ford, 80, 1:59'04.083
- United States, 7 October 1973, *Ronnie Peterson*, Lotus-Ford, 59, 1:41'15.799

- Argentina, 13 January 1974, *Denny Hulme*, McLaren-Ford, 53, 1:41'02.01
- Brazil, 27 January 1974, *Emerson Fittipaldi*, McLaren-Ford, 32, 1:24'37.06
- South Africa, 30 March 1974, *Carlos Reutemann*, Brabham-Ford, 78, 1:42'40.96
- Spain, 28 April 1974, *Niki Lauda*, Ferrari, 84, 2:00'29.56
- Belgium, 12 May 1974, *Emerson Fittipaldi*, McLaren-Ford, 85, 1:44'20.57
- Monaco, 26 May 1974, *Ronnie Peterson*, Lotus-Ford, 78, 1:58'03.7
- Sweden, 9 June 1974, *Jody Scheckter*, Tyrrell-Ford, 80, 1:58'31.391
- Netherlands, 23 June 1974, *Niki Lauda*, Ferrari, 75, 1:43'00.35
- Switzerland, 7 July 1974, *Ronnie Peterson*, Lotus-Ford, 80, 1:21'55.02
- Great Britain, 20 July 1974, *Jody Scheckter*, Tyrrell-Ford, 75, 1:43'02.2
- Germany, 4 August 1974, *Clay Regazzoni*, Ferrari, 14, 1:41'35.0
- Austria, 18 August 1974, *Carlos Reutemann*, Brabham-Ford, 54, 1:28'44.72
- Italy, 8 September 1974, *Ronnie Peterson*, Lotus-Ford, 52, 1:22'56.6
- Canada, 22 September 1974, *Emerson Fittipaldi*, McLaren-Ford, 80 1:40'26.136
- United States, 6 October 1974, *Carlos Reutemann*, Brabham-Ford, 59, 1:40'21.439

- Argentina, 12 January 1975, *Emerson Fittipaldi*, McLaren-Ford, 53, 1:39'26.29
- Brazil, 26 January 1975, *Carlos Pace*, Brabham-Ford, 40, 1:44'41.17
- South Africa, 1 March 1975, *Jody Scheckter*, Tyrrell-Ford, 78, 1:43'16.90
- Spain, 27 April 1975, *Jochen Mass*, McLaren-Ford, 29, 42'53.7
- Monaco, 11 May 1975, *Niki Lauda*, Ferrari, 75, 2:01'21.31
- Belgium, 25 May 1975, *Niki Lauda*, Ferrari, 70, 1:43'53.98
- Sweden, 8 June 1975, *Niki Lauda*, Ferrari, 80, 1:59'18.319
- Netherlands, 22 June 1975, *James Hunt*, Hesketh-Ford, 75, 1:46'57.40
- France, 6 July 1975, *Niki Lauda*, Ferrari, 54, 1:40'18.84
- Great Britain, 19 July 1975, *Emerson Fittipaldi*, McLaren-Ford, 56, 1:22'05.0
- Germany, 3 August 1975, *Carlos Reutemann*, Brabham-Ford, 14, 1:41'14.1
- Austria, 17 August 1975, *Vittorio Brambilla*, March-Ford, 29, 57'56.69
- Italy, 7 September 1975, *Clay Regazzoni*, Ferrari, 52, 1:22'42.6
- United States, 5 October 1975, *Niki Lauda*, Ferrari, 59, 1:42'58.175

- Brazil, 25 January 1976, *Niki Lauda*, Ferrari, 40, 1:45'16.78
- South Africa, 6 March 1976, *Niki Lauda*, Ferrari, 78, 1:42'18.4
- USA West, 28 March 1976, *Clay Regazzoni*, Ferrari, 80, 1:53'18.471
- Spain, 2 May 1976, *James Hunt*, McLaren-Ford, 75, 1:42'20.43
- Belgium, 16 May 1976, *Niki Lauda*, Ferrari, 70, 1:42'53.23
- Monaco, 30 May 1976, *Niki Lauda*, Ferrari, 78, 1:59'51.47
- Sweden, 13 June 1976, *Jody Scheckter*, Tyrrell-Ford, 72, 1:46'53.729
- France, 4 July 1976, *James Hunt*, McLaren-Ford, 54, 1:40'58.60
- Great Britain, 18 July 1976, *Niki Lauda*, Ferrari, 76, 1:44'19.66
- Germany, 1 August 1976, *James Hunt*, McLaren-Ford, 14, 1:41'42.7
- Austria, 15 August 1976, *John Watson*, Penske-Ford, 54, 1:30'07.86
- Netherlands, 29 August 1976, *James Hunt*, McLaren-Ford, 75, 1:44'52.09
- Italy, 12 September 1976, *Ronnie Peterson*, March-Ford, 52, 1:30'35.6
- Canada, 3 October 1976, *James Hunt*, McLaren-Ford, 80, 1:40'09.626
- USA East, 10 October 1976, *James Hunt*, McLaren-Ford, 59, 1:42'40.741
- Japan, 24 October 1976, Mario Andretti, Lotus-Ford, 73, 1:43'58.86

- Argentina, 9 January 1977, *Jody Scheckter*, Wolf-Ford, 53, 1:40'11.19
- Brazil, 23 January 1977, *Carlos Reutemann*, Ferrari, 40, 1:45'07.72
- South Africa, 5 March 1977, *Niki Lauda*, Ferrari, 78, 1:42'21.6
- USA West, 3 April 1977, *Mario Andretti*, Lotus-Ford, 80, 1:51'35.470
- Spain, 8 May 1977, *Mario Andretti*, Lotus-Ford, 75, 1:42'52.22
- Monaco, 22 May 1977, *Jody Scheckter*, Wolf-Ford, 76, 1:57'52.77
- Belgium, 5 June 1977, *Gunnar Nilsson*, Lotus-Ford, 70, 1:55'05.71
- Sweden, 19 June 1977, *Jacques Laffite*, Ligier-Matra, 72, 1:46'55.520
- France, 3 July 1977, *Mario Andretti*, Lotus-Ford, 80, 1:39'40.13
- Great Britain, 16 July 1977, *James Hunt*, McLaren-Ford, 68, 1:31'46.06
- Germany, 31 July 1977, *Niki Lauda*, Ferrari, 47, 1:31'48.62
- Austria, 14 August 1977, *Alan Jones*, Shadow-Ford, 54, 1:37'16.49
- Netherlands, 28 August 1977, *Niki Lauda*, Ferrari, 75, 1:41'45.93
- Italy, 11 September 1977, *Mario Andretti*, Lotus-Ford, 52, 1:27'50.30
- USA East, 2 October 1977, *James Hunt*, McLaren-Ford, 59, 1:58'23.267
- Canada, 9 October 1977, *Jody Scheckter*, Wolf-Ford, 80, 1:40'00.00
- Japan, 23 October 1977, *James Hunt*, McLaren-Ford, 73, 1:31'51.68

- Argentina, 15 January 1978, *Mario Andretti*, Lotus-Ford, 52, 1:37'04.47
- Brazil, 29 January 1978, *Carlos Reutemann*, Ferrari, 63, 1:49'59.86
- South Africa, 4 March 1978, *Ronnie Peterson*, Lotus-Ford, 78, 1:42'15.767
- USA West, 2 April 1978, *Carlos Reutemann*, Ferrari, 80, 1:52'01.301
- Monaco, 7 May 1978, *Patrick Depailler*, Tyrrell-Ford, 75, 1:55'14.66
- Belgium, 21 May 1978, *Mario Andretti*, Lotus-Ford, 70, 1:39'52.02
- Spain, 4 June 1978, Mario Andretti, Lotus-Ford, 75, 1:41'47.06
- Sweden, 17 June 1978, *Niki Lauda*, Brabham-Alfa Romeo, 70, 1:41'00.606
- France, 2 July 1978, *Mario Andretti*, Lotus-Ford, 54, 1:38'51.92
- Great Britain, 16 July 1978, *Carlos Reutemann*, Ferrari, 76, 1:42'12.39
- Germany, 30 July 1978, *Mario Andretti*, Lotus-Ford, 45, 1:28'00.90
- Austria, 13 August 1978, *Ronnie Peterson*, Lotus-Ford, 54, 1:41'21.57
- Netherlands, 27 August 1978, *Mario Andretti*, Lotus-Ford, 75, 1:41'04.23
- Italy, 10 September 1978, *Niki Lauda*, Brabham-Alfa Romeo, 40, 1:07'04.54
- USA East, 1 October 1978, *Carlos Reutemann*, Ferrari, 59, 1:40'48.800
- Canada, 8 October 1978, *Gilles Villeneuve*, Ferrari, 70, 1:57'49.196

- Argentina, 21 January 1979, *Jacques Laffite*, Ligier-Ford, 53, 1:36'03.21
- Brazil, 4 February 1979, *Jacques Laffite*, Ligier-Ford, 40, 1:40'09.64
- South Africa, 3 March 1979, *Gilles Villeneuve*, Ferrari, 78, 1:41'49.96
- USA West, 8 April 1979, *Gilles Villeneuve*, Ferrari, 80, 1:50'25.40
- Spain, 29 April 1979, *Patrick Depailler*, Ligier-Ford, 75, 1:39'11.84
- Belgium, 13 May 1979, *Jody Scheckter*, Ferrari, 70, 1:39'59.53
- Monaco, 27 May 1979, *Jody Scheckter*, Ferrari, 76, 1:55'22.48
- Switzerland, 1 July 1979, *Jean Pierre Jabouille*, Renault, 80, 1:35'20.42
- Great Britain, 14 July 1979, *Clay Regazzoni*, Williams-Ford, 68, 1:26'11.17
- Germany, 29 July 1979, *Alan Jones*, Williams-Ford, 45, 1:24'48.83
- Austria, 12 August 1979, *Alan Jones*, Williams-Ford, 54, 1:27'38.01
- Netherlands, 26 August 1979, *Alan Jones*, Williams-Ford, 75, 1:41'19.775
- Italy, 9 September 1979, *Jody Scheckter*, Ferrari, 50, 1:22'00.22
- Canada, 30 September 1979, *Alan Jones*, Williams-Ford, 72, 1:52'06.892
- USA East, 7 October 1979, *Gilles Villeneuve*, Ferrari, 59, 1:52'17.734

- Argentina, 13 January 1980, *Alan Jones*, Williams-Ford, 53, 1:43'24.38
- Brazil, 27 January 1980, *Rene Arnoux*, Renault, 40, 1:40'01.33
- South Africa, 1 March 1980, *Rene Arnoux*, Renault, 78, 1:36'52.54
- USA West, 30 March 1980, *Nelson Piquet*, Brabham-Ford, 80, 1:50'18.550
- Belgium, 4 May 1980, *Didier Pironi*, Ligier-Ford, 72, 1:38'46.51
- Monaco, 18 May 1980, *Carlos Reutemann*, Williams-Ford, 76, 1:55'34.365
- France, 29 June 1980, *Alan Jones*, Williams-Ford, 54, 1:32'43.42
- Great Britain, 13 July 1980, *Alan Jones*, Williams-Ford, 76, 1:34'49.228
- Germany, 10 August 1980, *Jacques Laffite*, Ligier-Ford, 45, 1:22'59.73
- Austria, 17 August 1980, *Jean Pierre Jabouille*, Renault, 54, 1:26'15.73
- Netherlands, 31 August 1980, *Nelson Piquet*, Brabham-Ford, 72, 1:38'13.83
- Italy, 14 September 1980, *Nelson Piquet*, Brabham-Ford, 60, 1:38'07.52
- Canada, 28 September 1980, *Alan Jones*, Williams-Ford, 70, 1:46'45.53
- USA East, 5 October 1980, *Alan Jones*, Williams-Ford, 59, 1:34'36.05

Statistics

- USA West, 15 March 1981, *Alan Jones*, Williams-Ford, 80, 1:50'41.33
- Brazil, 29 March 1981, *Carlos Reutemann*, Williams-Ford, 62, 2:00'23.66
- Argentina, 12 April 1981, *Nelson Piquet*, Brabham-Ford, 53, 1:34'32.74
- San Marino, 3 May 1981, *Nelson Piquet*, Brabham-Ford, 60, 1:51'23.97
- Belgium, 17 May 1981, *Carlos Reutemann*, Williams-Ford, 54, 1:16'31.61
- Monaco, 31 May 1981, *Gilles Villeneuve*, Ferrari, 76, 1:54'23.38
- Spain, 21 June 1981, *Gilles Villeneuve*, Ferrari, 80, 1:46'35.01
- Switzerland, 5 July 1981, *Alain Prost*, Renault, 80, 1:35'48.13
- Great Britain, 18 July 1981, *John Watson*, McLaren-Ford, 68, 1:26'54.80
- Germany, 2 August 1981, *Nelson Piquet*, Brabham-Ford, 45, 1:25'55.60
- Austria, 16 August 1981, *Jacques Laffite*, Ligier-Matra, 53, 1:27'36.47
- Netherlands, 30 August 1981, *Alain Prost*, Renault, 72, 1:40'22.43
- Italy, 13 September 1981, *Alain Prost*, Renault, 52, 1:26'33.897
- Canada, 27 September 1981, *Jacques Laffite*, Ligier-Matra, 63, 2:01'25.20
- Las Vegas, 17 October 1981, *Alan Jones*, Williams-Ford, 75, 1:44'09.077

- South Africa, 23 January 1982, *Alain Prost*, Renault, 77, 1:32'08.401
- Brazil, 21 March 1982, *Alain Prost*, Renault, 63, 1:44'33.134
- USA West, 4 April 1982, *Niki Lauda*, McLaren-Ford, 75, 1:58'25.318
- San Marino, 25 April 1982, *Didier Pironi*, Ferrari, 60, 1:36'38.887
- Belgium, 9 May 1982, *John Watson*, McLaren-Ford, 70, 1:35'41.995
- Monaco, 23 May 1982, *Riccardo Patrese*, Brabham-Ford, 76, 1:54'11.259
- USA East, 6 June 1982, *John Watson*, McLaren-Ford, 62, 1:58'41.043
- Canada, 13 June 1982, *Nelson Piquet*, Brabham-BMW, 70, 1:46'39.577
- Netherlands, 3 July 1982, *Didier Pironi*, Ferrari, 72, 1:38'03.254
- Great Britain, 18 July 1982, *Niki Lauda*, McLaren-Ford, 76, 1:35'33.812
- France, 25 July 1982, *Rene Arnoux*, Renault, 54, 1:33'33.217
- Germany, 8 August 1982, *Patrick Tambay*, Ferrari, 45, 1:27'25.178
- Austria, 15 August 1982, *Elio de Angelis*, Lotus-Ford, 53, 1:25'02.212
- Switzerland, 29 August 1982, *Keke Rosberg*, Williams-Ford, 80, 1:32'41.087
- Italy, 12 September 1982, *Rene Arnoux*, Renault, 52, 1:22'25.734
- Las Vegas, 25 September 1982, *Michele Alboreto*, Tyrrell-Ford, 75, 1:41'56.888

- Brazil, 13 March 1983, *Nelson Piquet*, Brabham-BMW, 63, 1:48'27.731
- USA West, 27 March 1983, *John Watson*, McLaren-Ford, 75, 1:53'34.889
- France, 17 April 1983, *Alain Prost*, Renault, 54, 1:34'13.913
- San Marino, 1 May 1983, *Patrick Tambay*, Ferrari, 60, 1:37'52.460
- Monaco, 15 May 1983, *Keke Rosberg*, Williams-Ford, 76, 1:56'38.121
- Belgium, 22 May 1983, *Alain Prost*, Renault, 40, 1:27'11.502
- United States, 5 June 1983, *Michele Alboreto*, Tyrrell-Ford, 60, 1:50'53.669
- Canada, 12 July 1983, *Rene Arnoux*, Ferrari, 70, 1:48'31.838
- Great Britain, 16 July 1983, *Alain Prost*, Renault, 67, 1:24'39.780
- Germany, 7 August 1983, *Rene Arnoux*, Ferrari, 45, 1:27'10.319
- Austria, 14 August 1983, *Alain Prost*, Renault, 53, 1:24'32.745
- Netherlands, 28 August 1983, *Rene Arnoux*, Ferrari, 72, 1:38'41.950
- Italy, 11 September 1983, *Nelson Piquet*, Brabham-BMW, 52, 1:23'10.880
- Europe, 25 September 1983, *Nelson Piquet*, Brabham-BMW, 76, 1:36'45.865
- South Africa, 15 October 1983, *Riccardo Patrese*, Brabham-BMW, 77, 1:33'25.708

- Brazil, 25 March 1984, *Alain Prost*, McLaren-TAG, 61, 1:42'34.492
- South Africa, 7 April 1984, *Niki Lauda*, McLaren-TAG, 75, 1:29'23.430
- Belgium, 29 April 1984, *Michele Alboreto*, Ferrari, 70, 1:36'32.048
- San Marino, 6 May 1984, *Alain Prost*, McLaren-TAG, 60, 1:36'53.679
- France, 20 May 1984, *Niki Lauda*, McLaren-TAG, 79, 1:31'11.951
- Monaco, 3 June 1984, *Alain Prost*, McLaren-TAG, 31, 1:01'07.740
- Canada, 17 June 1984, *Nelson Piquet*, Brabham-BMW, 70, 1:46'23.748
- USA East, 24 June 1984, *Nelson Piquet*, Brabham-BMW, 63, 1:55'41.842
- United States, 8 July 1984, *Keke Rosberg*, Williams-Honda, 67, 2:01'22.617
- Great Britain, 22 July 1984, *Niki Lauda*, McLaren-TAG, 71, 1:29'28.532
- Germany, 5 August 1984, *Alain Prost*, McLaren-TAG, 44, 1:24'43.210
- Austria, 19 August 1984, *Niki Lauda*, McLaren-TAG, 51, 1:21'12.851
- Netherlands, 26 August 1984, *Alain Prost*, McLaren-TAG, 71, 1:37'21.468
- Italy, 9 September 1984, *Niki Lauda*, McLaren-TAG, 51, 1:20'29.065
- Europe, 7 October 1984, *Alain Prost*, McLaren-TAG, 67, 1:35'13.284
- Portugal, 21 October 1984, *Alain Prost*, McLaren-TAG, 70, 1:41'11.753

- Brazil, 7 April 1985, *Alain Prost*, McLaren-TAG, 61, 1:41'26.115
- Portugal, 21 April 1985, *Ayrton Senna*, Lotus-Renault, 67, 2:00'28.006
- San Marino, 5 May 1985, *Elio de Angelis*, Lotus-Renault, 60, 1:34'35.955
- Monaco, 19 May 1985, *Alain Prost*, McLaren-TAG, 78, 1:51'58.034
- Canada, 16 June 1985, *Michele Alboreto*, Ferrari, 70, 1:46'01.813
- USA East, 23 June 1985, *Keke Rosberg*, Williams-Honda, 63, 1:55'39.851
- France, 7 July 1985, *Nelson Piquet*, Brabham-BMW, 53, 1:31'46.266
- Great Britain, 21 July 1985, *Alain Prost*, McLaren-TAG, 65, 1:18'10.436
- Germany, 4 August 1985, *Michele Alboreto*, Ferrari, 67, 1:35'31.337
- Austria, 18 August 1985, *Alain Prost*, McLaren-TAG, 52, 1:20'12.583
- Netherlands, 25 August 1985, *Niki Lauda*, McLaren-TAG, 70, 1:32'29.263
- Italy, 8 September 1985, *Alain Prost*, McLaren-TAG, 51, 1:17'59.451
- Belgium, 15 September 1985, *Ayrton Senna*, Lotus-Renault, 43, 1:34'19.893
- Europe, 6 October 1985, *Nigel Mansell*, Williams-Honda, 75, 1:32'58.109
- South Africa, 19 October 1985, *Nigel Mansell*, Williams-Honda, 75, 1:28'22.866
- Australia, 3 November 1985, *Keke Rosberg*, Williams-Honda, 82, 2:00'40.473

- Brazil, 23 March 1986, *Nelson Piquet*, Williams-Honda, 61, 1:39'32.583
- Spain, 13 April 1986, Ayrton Senna, Lotus-Renault, 72, 1:48'47.735
- San Marino, 27 April 1986, *Alain Prost*, McLaren-TAG, 60, 1:32'28.408
- Monaco, 11 May 1986, *Alain Prost*, McLaren-TAG, 78, 1:55'41.060
- Belgium, 25 May 1986, *Nigel Mansell*, Williams-Honda, 43, 1:27'57.925
- Canada, 15 June 1986, *Nigel Mansell*, Williams-Honda, 69, 1:42'26.415
- USA East, 22 June 1986, *Ayrton Senna*, Lotus-Renault, 63, 1:51'12.847
- France, 6 July 1986, *Nigel Mansell*, Williams-Honda, 80, 1:37'19.272
- Great Britain, 13 July 1986, *Nigel Mansell*, Williams-Honda, 75, 1:30'38.471
- Germany, 27 July 1986, *Nelson Piquet*, Williams-Honda, 44, 1:22'08.263
- Hungary, 10 August 1986, *Nelson Piquet*, Williams-Honda, 76, 2:00'34.508
- Austria, 17 August 1986, *Alain Prost*, McLaren-TAG, 52, 1:21'22.531
- Italy, 7 September 1986, *Nelson Piquet*, Williams-Honda, 51, 1:17'42.889
- Portugal, 21 September 1986, *Nigel Mansell*, Williams-Honda, 70, 1:37'21.900
- Mexico, 12 October 1986, *Gerhard Berger*, Benetton-BMW, 68, 1:33'18.700
- Australia, 26 October 1986, *Alain Prost*, McLaren-TAG, 82, 1:54'20.388

- Brazil, 12 April 1987, *Alain Prost*, McLaren-TAG, 61, 1:39'45.141
- San Marino, 3 May 1987, *Nigel Mansell*, Williams-Honda, 59, 1:31'24.076
- Belgium, 17 May 1987, *Alain Prost*, McLaren-TAG, 43, 1:27'03.217
- Monaco, 31 May 1987, *Ayrton Senna*, Lotus-Honda, 78, 1:57'54.085
- United States, 21 June 1987, *Ayrton Senna*, Lotus-Honda, 63, 1:50'16.358
- France, 5 July 1987, *Nigel Mansell*, Williams-Honda, 80, 1:37'03.839
- Great Britain, 12 July 1987, *Nigel Mansell*, Williams-Honda, 65, 1:19'11.780
- Germany, 26 July 1987, *Nelson Piquet*, Williams-Honda, 44, 1:21'25.091
- Hungary, 9 August 1987, *Nelson Piquet*, Williams-Honda, 76, 1:59'26.793
- Austria, 16 August 1987, *Nigel Mansell*, Williams-Honda, 52, 1:18'44.898
- Italy, 6 September 1987, *Nelson Piquet*, Williams-Honda, 50, 1:14'47.707
- Portugal, 20 September 1987, *Alain Prost*, McLaren-TAG, 70, 1:37'03.906
- Spain, 27 September 1987, *Nigel Mansell*, Williams-Honda, 72, 1:49'12.692
- Mexico, 18 October 1987, *Nigel Mansell*, Williams-Honda, 63, 1:26'24.207
- Japan, 1 November 1987, *Gerhard Berger*, Ferrari, 51, 1:32'58.072
- Australia, 15 November 1987, *Gerhard Berger*, Ferrari, 82, 1:52'56.144

- Brazil, 3 April 1988, *Alain Prost*, McLaren-Honda, 60, 1:36'06.857
- San Marino, 1 May 1988, *Ayrton Senna*, McLaren-Honda, 60, 1:32'41.264
- Monaco, 15 May 1988, *Alain Prost*, McLaren-Honda, 78, 1:57'17.077
- Mexico, 29 May 1988, *Alain Prost*, McLaren-Honda, 67, 1:30'15.737
- Canada, 12 June 1988, *Ayrton Senna*, McLaren-Honda, 69, 1:39'46.618
- United States, 19 June 1988, *Ayrton Senna*, McLaren-Honda, 63, 1:54'56.035
- France, 3 July 1988, *Alain Prost*, McLaren-Honda, 80, 1:37'37.328
- Great Britain, 10 July 1988, *Ayrton Senna*, McLaren-Honda, 65, 1:33'16.367
- Germany, 24 July 1988, *Ayrton Senna*, McLaren-Honda, 44, 1:32'54.188
- Hungary, 7 August 1988, *Ayrton Senna*, McLaren-Honda, 76, 1:57'47.081
- Belgium, 28 August 1988, *Ayrton Senna*, McLaren-Honda, 43, 1:28'00.549
- Italy, 11 September 1988, *Gerhard Berger*, Ferrari, 51, 1:17'39.744
- Portugal, 25 September 1988, *Alain Prost*, McLaren-Honda, 70, 1:37'40.958
- Spain, 2 October 1988, *Alain Prost*, McLaren-Honda, 72, 1:48'43.851
- Japan, 30 October 1988, *Ayrton Senna*, McLaren-Honda, 51, 1:33'26.173
- Australia, 13 November 1988, *Alain Prost*, McLaren-Honda, 82, 1:53'14.676

- Brazil, 26 March 1989, *Nigel Mansell*, Ferrari, 61, 1:38'58.744
- San Marino, 23 April 1989, *Ayrton Senna*, McLaren-Honda, 58, 1:26'51.245
- Monaco, 7 May 1989, *Ayrton Senna*, McLaren-Honda, 77, 1:53'33.251
- Mexico, 28 May 1989, *Ayrton Senna*, McLaren-Honda, 69, 1:35'21.431
- United States, 4 June 1989, *Alain Prost*, McLaren-Honda, 75, 2:01'33.133
- Canada, 18 June 1989, *Thierry Boutsen*, Williams-Renault, 69, 2:01'24.073
- France, 9 July 1989, *Alain Prost*, McLaren-Honda, 80, 1:38'29.411
- Great Britain, 16 July 1989, *Alain Prost*, McLaren-Honda, 64, 1:19'22.131
- Germany, 30 July 1989, *Ayrton Senna*, McLaren-Honda, 42, 1:21'43.302
- Hungary, 13 August 1989, *Nigel Mansell*, Ferrari, 77, 1:49'38.650
- Belgium, 27 August 1989, *Ayrton Senna*, McLaren-Honda, 44, 1:40'54.196
- Italy, 10 September 1989, *Alain Prost*, McLaren-Honda, 53, 1:19'27.550
- Portugal, 24 September 1989, *Gerhard Berger*, Ferrari, 71, 1:36'48.546
- Spain, 1 October 1989, *Ayrton Senna*, McLaren-Honda, 73, 1:47'48.264
- Japan, 22 October 1989, *Alessandro Nannini*, Benetton-Ford, 53, 1:35'06.277
- Australia, 5 November 1989, *Thierry Boutsen*, Williams-Renault, 70, 2:00'17.421

- United States, 11 March 1990, *Ayrton Senna*, McLaren-Honda, 72, 1:52'32.829
- Brazil, 25 March 1990, *Alain Prost*, Ferrari, 71, 1:37'21.258
- San Marino, 13 May 1990, *Riccardo Patrese*, Williams-Renault, 61, 1:30'55.478
- Monaco, 27 May 1990, *Ayrton Senna*, McLaren-Honda, 78, 1:52'46.982
- Canada 10 June 1990, *Ayrton Senna*, McLaren-Honda, 70, 1:42'56.400
- Mexico, 24 June 1990, *Alain Prost*, Ferrari, 69, 1:32'35.783
- France, 8 July 1990, *Alain Prost*, Ferrari, 80, 1:33'29.606
- Great Britain, 15 July 1990, *Alain Prost*, Ferrari, 64, 1:18'30.999
- Germany, 29 July 1990, *Ayrton Senna*, McLaren-Honda, 45, 1:20'47.164
- Hungary, 12 August 1990, *Thierry Boutsen*, Williams-Renault, 77, 1:49'30.597
- Belgium, 26 August 1990, *Ayrton Senna*, McLaren-Honda, 44, 1:26'31.997
- Italy, 9 September 1990, *Ayrton Senna*, McLaren-Honda, 53, 1:17'57.878
- Portugal, 23 September 1990, *Nigel Mansell*, Ferrari, 61, 1:22'11.014
- Spain, 30 September 1990, *Alain Prost*, Ferrari, 73, 1:48'01.461
- Japan, 21 October 1990, *Nelson Piquet*, Benetton-Ford, 53, 1:34'36.824
- Australia, 4 November 1990, *Nelson Piquet*, Benetton-Ford, 81, 1:49'44.570

- United States, 10 March 1991, *Ayrton Senna*, McLaren-Honda, 81, 2:00'47.828
- Brazil, 24 March 1991, *Ayrton Senna*, McLaren-Honda, 71, 1:38'28.128
- San Marino, 28 April 1991, *Ayrton Senna*, McLaren-Honda, 61, 1:35'14.750
- Monaco, 12 May 1991, *Ayrton Senna*, McLaren-Honda, 78, 1:53'02.334
- Canada, 2 June 1991, *Nelson Piquet*, Benetton-Ford, 69, 1:38'51.490
- Mexico, 16 June 1991, *Riccardo Patrese*, Williams-Renault, 67, 1:29'52.205
- France, 7 July 1991, *Nigel Mansell*, Williams-Renault, 72, 1:38'00.056
- Great Britain, 14 July 1991, *Nigel Mansell*, Williams-Renault, 59, 1:27'35.479
- Germany, 28 July 1991, *Nigel Mansell*, Williams-Renault, 45, 1:19'29.661
- Hungary, 11 August 1991, *Ayrton Senna*, McLaren-Honda, 77, 1:49'12.796
- Belgium, 25 August 1991, *Ayrton Senna*, McLaren-Honda, 44, 1:27'17.669
- Italy, 8 September 1991, *Nigel Mansell*, Williams-Renault, 53, 1:17'54.319
- Portugal, 22 September 1991, *Riccardo Patrese*, Williams-Renault, 71, 1:35'42.304
- Spain, 29 September 1991, *Nigel Mansell*, Williams-Renault, 65, 1:38'41.541
- Japan, 20 October 1991, *Gerhard Berger*, McLaren-Honda, 53, 1:32'10.695
- Australia, 3 November 1991, *Ayrton Senna*, McLaren-Honda, 14, 24'34.899

- South Africa, 1 March 1992, *Nigel Mansell*, Williams-Renault, 72, 1:36'45.320
- Mexico, 22 March 1992, *Nigel Mansell*, Williams-Renault, 69, 1:31'53.587
- Brazil, 5 April 1992, *Nigel Mansell*, Williams-Renault, 71, 1:36'51.85
- Spain, 3 May 1992, *Nigel Mansell*, Williams-Renault, 65, 1:56'10.674
- San Marino, 17 May 1992, *Nigel Mansell*, Williams-Renault, 60, 1:28'40.927
- Monaco, 31 May 1992, *Ayrton Senna*, McLaren-Honda, 78, 1:50'59.372
- Canada, 14 June 1992, *Gerhard Berger*, McLaren-Honda, 69, 1:37'08.299
- France, 5 July 1992, *Nigel Mansell*, Williams-Renault, 69, 1:38'08.459
- Great Britain, 12 July 1992, *Nigel Mansell*, Williams-Renault, 59, 1:25'42.991
- Germany, 26 July 1992, *Nigel Mansell*, Williams-Renault, 45, 1:18'22.032
- Hungary, 16 August 1992, *Ayrton Senna*, McLaren-Honda, 77, 1:46'19.216
- Belgium, 30 August 1992, *Michael Schumacher*, Benetton-Ford, 44, 1:36'10.721
- Italy, 13 September 1992, *Ayrton Senna*, McLaren-Honda, 53, 1:18'15.349
- Portugal, 27 September 1992, *Nigel Mansell*, Williams-Renault, 71, 1:34'46.659
- Japan, 25 October 1992, *Riccardo Patrese*, Williams-Renault, 53, 1:33'09.533
- Australia, 8 November 1992, *Gerhard Berger*, McLaren-Honda, 81, 1:46'54.786

- South Africa, 14 March 1993, *Alain Prost*, Williams-Renault, 72, 1:38'45.082
- Brazil, 28 March 1993, *Ayrton Senna*, McLaren-Ford, 71, 1:51'15.485
- Europe, 11 April 1993, *Ayrton Senna*, McLaren-Ford, 76, 1:50'46.570
- San Marino, 25 April 1993, *Alain Prost*, Williams-Renault, 61, 1:33'20.413
- Spain, 9 May 1993, *Alain Prost*, Williams-Renault, 65, 1:32'27.685
- Monaco, 23 May 1993, *Ayrton Senna*, McLaren-Ford, 78, 1:52'10.947
- Canada, 13 June 1993, *Alain Prost*, Williams-Renault, 69, 1:36'41.822
- France, 4 July 1993, *Alain Prost*, Williams-Renault, 72, 1:38'35.241
- Great Britain, 11 July 1993, *Alain Prost*, Williams-Renault, 59, 1:25'38.189
- Germany, 25 July 1993, *Alain Prost*, Williams-Renault, 45, 1:18'40.885
- Hungary, 15 August 1993, *Damon Hill*, Williams-Renault, 77, 1:47'39.09
- Belgium, 29 August 1993, *Damon Hill*, Williams-Renault, 44, 1:24'32.124
- Italy, 12 September 1993, *Damon Hill*, Williams-Renault, 53, 1:17'07.509
- Portugal, 26 September 1993, *Michael Schumacher*, Benetton-Ford, 71, 1:32'46.309
- Japan, 24 October 1993, *Ayrton Senna*, McLaren-Ford, 53, 1:40'27.912
- Australia, 7 November 1993, *Ayrton Senna*, McLaren-Ford, 79, 1:43'27.476

- Brazil, 27 March 1994, *Michael Schumacher*, Benetton-Ford, 71, 1:35'38.759
- Pacific, 17 April 1994, *Michael Schumacher*, Benetton-Ford, 83, 1:46'01.693
- San Marino, 1 May 1994, *Michael Schumacher*, Benetton-Ford, 58, 1:28'28.642

- Monaco, 15 May 1994, *Michael Schumacher*, Benetton-Ford, 78, 1:49'55.372
- Spain, 29 May 1994, *Damon Hill*, Williams-Renault, 65, 1:36'14.374
- Canada, 12 June 1994, *Michael Schumacher*, Benetton-Ford, 69, 1:44'31.887
- France, 3 July 1994, *Michael Schumacher*, Benetton-Ford, 72, 1:38'35.704
- Great Britain, 10 July 1994, *Damon Hill*, Williams-Renault, 60, 1:30'03.640
- Germany, 31 July 1994, *Gerhard Berger*, Ferrari, 45, 1:22'37.272
- Hungary, 14 August 1994, *Michael Schumacher*, Benetton-Ford, 77, 1:48'00.185
- Belgium, 28 August 1994, *Damon Hill*, Williams-Renault, 44, 1:28'47.170
- Italy, 11 September 1994, *Damon Hill*, Williams-Renault, 53, 1:18'02.754
- Portugal, 25 September 1994, *Damon Hill*, Williams-Renault, 71, 1:41'10.165
- Europe, 16 October 1994, *Michael Schumacher*, Benetton-Ford, 69, 1:40'26.689
- Japan, 6 November 1994, *Damon Hill*, Williams-Renault, 50, 1:55'53.532
- Australia, 13 November 1994, *Nigel Mansell*, Williams-Renault, 81, 1:47'51.480

- Brazil, 26 March 1995, *Michael Schumacher*, Benetton-Renault, 71, 1:38'34.154
- Argentina, 9 April 1995, *Damon Hill*, Williams-Renault, 72, 1:53'14.532
- San Marino, 30 April 1995, *Damon Hill*, Williams-Renault, 63, 1:41'42.522
- Spain, 14 May 1995, *Michael Schumacher*, Benetton-Renault, 65, 1:34'20.507
- Monaco, 28 May 1995, *Michael Schumacher*, Benetton-Renault, 78, 1:53'11.258
- Canada, 11 June 1995, *Jean Alesi*, Ferrari, 68, 1:44'54.171
- France, 2 July 1995, *Michael Schumacher*, Benetton-Renault, 72, 1:38'28.429
- Great Britain, 16 July 1995, *Johnny Herbert*, Benetton-Renault, 61, 1:34'35.093
- Germany, 30 July 1995, *Michael Schumacher*, Benetton-Renault, 45, 1:22'56.043
- Hungary, 13 August 1995, *Damon Hill*, Williams-Renault, 77, 1:46'25.721
- Belgium, 27 August 1995, *Michael Schumacher*, Benetton-Renault, 44, 1:36'47.875
- Italy, 10 September 1995, *Johnny Herbert*, Benetton-Renault, 53, 1:18'27.916
- Portugal, 24 September 1995, *David Coulthard*, Williams-Renault, 71, 1:41'52.145
- Europe, 1 October 1995, *Michael Schumacher*, Benetton-Renault, 67, 1:39'59.044
- Pacific, 22 October 1995, *Michael Schumacher*, Benetton-Renault, 83, 1:48'49.972
- Japan, 29 October 1995, *Michael Schumacher*, Benetton-Renault, 53, 1:36'52.930
- Australia, 12 November 1995, *Damon Hill*, Williams-Renault, 81, 1:49'15.946

Statistics

- Australia, 10 March 1996, *Damon Hill*, Williams-Renault, 58, 1:32'50.491
- Brazil, 31 March 1996, *Damon Hill*, Williams-Renault, 71, 1:49'52.976
- Argentina, 7 April 1996, *Damon Hill*, Williams-Renault, 72, 1:54'55.322
- Europe, 28 April 1996, *Jacques Villeneuve*, Williams-Renault, 67, 1:33'26.473
- San Marino, 5 May 1996, *Damon Hill*, Williams-Renault, 63, 1:35'26.156
- Monaco, 19 May 1996, *Olivier Panis*, Ligier-Mugen-Honda, 75, 2:00'45.629
- Spain, 2 June 1996, *Michael Schumacher*, Ferrari, 65, 1:59'49.307
- Canada, 16 June 1996, *Damon Hill*, Williams-Renault, 69, 1:36'03.465
- France, 30 June 1996, *Damon Hill*, Williams-Renault, 72, 1:36'28.795
- Great Britain, 14 July 1996, *Jacques Villeneuve*, Williams-Renault, 61, 1:33'00.874
- Germany, 28 July 1996, *Damon Hill*, Williams-Renault, 45, 1:21'43.417
- Hungary, 11 August 1996, *Jacques Villeneuve*, Williams-Renault, 77, 1:46'21.134
- Belgium, 25 August 1996, *Michael Schumacher*, Ferrari, 44, 1:28'15.125
- Italy, 8 September 1996, *Michael Schumacher*, Ferrari, 53, 1:17'43.632
- Portugal, 22 September 1996, *Jacques Villeneuve*, Williams-Renault 70, 1:40'22.915
- Japan, 13 October 1996, *Damon Hill*, Williams-Renault, 52, 1:32'33.791

- Australia, 9 March 1997, *David Coulthard*, McLaren-Mercedes 58, 1:30'28.718
- Brazil, 30 March 1997, *Jacques Villeneuve*, Williams-Renault, 72, 1:36'06.990
- Argentina, 13 April 1997, *Jacques Villeneuve*, Williams-Renault, 72, 1:52'01.715
- San Marino, 27 April 1997, *Heinz-Harald Frentzen*, Williams-Renault, 62, 1:31'00.673
- Monaco, 11 May 1997, *Michael Schumacher*, Ferrari, 62, 2:00'05.654
- Spain, 25 May 1997, *Jacques Villeneuve*, Williams-Renault, 64, 1:30'35.896
- Canada, 15 June 1997, *Michael Schumacher*, Ferrari, 54, 1:17'40.646
- France, 29 June 1997, *Michael Schumacher*, Ferrari, 72, 1:38'50.492
- Great Britain, 13 July 1997, *Jacques Villeneuve*, Williams-Renault, 59, 1:28'01.665
- Germany, 27 July 1997, *Gerhard Berger*, Benetton-Renault, 45, 1:20'59.046
- Hungary, 10 August 1997, *Jacques Villeneuve*, Williams-Renault, 77, 1:45'47.149
- Belgium, 24 August 1997, *Michael Schumacher*, Ferrari, 44, 1:33'46.717
- Italy, 7 September 1997, *David Coulthard*, McLaren-Mercedes, 53, 1:17'04.609
- Austria, 21 September 1997, *Jacques Villeneuve*, Williams-Renault, 71, 1:27'35.999
- Luxembourg, 28 September 1997, *Jacques Villeneuve*, Williams-Renault, 67, 1:31'27.843
- Japan, 12 October 1997, *Michael Schumacher*, Ferrari, 53, 1:29'48.446
- Europe, 26 October 1997, *Mika Häkkinen*, McLaren-Mercedes, 69, 1:38'57.771

- Australia, 8 March 1998, *Mika Häkkinen*, McLaren-Mercedes, 58, 1:31'45.996
- Brazil, 29 March 1998, *Mika Häkkinen*, McLaren-Mercedes, 72, 1:37'11.747
- Argentina, 12 April 1998, *Michael Schumacher*, Ferrari, 72, 1:48'36.175
- San Marino, 26 April 1998, *David Coulthard*, McLaren-Mercedes, 62, 1:34'24.593
- Spain, 10 May 1998, *Mika Häkkinen*, McLaren-Mercedes, 65, 1:33'37.621
- Monaco, 24 May 1998, *Mika Häkkinen*, McLaren-Mercedes, 78, 1:51'23.595
- Canada, 7 June 1998, *Michael Schumacher*, Ferrari, 69 1:40'57.355
- France, 28 June 1998, *Michael Schumacher*, Ferrari, 71, 1:34'45.026
- Great Britain, 12 July 1998, *Michael Schumacher*, Ferrari, 60, 1:47'02.450
- Austria, 26 July 1998, *Mika Häkkinen*, McLaren-Mercedes, 71, 1:30'44.086
- Germany, 2 August 1998, *Mika Häkkinen*, McLaren-Mercedes, 45, 1:20'47.984
- Hungary, 16 August 1998, *Michael Schumacher*, Ferrari, 77, 1:45'25.550
- Belgium, 30 August 1998, *Damon Hill*, Jordan-Mugen-Honda, 44, 1:43'47.407
- Italy, 13 September 1998, *Michael Schumacher*, Ferrari, 53, 1:17'09.672
- Luxembourg, 27 September 1998, *Mika Häkkinen*, McLaren-Mercedes, 67, 1:32'14.789
- Japan, 1 November 1998, *Mika Häkkinen*, McLaren-Mercedes, 51, 1:27'22.535

- Australia, 7 March 1999, *Eddie Irvine*, Ferrari, 57, 1:35'01.659
- Brazil, 11 April 1999, *Mika Häkkinen*, McLaren-Mercedes, 72, 1:36'03.785
- San Marino, 2 May 1999, *Michael Schumacher*, Ferrari, 62, 1:33'44.792
- Monaco, 16 May 1999, *Michael Schumacher*, Ferrari, 78, 1:49'31.812
- Spain, 30 May 1999, *Mika Häkkinen*, McLaren-Mercedes, 65, 1:34'13.665
- Canada, 13 June 1999, *Mika Häkkinen*, McLaren-Mercedes, 69, 1:41'35.727
- France, 27 June 1999, *Heinz-Harald Frentzen*, Jordan-Mugen-Honda, 72, 1:58'24.343
- Great Britain, 11 July 1999, *David Coulthard*, McLaren-Mercedes, 60, 1:32'30.144
- Austria, 25 July 1999, *Eddie Irvine*, Ferrari, 71, 1:28'12.438
- Germany, 1 August 1999, *Eddie Irvine*, Ferrari, 45, 1:21'58.594
- Hungary, 15 August 1999, *Mika Häkkinen*, McLaren-Mercedes, 77, 1:46'23.536
- Belgium, 29 August 1999, *David Coulthard*, McLaren-Mercedes, 44, 1:25'43.057
- Italy, 12 September 1999, *Heinz-Harald Frentzen*, Jordan-Mugen-Honda, 53, 1:17'02.923
- Europe, 26 September 1999, *Johnny Herbert*, Stewart-Ford, 66, 1:41'54.314
- Malaysia, 17 October 1999, *Eddie Irvine*, Ferrari, 56, 1:36'38.494
- Japan, 31 October 1999, *Mika Häkkinen*, McLaren-Mercedes, 53, 1:31'18.785

- Australia, 12 March 2000, *Michael Schumacher*, Ferrari, 58, 1:34'01.987
- Brazil, 26 March 2000, *Michael Schumacher*, Ferrari, 71, 1:31'35.271
- San Marino, 9 April 2000, *Michael Schumacher*, Ferrari, 62, 1:31'39.776
- Great Britain, 23 April 2000, *David Coulthard*, McLaren-Mercedes, 60, 1:28'50.108
- Spain, 7 May 2000, *Mika Häkkinen*, McLaren-Mercedes, 65, 1:33'55.390
- Europe, 21 May 2000, *Michael Schumacher*, Ferrari, 67, 1:42'00.307
- Monaco, 4 June 2000, *David Coulthard*, McLaren-Mercedes, 78, 1:49'28.213
- Canada, 18 June 2000, *Michael Schumacher*, Ferrari, 69, 1:41'12.313
- France, 2 July 2000, *David Coulthard*, McLaren-Mercedes, 72, 1:38'05.538
- Austria, 16 July 2000, *Mika Häkkinen*, McLaren-Mercedes, 71, 1:28'15.818
- Germany, 30 July 2000, *Rubens Barrichello*, Ferrari, 45, 1:25'34.418
- Hungary, 13 August 2000, *Mika Häkkinen*, McLaren-Mercedes, 77, 1:45'33.869
- Belgium, 27 August 2000, *Mika Häkkinen*, McLaren-Mercedes, 44, 1:28'14.494
- Italy, 10 September 2000, *Michael Schumacher*, Ferrari, 53, 1:27'31.638
- United States, 24 September 2000, *Michael Schumacher*, Ferrari, 73, 1:36'30.883
- Japan, 8 October 2000, *Michael Schumacher*, Ferrari, 53, 1:38'26.533
- Malaysia, 22 October 2000, *Michael Schumacher*, Ferrari, 56, 1:35'54.235

- Australia, 4 March 2001, *Michael Schumacher*, Ferrari, 58, 1:38'26.533
- Malaysia, 18 March 2001, *Michael Schumacher*, Ferrari, 55, 1:47'34.801
- Brazil, 1 April 2001, *David Coulthard*, McLaren-Mercedes, 71, 1:39'00.834
- San Marino, 15 April 2001, *Ralf Schumacher*, Williams-BMW, 62, 1:30'44.817
- Spain, 29 April 2001, *Michael Schumacher*, Ferrari, 65, 1:31'03.305
- Austria, 13 May 2001, *David Coulthard*, McLaren-Mercedes, 71, 1:27'45.927
- Monaco, 27 May 2001, *Michael Schumacher*, Ferrari, 78, 1:47'22.561
- Canada, 10 June 2001, *Ralf Schumacher*, Williams-BMW, 69, 1:34'31.522
- Europe, 24 June 2001, *Michael Schumacher*, Ferrari, 67, 1:29'42.724
- France, 1 July 2001, *Michael Schumacher*, Ferrari, 72, 1:33'35.636
- Great Britain, 15 July 2001, *Mika Häkkinen*, McLaren-Mercedes, 60, 1:25'33.770
- Germany, 29 July 2001, *Ralf Schumacher*, Williams-BMW, 45, 1:18'17.873
- Hungary, 19 August 2001, *Michael Schumacher*, Ferrari, 77, 1:41'49.675
- Belgium, 2 September 2001, *Michael Schumacher*, Ferrari, 36, 1:08'05.002
- Italy, 16 September 2001, *Juan Pablo Montoya*, Williams-BMW, 53, 1:16'58.493
- United States, 30 September 2001, *Mika Häkkinen*, McLaren-Mercedes, 73, 1:32'42.840
- Japan, 14 October 2001, *Michael Schumacher*, Ferrari, 53, 1:27'33.298

- Australia, 3 March 2002, *Michael Schumacher*, Ferrari, 58, 1:35'36.792
- Malaysia, 17 March 2002, *Ralf Schumacher*, Williams-BMW, 56, 1:34'12.912
- Brazil, 31 March 2002, *Michael Schumacher*, Ferrari, 71, 1:31'43.663
- San Marino, 14 April 2002, *Michael Schumacher*, Ferrari, 62, 1:29'10.789
- Spain, 28 April 2002, *Michael Schumacher*, Ferrari, 65, 1:30'29.981
- Austria, 12 May 2002, *Michael Schumacher*, Ferrari, 71, 1:33'51.562
- Monaco, 26 May 2002, *David Coulthard*, McLaren-Mercedes, 78, 1:45'39.055
- Canada, 9 June 2002, *Michael Schumacher*, Ferrari, 70, 1:33'36.111
- Europe, 23 June 2002, *Rubens Barrichello*, Ferrari, 60, 1:35'07.426
- Great Britain, 7 July 2002, *Michael Schumacher*, Ferrari, 60, 1:31'45.015
- France, 21 July 2002, *Michael Schumacher*, Ferrari, 72, 1:32'09.837
- Germany, 28 July 2002, *Michael Schumacher*, Ferrari, 67, 1:27'52.078
- Hungary, 18 August 2002, *Rubens Barrichello*, Ferrari, 77, 1:41'49.001
- Belgium, 1 September 2002, *Michael Schumacher*, Ferrari, 44, 1:21'20.634
- Italy, 15 September 2002, *Rubens Barrichello*, Ferrari, 53, 1:16'19.982
- United States, 29 September 2002, *Rubens Barrichello*, Ferrari, 73, 1:31'07.934
- Japan, 13 October 2002, *Michael Schumacher*, Ferrari, 53, 1:26'59.698

- Australia, 9 March 2003, *David Coulthard*, McLaren-Mercedes, 58, 1:34'42.124
- Malaysia, 23 March 2003, *Kimi Räikkönen*, McLaren-Mercedes, 56, 1:32'22.195
- Brazil, 6 April 2003, *Giancarlo Fisichella*, Jordan-Ford, 54, 1:31'17.748
- San Marino, 20 April 2003, *Michael Schumacher*, Ferrari, 62, 1:28'12.058

- Spain, 4 May 2003, *Michael Schumacher*, Ferrari, 65, 1:33'46.933
- Austria, 18 May 2003, *Michael Schumacher*, Ferrari, 69, 1:24'04.888
- Monaco, 1 June 2003, *Juan Pablo Montoya*, Williams-BMW, 78, 1:42'19.010
- Canada, 15 June 2003, *Michael Schumacher*, Ferrari, 70, 1:31'13.591
- Europe, 29 June 2003, *Ralf Schumacher*, Williams-BMW, 60, 1:34'43.622
- France, 6 July 2003, *Ralf Schumacher*, Williams-BMW, 70, 1:30'49.213
- Great Britain, 20 July 2003, *Rubens Barrichello*, Ferrari, 60, 1:28'37.554
- Germany, 3 August 2003, *Juan Pablo Montoya*, Williams-BMW, 67, 1:28'48.769
- Hungary, 24 August 2003, *Fernando Alonso*, Renault, 70, 1:39'01.460
- Italy, 14 September 2003, *Michael Schumacher*, Ferrari, 53, 1:14'19.838
- United States, 28 September 2003, *Michael Schumacher*, Ferrari, 73, 1:33'35.997
- Japan, 12 October 2003, *Rubens Barrichello*, Ferrari, 53, 1:25'11.743

- Australia, 7 March 2004, *Michael Schumacher*, Ferrari, 58, 1:24'15.757
- Malaysia, 21 March 2004, *Michael Schumacher*, Ferrari, 56, 1:31'07.490
- Bahrain, 4 April 2004, *Michael Schumacher*, Ferrari, 57, 1:28'34.875
- San Marino, 25 April 2004, *Michael Schumacher*, Ferrari, 62, 1:26'19.670
- Spain, 9 May 2004, *Michael Schumacher*, Ferrari, 66, 1:27'32.841
- Monaco, 23 May 2004, *Jarno Trulli*, Renault, 77, 1:45'46.601
- Europe, 30 May 2004, *Michael Schumacher*, Ferrari, 60, 1:32'35.101
- Canada, 13 June 2004, *Michael Schumacher*, Ferrari, 70, 1:28'24.803
- United States, 20 June 2004, *Michael Schumacher*, Ferrari, 73, 1:40'29.914
- France, 4 July 2004, *Michael Schumacher*, Ferrari, 70, 1:30'18.133
- Great Britain, 11 July 2004, *Michael Schumacher*, Ferrari, 60, 1:24'42.700
- Germany, 25 July 2004, *Michael Schumacher*, Ferrari, 66, 1:23'54.848
- Hungary, 15 August 2004, *Michael Schumacher*, Ferrari, 70, 1:35'26.131
- Belgium, 29 August 2004, *Kimi Räikkönen*, McLaren-Mercedes, 44, 1:32'35.274
- Italy, 12 September 2004, *Rubens Barrichello*, Ferrari, 53, 1:15'18.448
- China, 26 September 2004, *Rubens Barrichello*, Ferrari, 56, 1:29'12.420
- Japan, 10 October 2004, *Michael Schumacher*, Ferrari, 53, 1:24'26.985
- Brazil, 24 October 2004, *Juan Pablo Montoya*, Williams-BMW, 71, 1:28'01.451

- Australia, 6 March 2005, *Giancarlo Fisichella*, Renault, 57, 1:24'17.336
- Malaysia, 20 March 2005, *Fernando Alonso*, Renault, 56, 1:31'33.736
- Bahrain, 3 April 2005, *Fernando Alonso*, Renault, 57, 1:29'18.531
- San Marino, 24 April 2005, *Fernando Alonso*, Renault, 62, 1:27'41.921
- Spain, 8 May 2005, *Kimi Räikkönen*, McLaren-Mercedes, 66, 1:27'16.830
- Monaco, 22 May 2005, *Kimi Räikkönen*, McLaren-Mercedes, 78, 1:45'15.556
- Europe, 29 May 2005, *Fernando Alonso*, Renault, 59, 1:31'46.648
- Canada, 12 June 2005, *Kimi Räikkönen*, McLaren-Mercedes, 70, 1:32'09.290
- United States, 19 June 2005, *Michael Schumacher*, Ferrari, 73, 1:29'43.181
- France, 3 July 2005, *Fernando Alonso*, Renault, 70, 1:31'22.233
- Great Britain, 10 July 2005, *Juan Pablo Montoya*, McLaren-Mercedes, 60, 1:24'29.588
- Germany, 24 July 2005, *Fernando Alonso*, Renault, 67, 1:26'28.599
- Hungary, 31 July 2005, *Kimi Räikkönen*, McLaren-Mercedes, 70, 1:37'25.552
- Turkey, 21 August 2005, *Kimi Räikkönen*, McLaren-Mercedes, 58, 1:24'34.454
- Italy, 4 September 2005, *Juan Pablo Montoya*, McLaren-Mercedes, 53, 1:14'28.659
- Belgium, 11 September 2005, *Kimi Räikkönen*, McLaren-Mercedes, 44, 1:30'01.295
- Brazil, 25 September 2005, *Juan Pablo Montoya*, McLaren-Mercedes, 71, 1:29'20.574
- Japan, 9 October 2005, *Kimi Räikkönen*, McLaren-Mercedes, 53, 1:29'02.212
- China, 16 October 2005, *Fernando Alonso*, Renault, 56, 1:39'53.618

- Bahrain, 12 March 2006, *Fernando Alonso*, Renault, 57, 1:29'46.205
- Malaysia, 19 March 2006, *Giancarlo Fisichella*, Renault, 56, 1:30'40.529
- Australia, 2 April 2006, *Fernando Alonso* Renault, 57, 1:34'27.870
- San Marino, 23 April 2006, *Michael Schumacher*, Ferrari, 62, 1:31'06.486
- Europe, 7 May 2006, *Michael Schumacher*, Ferrari, 60, 1:35'58.765
- Spain, 14 May 2006, *Fernando Alonso*, Renault, 66, 1:26'21.759
- Monaco, 28 May 2006, *Fernando Alonso*, Renault, 78, 1:43'43.116
- Great Britain, 11 June 2006, *Fernando Alonso*, Renault, 60, 1:25'51.927
- Canada, 25 June 2006, *Fernando Alonso*, Renault, 70, 1:34'37.308
- United States, 2 July 2006, *Michael Schumacher*, Ferrari, 73, 1:34'35.199
- France, 16 July 2006, *Michael Schumacher*, Ferrari, 70, 1:32'07.803
- Germany, 30 July 2006, *Michael Schumacher*, Ferrari, 67, 1:27'51.693
- Hungary, 6 August 2006, *Jenson Button*, Honda, 70, 1:52'20.941
- Turkey, 27 August 2006, *Felipe Massa*, Ferrari, 58, 1:28'51.082
- Italy, 10 September 2006, *Michael Schumacher*, Ferrari, 53, 1:14'51.975
- China, 1 October 2006, *Michael Schumacher*, Ferrari, 56, 1:37'32.747
- Japan, 8 October 2006, *Fernando Alonso*, Renault, 53, 1:23'53.413
- Brazil, 22 October 2006, *Felipe Massa*, Ferrari, 71, 1:31'53.751

- Australia, 18 March 2007, *Kimi Räikkönen*, Ferrari, 58, 1:25'28.770
- Malaysia, 8 April 2007, *Fernando Alonso*, McLaren-Mercedes, 56, 1:32'14.930
- Bahrain, 15 April 2007, *Felipe Massa*, Ferrari, 57, 1:33'27.515
- Spain, 13 May 2007, *Felipe Massa*, Ferrari, 65, 1:31'36.230
- Monaco, 27 May 2007, *Fernando Alonso*, McLaren-Mercedes, 78, 1:40'29.329
- Canada, 10 June 2007, *Lewis Hamilton*, McLaren-Mercedes, 70, 1:44'11.292
- United States, 17 June 2007, *Lewis Hamilton*, McLaren-Mercedes, 73, 1:31'09.965
- France, 1 July 2007, *Kimi Räikkönen*, Ferrari, 70, 1:30'54.200
- Great Britain, 8 July 2007, *Kimi Räikkönen*, Ferrari, 59, 1:21'43.074
- Europe, 22 July 2007, *Fernando Alonso*, McLaren-Mercedes, 60, 2:06'26.358
- Hungary, 5 August 2007, *Lewis Hamilton*, McLaren-Mercedes, 70, 1:35'52.991
- Turkey, 26 August 2007, *Felipe Massa*, Ferrari, 58, 1:26'42.161
- Italy, 9 September 2007, *Fernando Alonso*, McLaren-Mercedes, 53, 1:18'37.806
- Belgium, 16 September 2007, *Kimi Räikkönen*, Ferrari, 44, 1:20'39.066
- Japan, 30 September 2007, *Lewis Hamilton*, McLaren-Mercedes, 67, 2:00'34.579
- China, 7 October 2007, *Kimi Räikkönen*, Ferrari, 56, 1:37'58.395
- Brazil, 21 October 2007, *Kimi Räikkönen*, Ferrari, 71, 1:28'15.270

- Australia, 16 March 2008, *Lewis Hamilton*, McLaren-Mercedes, 58, 1:34'50.616
- Malaysia, 23 March 2008, *Kimi Räikkönen*, Ferrari, 56, 1:31'18.555
- Bahrain, 6 April 2008, *Felipe Massa*, Ferrari, 57, 1:31'06.970
- Spain, 27 April 2008, *Kimi Räikkönen*, Ferrari, 66, 1:38'19.051
- Turkey, 11 May 2008, *Felipe Massa*, Ferrari, 58, 1:26'49.451
- Monaco, 25 May 2008, *Lewis Hamilton*, McLaren-Mercedes, 76, 2:00'42.742
- Canada, 8 June 2008, *Robert Kubica*, BMW Sauber, 70, 1:36'24.447
- France, 22 June 2008, *Felipe Massa*, Ferrari, 70, 1:31'50.245
- Great Britain, 6 July 2008, *Lewis Hamilton*, McLaren-Mercedes, 60, 1:39'09.440
- Germany, 20 July 2008, *Lewis Hamilton*, McLaren-Mercedes, 67, 1:31'20.874
- Hungary, 3 August 2008, *Heikki Kovalainen*, McLaren-Mercedes, 70, 1:37'27.067
- Europe, 24 August 2008, *Felipe Massa*, Ferrari, 57, 1:35'32.339
- Belgium, 7 September 2008, *Felipe Massa*, Ferrari, 44, 1:22'59.394
- Italy, 14 September 2008, *Sebastian Vettel*, STR-Ferrari, 53, 1:26'47.494
- Singapore, 28 September 2008, *Fernando Alonso*, Renault, 61, 1:57'16.304
- Japan, 12 October 2008, *Fernando Alonso*, Renault, 67, 1:30'21.892
- China, 19 October 2008, *Lewis Hamilton*, McLaren-Mercedes, 56, 1:31'57.403
- Brazil, 2 November 2008, *Felipe Massa*, Ferrari, 71, 1:34'11.435

Glossary

ACTIVE SUSPENSION
A system that automatically adjusts the suspension to suit different parts of the track, making it firmer when going around corners, for instance, to stop the car from rolling. Active suspension is currently banned in Formula 1 racing.

AERODYNAMICS
How air behaves when it passes over an object. Engineers can alter the shape of a car to affect how the air behaves, allowing the car to travel faster while creating more downforce at the same time.

APEX
The point of the corner that drivers aim for to allow the straightest line through a corner, maintaining maximum speed. This is usually at the geometric centre of the turn.

BARGEBOARD
A piece of a Formula 1 car's bodywork found in front of the sidepods and used to improve airflow around the car.

BUDGET CAP
A restriction on the amount of money that can be spent.

CAMBER
The curve on a road's surface where the middle of the road is usually higher than the outsides.

CC
Short for 'cubic centimetre', this is a unit used to measure the total volume of an engine's cylinders.

CFD
Short for 'Computational Fluid Dynamics', this is the software that designers can use to see how changes in a car's shape will affect airflow and temperature before having to build a model or any parts.

CHASSIS
The frame of a car to which wheels, engine, and body are attached.

COMPOUND
The type of rubber used to make a tyre. There are usually two types of compound used for each race, one of which is harder than the other.

CONSTRUCTORS' CHAMPIONSHIP
The prize awarded to the team that has scored the most points over an entire Formula 1 season.

DIFFUSER
Part of the underneath of a car that affects the airflow, improving its aerodynamics.

DIRTY AIR
The term used to describe swirling, turbulent air coming off the car in front that adversely affects any cars following closely behind.

DOWNFORCE
The force that pushes the car down onto the track. It is created by air passing over the car's wings and body, forming areas of high pressure above the car and low pressure below the car. This difference in air pressure pushes the car down onto the track.

DRAG
The force created by air turbulence behind a car. A car with poor aerodynamics will create a lot of drag and this will slow the car down.

DRIVERS' CHAMPIONSHIP
The prize awarded to the driver who has scored the most points over an entire Formula 1 season.

FORMULA
The set of rules which every car must adhere to in a motor racing championship.

GARAGISTE
The term used to describe a small, independent team, usually owned or started by an individual, as opposed to a team owned and run by a large company.

GRAND PRIX
Meaning 'large prize', this is the term used to describe the races that make up a Formula 1 season.

GRID
The line-up of cars at the start of a race. In a Formula 1 race, cars form a grid in two staggered columns.

GRIP
A car's ability to transfer its power onto the track. Too little grip will see the car skid and slide.

GROUND-EFFECT
To create an area of low pressure beneath a car so that it is pushed down onto the track. In the past, this has been achieved by using large fans or by shaping the underside of the car's body.

HP
Short for 'horsepower', this is the unit used to measure the power produced by an engine.

INTERMEDIATE TYRES
Tyres with a small tread pattern on them. They will disperse a small amount of water and are used during light rain.

KERS
Short for 'Kinetic Energy Recovery System', this device converts energy that is usually lost during braking and stores it, either in a battery or a flywheel. Drivers can then release this energy to produce a surge of power.

MONOCOQUE
A type of body, or chassis, that is made from a single piece, rather than lots of different parts. A monocoque chassis is very light and very strong.

NOMEX®
The flameproof material used to make drivers' undergarments and racing suits.

PADDOCK
The name given to the part of the track where the pitlane is and where the teams set up their garages and motorhomes.

PIT CREW
The members of a Formula 1 team who work on the car during a pit stop. They will change the wheels, refuel the car, and replace any parts that are damaged.

PITLANE
The part of the track where the teams' garages are. It is usually found running alongside the start/finish straight.

PITLANE LIMITER
A switch on the steering wheel which, when activated, restricts the car's speed as it enters and exits the pitlane.

PIT STOP
The period when a driver pulls into the pitlane and stops outside his team's garage to refuel and change his tyres. It is also an opportunity to replace any damaged parts on the car.

PODIUM
The three-tiered stand on which the first three finishers celebrate their success.

POLE POSITION
The position at the front of the starting grid.

ROLL BARS
Strong metal bars placed over the driver's head to protect him should his car roll over.

RPM
Short for 'Revolutions Per Minute', it is used to describe how quickly the driveshaft of an engine spins.

RUN-OFF AREA
An area to one side of a track, usually by a bend or corner. Run-off areas are usually covered in gravel to slow a car down should a driver misjudge a bend.

SEASON
The duration of a single championship year.

SIDEPODS
The outer bodywork fitted around a car's radiators and engine systems.

SLICK TYRES
Tyres with no tread pattern on them. They offer the most amount of grip in dry conditions, but are useless in the wet because they do not disperse any water.

SPONSORS
Companies or individuals who pay teams to show their names or logos on cars.

TEAM PRINCIPAL
The person who runs a Formula 1 team.

TELEMETRY
Information that is collected by sensors on the car and sent back via radio to the team in the pitlane so that they can see how the car and the driver are performing.

TEST RIG
Also called a 'shaker', this is a series of vibrating posts to which a car is attached to simulate racing conditions.

TURBO
A fan used to push more air into an engine to increase the pressure inside the cylinders. This increases the power output of the engine. The fan on a turbo is powered by the exhaust gases leaving the engine. Currently illegal in Formula 1 racing.

WET-WEATHER TYRES
Tyres with a deep tread pattern on them that will disperse a lot of water and are used in heavy rainfall.

WHEELBASE
The distance between the front and rear wheels.

WIND TUNNEL
A large room with a fan at one end. The fan blows air over a model of a car to mimic the car driving forwards. Engineers can then see how the air behaves as it moves over the car.

WING
Part of a Formula 1 car that is used to create downforce. The shape of the wing is such that air passing under the wing travels faster than air travelling over the wing. This creates low pressure below the wing and high pressure above. The higher air pressure pushes down on the car, creating downforce.

Red Bull
15

Sebastian Vettel passes the grandstand in a blur during qualifying for the 2009 FORMULA 1 SANTANDER BRITISH GRAND PRIX.

Index

Credits

THE PUBLISHER WOULD LIKE TO THANK THE FOLLOWING FOR THEIR KIND PERMISSION TO REPRODUCE THEIR PHOTOGRAPHS:

Key:
a–above; b–below/bottom; c–centre; f–far; l–left; r–right; t–top

1 Getty Images: ROSLAN RAHMAN/AFP. 2-3 Getty Images: WILLIAM WEST. 4-5 Getty Images: Clive Mason. 6-7 Getty Images: Clive Mason. 8-9 Getty Images. 10-11 Getty Images: BERTRAND GUAY/AFP. 12 Corbis: Gianni Dagli Orti (br). Getty Images: Hulton Archive (tr); Manu Fernandez/AFP (bl). 13 Corbis: Bettmann (tl). Getty Images: Hulton Archive (tr); Popperfoto (b). 14 Getty Images: (cl); Popperfoto (br). 15 Corbis: Schlegelmilch (t) (cl). Getty Images: Central Press (bl); Victor Blackman/Express (cr). 16 Getty Images: Clive Mason (t); Mark Thompson (bl); Paul Gilham (br). 17 Corbis: Tim Tadder (t). Getty Images: (b). 18 Corbis: Schlegelmilch (t). Getty Images: (cra); Mark Thompson (b); OLIVIER LABAN-MATTEI/AFP (crb). 19 Getty Images: (b); Clive Mason (cr). 20-21 Getty Images. 22 Corbis: Hulton-Deutsch Collection (bc). Getty Images: Clive Mason (t); Mark Thompson (cr); Robert Riger (br). 23 Corbis: Gianni Giansanti/Sygma (br). Getty Images: Clive Mason (fbr); Keystone (fbl) (bl); Mark Thompson (tl) (cr); Serge Thomann (cl). 24 Getty Images: (b); SHAUN CURRY/AFP (t). 25 Corbis: Hulton-Deutsch Collection (tl). Getty Images: Alvis Upitis (tr); Mark Thompson (b); Paul Gilham (c). 26-27 Getty Images. 28-29 NASA. 30 Getty Images: (cr); ANTONIO SCORZA (bl). 30-31 Getty Images: Christian Fischer/Bongarts. 31 Getty Images: (c); AFP (cl). 32 Corbis: Bettmann (fcla). Getty Images: AllsportUK (fclb); Alvis Upitis (cla); Clive Mason /Allsport (ca); Hulton Archive (cr); Keystone/ Hulton Archive (clb); Popperfoto (br); VANDERLEI ALMEIDA/AFP (cb). 32-32 Getty Images: Popperfoto (c). 32-33 Getty Images: Mark Thompson. 33 Getty Images: Clive Mason/ALLSPORT (cb); MARCUS BRANDT/AFP (bl); MUSTAFA OZER/AFP (tr). 34 Getty Images: (bl). 35 Getty Images: Robert Cianflone/ALLSPORT (tr). 36 Getty Images: AFP (bl). 37 Corbis: Bryn Williams/Handoout/Reuters (tl). 38 Corbis: Schlegelmilch (br). 39 Getty Images: Mark Thompson (b). 40 Getty Images: BERTRAND GUAY/AFP (tl). 41 Getty Images: (b). 42 Getty Images: (tl). 43 Getty Images: Mike Cooper /Allsport (tl). 44 Getty Images: Bongarts (b). 45 Getty Images: Popperfoto (t). 46 Corbis: HOW HWEE YOUNG/epa (b). 47 Getty Images: (t). 48 Getty Images: VANDERLEI ALMEIDA/AFP (bl). 49 courtesy of Yas Marina circuit: (br). 50-51 Getty Images: BERTRAND GUAY/AFP. 52 Getty Images: Paul Gilham (cl) (bl); VINCENZO PINTO/AFP (cr); Vladimir Rys/Bongarts (tr). 52-53 Getty Images: (bc). 53 Corbis: Kirsty Umback (c). Getty Images: Reg Lancaster/Express (tl); Tom Shaw (tr). 54 Getty Images: Mark Thompson (b) (tr); Michael Cooper /Allsport (cr); Oli Scarff (cl). 55 Corbis: Terry Cryer (tr). Getty Images: Michael Steele (c); PASCAL GUYOT/AFP (bc); Peter Macdiarmid (tl). 56 BMW AG: (t) (cr). Getty Images: Jasper Juinen (cl). 56-57 BMW AG: (b). 57 BMW AG: (cl) (crb). Getty Images: Mark Thompson (t). 58 Corbis: Vittoriano Rastelli (crb). courtesy of Williams F1: (cl). Getty Images: Mark Thompson (tc) (cr). 58-59 courtesy of Williams F1: (b). 59 Corbis: Alberto Pizzoli/Sygma (c); STR/epa (t). 60 Getty Images: Peter Fox (tr) (tc); ROSLAN RAHMAN/AFP (cl). 60-61 Getty Images: Peter Fox (b). 61 Getty Images: Clive Mason (t) (c); Mark Thompson (clb); Mark Thompson (bl). 62 Getty Images: Mark Thompson/ALLSPORT (t) (clb); Robert Cianflone (cr). 62-63 Getty Images: Mark Thompson (b). 63 Getty Images: ANTONIO SCORZA/AFP (c); Vladimir Rys/ Bongarts (tl). 64 courtesy of Toyota Motorsport: (cl). Getty Images: (b); Lars Baron/ Bongarts (tc) (tr). 65 Getty Images: (cl); Bryn Lennon (bc); PETER KOHALMI/AFP (tl); Vladimir Rys/Bongarts (tr). 66 Getty Images: Clive Mason (tc); Mark Thompson (cl) (cr). 66-67 Getty Images: Mark Thompson (b); Clive Mason (cl). 67 Getty Images: Clive Mason/ALLSPORT (c); Dave M. Benett (tr); MAURICIO LIMA/AFP (tl). 68 Getty Images: BERTRAND GUAY/AFP/ (tc); LLUIS GENE/AFP (tr); Mark Thompson (cl). 68-69 courtesy of Brawn GP: (b). 69 Getty Images: BERTRAND GUAY/AFP (bc); GREG WOOD/AFP (tl); PAUL CROCK/AFP (tr). 70 Getty Images: Clive Mason (tr); DIEGO TUSON/AFP (cr); Paul Gilham (cl). 70-71 Getty Images: (b). 71 Getty Images: ORLANDO KISSNER/AFP (cl); PAL PILLAI/AFP (bc); Paul Gilham (t). 72-73 Getty Images: Rolls Press/Popperfoto. 74-75 Getty Images: Michael Cooper / Allsport. 76-77 Corbis: Jean-Yves Ruszniewski/TempSport. 78-79 Getty Images: Klemantaski Collection. 80-81 Getty Images: Alvis Upitis. 82-83 Corbis: Schlegelmilch. 84 Getty Images: (t). 84-85 Getty Images. 85 Getty Images: (cl) (cr). 86 Getty Images: (bl); Popperfoto (br). 87 Corbis: Martyn Goddard / TRANSTOCK (t). Getty Images: (br). 88 Getty Images: Alvis Upitis (tr); Popperfoto (bl). 88-89 Getty Images: Bob Thomas (c). 89 Getty Images: (br) (tl). 90 Corbis: Schlegelmilch (cl). Getty Images: (bl) (br). 91 Getty Images: Pascal Rondeau/Allsport (b); Simon Bruty/ Allsport (t). 92 Getty Images: (br); Pascal Rondeau/Allsport (cl) (bl). 93 Getty Images: Andreas Rentz/Bongarts (b); KAZUHIRO NOGI/AFP (t). 94 Getty Images: EMMANUEL DUNAND/AFP (bl); Mark Thompson /Allsport (cl); Mark Thompson/ ALLSPORT (tr). 95 Getty Images: Paul Gilham (b); THIERRY ZOCCOLAN/AFP (t). 96-97 BMW AG. 98 BMW AG: (b). courtesy of Williams F1: (cl) (cr). 99 BMW AG: (t). Getty Images: Stuart Franklin (b). 100 BMW AG: (b). 101 Getty Images: (cr) (br); Force India F1 (cl); Mark Thompson (t); Peter Fox (bl). 102 Getty Images: ANTONIO SCORZA (tr); Toyota (br). 103 Getty Images: Alvis Upitis (cr); ATTILA KISBENEDEK/AFP (cl); PETER PARKS/AFP (tl); ROSLAN RAHMAN/AFP (b). 104 Getty Images: MARK RALSTON/AFP (tr); Toyota Motorsport (bl). 104-105 BMW AG: (bc). 105 Getty Images: Bryn Lennon (br); Hoch Zwei (tl). 106 Getty Images: ANTONIO SCORZA/AFP (c); PAUL CROCK/AFP (br). 107 BMW AG: (t). courtesy of Williams F1: (bl) (bc). 108-109 Getty Images: SAEED KHAN/AFP (b). 109 Getty Images: Paul Gilham (cra); Peter Fox (crb); Robert Cianflone (tr). 110-111 Getty Images: Paul Gilham. 112 Getty Images: Popperfoto (cl) (br). 112-113 Getty Images: Popperfoto. 113 Getty Images: Popperfoto (bl) (tr). 114 Getty Images: Keystone (tr). 114-115 Getty Images: Keystone. 115 Getty Images: Evening Standard (tl); George Stroud/Express/Hulton Archive (tr). 116 Getty Images: Alvis Upitis (bl); Bentley Archive/Popperfoto (br). 117 Getty Images: Keystone (cl); Robert Riger (t); Rolls Press/Popperfoto (cb). 118 Getty Images: Allsport UK /Allsport (c); GAUTREA/AFP (r). 119 Getty Images: AFP (bc); MAURICIO LIMA/AFP (cl); Pascal Rondeau/Allsport (tl). 120 Getty Images: Allsport UK /Allsport (tc). 120-121 Getty Images: Mike King (b). 121 Getty Images: CYRIL VILLEMAIN/AFP (cb); Pascal Rondeau/Allsport (tr) (cla). 122 Getty Images: STF/AFP (b); TOSHIFUMI KITAMURA/AFP (t). 123 Getty Images: AFP (b); Allsport UK /Allsport (t). 124 Getty Images: Allsport UK /Allsport (bl) (crb). 124-125 Getty Images: Allsport UK / Allsport (t). 125 Getty Images: Bob Thomas (clb); JOE KLAMAR/AFP (bc). 126 Getty Images: Pascal Rondeau /Allsport (cra); Paul Gilham (b). 127 Getty Images: Mark Sandten/Bongarts (tr); Robert Cianflone (bl); Tobias Heyer/Bongarts (c). 128 Getty Images: Ben Radford/Allsport (tr). 128-129 Getty Images: PASCAL PAVANI/ AFP. 129 Getty Images: Mike Cooper /Allsport (t). 130 Getty Images: Bentley Archive/Popperfoto (clb); Bob Thomas (tr). 130-131 Getty Images: Alvis Upitis (bc). 131 Getty Images: Keystone (tl); PATRICK HERTZOG/AFP (cla). 132 Getty Images: Bob Thomas (clb); David Cannon /Allsport (tr); Pascal Rondeau/Allsport (bl); SimonBruty/Allsport (br). 133 Getty Images: Pascal Rondeau (l). 134 BMW AG: (tl). Getty Images: BERTRAND GUAY/AFP (bl). 135 Getty Images: ROSLAN RAHMAN/ AFP (tr) (b). 136 Getty Images: Paul Gilham (bl) (r). 137 BMW AG: (br). Getty Images: Paul Gilham (tr). 138 courtesy of Williams F1: (br). Getty Images: Jasper Juinen (tr); Keystone (clb). 139 courtesy of Williams F1: (l). Getty Images: ANTONIO SCORZA/AFP (cb); Lars Baron/Bongarts (br); Mark Thompson (tr). 140-141 Getty Images. 142-143 Getty Images. 144 Getty Images: Vodafone (tr). 144-145 Getty Images: VANDERLEI ALMEIDA/AFP (b). 145 Getty Images: ROSLAN RAHMAN/AFP (tr). 146-147 Getty Images: Clive Mason. 148 BMW AG: (bl). Getty Images: Bentley Archive/Popperfoto (cla). 148-149 Getty Images: Shell (b). 149 Getty Images: Clive Mason (cra). 150-151 Getty Images: BAY ISMOYO/AFP. 152 BMW AG: (cl) (bc) (bl) (cr) (tr). 153 BMW AG: (tl) (cl) (tr). Getty Images: BERTRAND GUAY/AFP (b). 154 Getty Images: EVARISTO SA/AFP/ (tl); Frank Robichon/AFP (b). 155 Corbis: JENS BUETTNER/epa (tl). Getty Images: Frank Robichon/AFP (bc); Robert Cianflone (tr); Vladimir Rys/Bongarts (cl). 156 Getty Images: Mark Thompson (cl); Vladimir Rys/Bongarts (tr). 156-157 Getty Images: Pascal Rondeau/Allsport (b). 157 Getty Images: Central Press/Hulton Archive (tl); Mark Thompson (tr). 158 Getty Images: BULENT KILIC/AFP (br). 158-159 Getty Images: Vladimir Rys/Bongarts (t). 159 Getty Images: ALY SONG/AFP (bl); GUILLAUME BAPTISTE/AFP (crb). 160-161 Getty Images: BAY ISMOYO/AFP. 162 Getty Images: Frank Robichon/AFP (cra). 162-163 Getty Images: PAUL CROCK/ AFP (b). 163 Getty Images: Bryn Lennon (tl); JOSEP LAGO/AFP (cra). 164 Getty Images: Clive Mason (crb); GOH CHAI HIN/AFP (l); JOSEP LAGO/AFP (bl). 165 Getty Images: Clive Mason (br); GREG WOOD/AFP (t); Mark Thompson (bl). 166-167 Getty Images: Vladimir Rys/Bongarts. 168 Getty Images: J. Adam Huggins (clb); Ker Robertson (cra); PATRICK KOVARIK/AFP (bc). 169 Getty Images: ANDREAS SOLARO/AFP (b); ARTYOM KOROTAYEV/AFP (tr); Chung Sung-Jun (cla). 170 courtesy of GP2 Media Service: (tc). 170-171 courtesy of GP2 Media Service: (b). 171 Getty Images: Duif du Toit/Gallo Images (cra). Lat Photographic: Andrew Ferraro (tc); Nigel Kinrade, USA LAT Photographic (bc). 172 Getty Images: Jasper Juinen (bl); Peter Fox (tr). 172-173 Getty Images: SAEED KHAN/AFP (b). 173 Getty Images: Mark Thompson (tr). 174 Getty Images: Mark Thompson (tr); Robert Laberge (crb). 175 Getty Images: Mark Thompson (tl) (bl); Massimo Bettiol (br); Robert Cianflone (tr); VINCENZO PINTO/AFP (crb). 176-177 Getty Images: Paul Gilham. 178 Getty Images: Paul Gilham. 179 Getty Images: Bentley Archive/ Popperfoto. 180 Getty Images: Alvis Upitis. 182 Getty Images: Allsport UK /Allsport. 183 Getty Images: Pascal Rondeau. 185 Getty Images: ANTONIO SCORZA. 187 Getty Images: STF/AFP. 188-189 Getty Images: Clive Mason. 190 Getty Images: SAEED KHAN/AFP (l)

Front and Back Endpapers: Getty Images: Clive Mason

Jacket images: Back: Corbis: Schlegelmilch bl, br, fbl, fbr. Back Flaps: Nacym Bouras